PENGUIN BOOKS
SOMERVILLE AND

Gifford Lewis is half Scots   training in lettering and graphics an   ...iand from 1968. She was designer at the Ir   ...ty Press until 1972, when she founded, with Clare Craven, the firm of Gifford & Craven, publishing mainly art history and special editions. She started to read and collect Somerville and Ross in 1968 and to work on their papers in 1977. She has edited (with Dr Hilary Robinson) *The Buddh Dictionary*, Somerville and Ross's first manuscript written in collaboration. She is now completing an edition of the letters of Somerville and Ross.

Gifford Lewis married an Oxford historian in 1975, and they have two sons. She has published research into Scots and Irish genealogy and palaeography.

GIFFORD LEWIS

Somerville and Ross

THE WORLD OF THE IRISH R. M.

PENGUIN BOOKS

For Thomas Charles-Edwards

Penguin Books Ltd, Harmondsworth, Middlesex, England
Viking Penguin Inc., 40 West 23rd Street, New York, New York 10010, U.S.A.
Penguin Books Australia Ltd, Ringwood, Victoria, Australia
Penguin Books Canada Ltd, 2801 John Street, Markham, Ontario, Canada L3R 1B4
Penguin Books (N.Z.) Ltd, 182–190 Wairau Road, Auckland 10, New Zealand

First published by Viking 1985
Published in Penguin Books 1987

Made and printed in Great Britain by
Butler & Tanner Ltd, Frome and London

Contents

Introduction

In England during the, 1890s there was a pronounced interest in the Celtic Revival and a flourishing market for literary products from the fringe. Two books were published in this decade that have weathered well: *The Real Charlotte* (1894) and *Some Experiences of an Irish R.M.* (1899), both by the Irish writers Somerville and Ross. Reviewers quickly overcame their surprise at two women writing together and acclaimed these books, although they are utterly unlike other Revival books of the time, which were full of overdone dialect and theatrical 'PQ' (peasant quality).

Edith Œnone Somerville was born on 2 May 1858 at Corfu, where her father, Colonel Henry Somerville, was stationed as Colonel of the Buffs. She was brought up at Drishane House, Castletownshend, County Cork. Violet Martin, who wrote under the pen name of 'Martin Ross', was born at Ross House, County Galway, on 11 June 1862. She was brought up at Ross, moving for a time to Dublin with her mother shortly after her father, James Martin of Ross, died in 1872. Although Edith and Martin were cousins they did not meet until 1886; a brilliantly matched pair of minds, they took just over a year to decide to essay a literary career together.

In childhood neither Edith nor Martin had recognized social and class barriers and both spoke naturally to those who in England would have been termed their 'inferiors'. So that although they were from the privileged Anglo-Irish gentry, they were at home in the native Irish world to the extent that their record of native speech in English is uniquely impressive. They knew that in their novels they were recording the death-throes of their class - they made an unequalled portrait of the collapse of Anglo-Ireland and the rise through it of the new Irish middle class.

Somerville and Ross lived and wrote at the same time as writers of the Celtic Revival such as Lady Gregory and J.M. Synge, yet they kept apart from them. They, too, learned Irish, but Somerville and Ross did not feel the need to reach back into a heroic past, or to journey, notebook in hand, into the depths of the *Gaeltacht*. Rather they made a study of the speech and manners of those around them, many of whom still spoke Irish. They had been familiar from child-hood with the works of Scott and Edgeworth, which were read aloud. It seems possible that their system of building their books around

Castletownshend harbour from the terrace of Glen Barrahane during the mackerel-fishing season. The fleet is French: French-speaking sailors enlivened Castletownshend at such times. The photograph is by Martin Ross; the seated figure is Edith Somerville's sister Hildegarde.

The Ireland of Somerville and Ross.

recorded speech may have been influenced by Edgeworth's habit of footnoting her best speeches (as in *Castle Rackrent*), as '★verbatim'. Edgeworth was an idol to Edith and Martin; her influence on them was strong. They had too a strong personal connection, in that Edgeworth had been a close friend of Nancy Crampton, Edith and Martin's great-grandmother, and Martin had inherited their correspondence.

Ross. A view of the house across Ross Lake.

Maria Edgeworth was the first to portray the true contrast between Irish manners and intelligence and English manners and intelligence, to the detriment of England. *The Absentee*, particularly in the portrayal of Count O'Halloran and Larry Brady and his family, shows with absolute sympathy and clarity an Irishness that had never before been presented to the English reading public. Sir Walter Scott, a great admirer of Maria Edgeworth and her works, hoped to present the native Scot in the same way: 'not by a caricatured and exaggerated use of the national dialect, but by their habits, manners and feelings; so as in some way to emulate the admirable Irish portraits drawn by Miss Edgeworth'.

In literature, authenticity of scene and dialogue in portraying Ireland to the English reading public was rare; convincing portrayal of a society requires some degree of sympathy with that society, and Ireland in its duality posed a problem. Those writers from the class termed 'Anglo-Irish' experienced difficulty in describing a native world in many ways closed to them, and vice versa. Somerville and Ross bridged those two resolutely separate worlds, and they sold their intimate knowledge of Ireland in order to remain living in it.

Gladstone, in a series of Land Acts, dismantled the landownership system of the landlords and began re-distribution. The gentry – deprived of rents – had to reorganize. Their reduced circumstances forced

them into the professions: now not only the younger sons, but the eldest son, without patrimony, went into the army, the navy or the church. Ireland became a place for holidays. Unusually, as women, Edith Somerville and Violet Martin chose to continue to live in Ireland and work rather than marry. Their self-supporting literary lives curiously pre-figure the description given by Virginia Woolf in *A Room of One's Own* of the sort of life that intelligent women should work towards.

Edith's decision to work, taken long before her meeting with Martin, was tied to her wish to maintain the Somerville family home, Drishane; but for her efforts Drishane would have passed from Somerville hands. Financial strains absorbed her life. Edith and Martin's love of place, and particularly of their homes, Drishane and Ross, were the strongest fixed emotions of their lives. Edith was officially based at Drishane, in West Cork, and Martin at Ross, near Galway, until the death of Martin's mother in 1906. It was only for the last nine years of her life that Martin lived at Drishane and their writing could be a full-time, though much interrupted, occupation.

Castle Townshend lies in an area once called simply Castlehaven, after the safe harbour which lay below the cliffside O'Driscoll Castle. It was acquired, with a tract of surrounding countryside, by Colonel Richard Townshend, a Cromwellian officer. The family settled and thrived. Brian, son of Colonel Townshend, built the small star fort still standing on the rise behind the present Castle that overlooks the harbour. The Townshends were well established when Thomas Somerville was appointed rector of Castlehaven and Myross in 1732. Edith Somerville described the nexus of families in the village in *Irish Memories*: 'Somervilles and Townshends had been living and intermarrying in Castlehaven Parish, with none to molest their ancient solitary reign' until Charles Bushe, second son of Chief Justice Bushe, came as

Panoramic view of Castlehaven inlet, showing Horse Island, Toe Head and the peninsula of Reen. Drishane lies in the woods to the left.

rector with his wife Emmeline Coghill, whom he married in 1839, and many Coghill siblings came in Emmeline's wake. Her brother Joscelyn settled at Glen Barrahane and her sister Adelaide married Henry Somerville of Drishane.

Constance Bushe, daughter of Rector Charles, and mentor of young Edith Somerville, made a cartoon showing the arrival of the Coghills as an invasion of Palefaces upon aboriginal Red men. Edith describes it:

> A picture in which is depicted the supposed indignation of the Aboriginal Red men at the apostasy of my father in departing from the family habit of marrying a Townshend, and in allying himself with a Paleface ... The Red men and women are armed with clubs, the Palefaces with croquet mallets ... My grandmother (née Townshend of Castletownshend) one of my great aunts and other female relatives are profanely represented capering with fury in rabbit skins. The Paleface females surge in vast crinolines ... My grandfather swings a tomahawk, and is faced by my uncle, Sir Joscelyn Coghill, leader of the second wave of invasion, with a photographic camera (the first ever seen in West Carbery) and a tripod.

The world that they wrote of is not a world that we find described elsewhere in Anglo-Irish literature. It is an ephemeral world, where the failing Anglo-Irish mingled temporarily with the resurgent Irish native, as though the drawing room, devoid of men, and below-stairs had been compelled by circumstance to spend a decade or two together in a waiting room. It is not a world that could have engaged the attention of a man at that time, but writing from the inside, Somerville and Ross have given it perfect preservation.

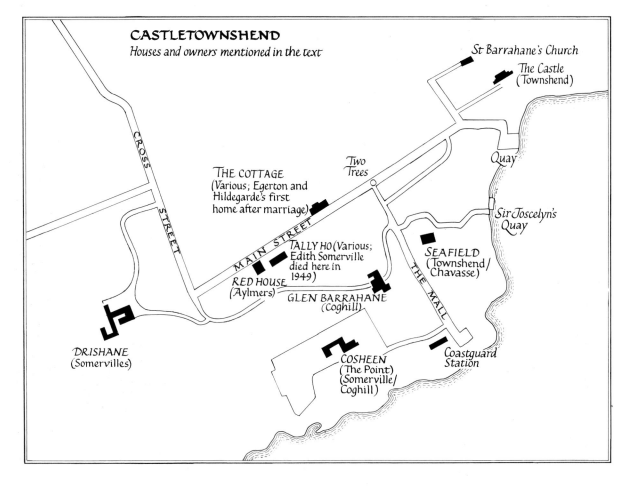

CASTLETOWNSHEND
Houses and owners mentioned in the text

St Barrahane's Church

The Castle
(Townshend)

CROSS STREET

Two
Trees

Quay

THE COTTAGE
(Various; Egerton and
Hildegarde's first
home after marriage)

Sir Joscelyn's
Quay

MAIN STREET

TALLY HO (Various;
Edith Somerville
died here in
1949)

SEAFIELD
(Townshend/
Chavasse)

RED HOUSE
(Aylmers)

GLEN BARRAHANE
(Coghill)

THE MALL

DRISHANE
(Somervilles)

COSHEEN
(The Point)
(Somerville/
Coghill)

Coastguard
Station

Plan of Castletownshend and the houses inhabited by Edith's relations.

It was an unstable broth of Anglo-Irish, in various stages of decay; Hiberno-Saxon, vulgarly called West British, in various stages of bloom; gombeen men, real native and affected, all grappling with the lack of substance, of any real wealth, and getting by with the bluff and counter-bluff of airy ostentations.

As writers, they are worthy of note not only for their superb style, realism and accuracy of dialogue, but also because they were in that very first wave of New Women to be independent of men and to have successful professional lives. The supressed sexuality of those lives has been mistaken for suppressed homosexuality, a misreading of character that has devalued their observations on men and on the relationships between men and women, which are, in fact, chillingly accurate, and boldly outspoken in comparison with their contemporaries in Anglo-Irish literature. *The Real Charlotte*, published in 1894, contains a study of sexual passion and jealousy that can stun the reader to this day.

To write off their partnership as one based on adolescent homosexuality is to devalue and misunderstand the entire nature of their

The Castle, Castletownshend, with St
Barrahane's Church on the hill above. St
Barrahane's was built in 1827 to replace the
old Castlehaven church, which had become
ruinous. The Castle, a rebuilding and
extension of the old Rectory, is of a slightly
later date and became the Townshend
residence after Madam Townshend, Edith
Somerville's great-grandmother, accidentally
demolished the family mansion on the level
ground between Brian's star fort and the sea.

collaboration and achievements. Their published works are the creations of a pair of emancipated and adult women who achieved their
emancipation and adulthood in adverse circumstances.

Their novels can be read for period detail on social customs, manners and habits of all classes in Ireland in that most fascinating period
of social change between 1880 and 1920. They deal with a wide range
of subjects: *The Real Charlotte* with land hunger and the drive for
possession; *Mount Music* with the Catholic versus Protestant crisis; *The
Big House of Inver* with the defeat of decadence by vulgarity; *Naboth's
Vineyard* with the land war and Land League tactics; *The Enthusiast*
with the hopelessness of the position of the Anglo-Irish. Their memoirs, *Wheel-Tracks* and *Irish Memories*, are meticulous and loving records of the raw material of their Castletownshend and Ross lives.

A Leech illustration from Surtees' Handley Cross *called 'Pigg in the Melon Frame'. Leech had a great influence on Edith Somerville as an illustrator. Her ludicrous scenes from Irish hunting life such as we see in* A Patrick's Day Hunt *have a strong family resemblance to Leech.*

They have been associated, unjustly, with a supercilious Ascendancy portrayal of stage Irish characters. 'Ah, they made great fun of us,' is an opinion of Somerville and Ross still to be met with today in West Cork. The *forte* humour of their most successful books, *Some Experiences of an Irish R.M.* (Resident Magistrate) and its sequels, mistaken for satire, is responsible for this opinion. Describing, in *Irish Memories* (1917), the good reception by critics of their first novel, *An Irish Cousin* (1889), Edith wrote:

> Miss Edgeworth had been the last to write of Irish country life with sincerity and originality, dealing with both the upper and lower classes, and dealing with both unconventionally. Lever's brilliant and extravagant books, with their ever enchanting Micky Frees and Corney Delaneys, merely created and throned the stage Irishman, the apotheosis of the English ideal. It was of Lever's period to be extravagant. The Handley Cross series is a case in point. Let me humbly and hurriedly disclaim any impious thought of deprecating Surtees. No one who has ever ridden a hunt, or loved a hound, but must admit that he has his unsurpassable moments ... But I think it is undeniable that the hunting people of Handley Cross, like Lever's dragoons, were always at full gallop. With Surtees as with Lever, every one is 'all out', there is nothing in hand – save perhaps a pair of duelling pistols or a tandem whip – and the height of the spirits is only equalled by the tallness of the hero's talk. That intolerable adjective 'rollicking' is consecrated to Lever; if certain of the rank and file of the reviewers of our later books could have realised with what

abhorrence we found it applied to ourselves, and could have known how rigorously we had endeavoured to purge our work of anything that might justify it, they might, out of the kindness that they had already shown us, have been more sparing of it. Lever was a Dublin man, who lived most of his life on the Continent, and worked like a scene painter, by artificial light from memoranda. Miss Edgeworth had the privilege, which was also ours, of living in Ireland, in the country, and among the people of whom she wrote.

CHAPTER 1

Somervilles and Martins – Cousins Innumerable

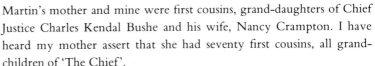

Martin's mother and mine were first cousins, grand-daughters of Chief Justice Charles Kendal Bushe and his wife, Nancy Crampton. I have heard my mother assert that she had seventy first cousins, all grand-children of 'The Chief'.

From *Irish Memories*, 1917

The Somerville family was of Norman origin and had settled in lowland Scotland with large estates by the late twelfth century. The Drishane Somervilles belonged to that class George Bernard Shaw calls 'downstarts'. They descend from Thomas, the brother of John, second Lord Somerville. By marriage Thomas acquired a small estate in Stirlingshire called Plane. He lived in a strong tower house; but his descendants continued slowly downwards until, by 1599, David Somerville of Plane, with little to pass on to his son, allowed him to become a merchant. He, Robert, became moderately wealthy and established himself at a large farmstead called Auchingray, near Carnwath in Lanark. His great-grandson, William, was the Somerville who in 1690 crossed over to Ireland. He was an Episcopalian minister, forced to flee from his manse when it was attacked by Covenanters. He took his family to safety with relatives in Ireland.

Two sons had crossed to Ireland with him; the elder, William, returned to Edinburgh, where he became a merchant burgess, like his grandfather, John. The other son, Thomas, had been a baby at the time of the flight to Ireland, and was educated there. He went to Trinity College, and took his B.A. in 1711. He entered the Church and was ordained in Cloyne Cathedral in 1715. He served as a curate in Cork and in 1732 was made rector of Myross and Castlehaven, a rich parish which included Castletownshend.

It was his son Thomas who, by becoming a very successful merchant trading with Newfoundland and the West Indies, was able to build up again the estate of his family. He bought land, and built two beautiful

Castletownshend village street climbs up the hill behind the Quay Stores. Sir Joscelyn's Quay is to the left.

houses. We see his hand in many places in Castletownshend. He used
excellent masons, and they built for him not only the Mall House and
Drishane, but the watch and signal towers, storehouses and quays
necessary to his shipping trade. The tower on Horse Island signalled
home port to his returning ships, which brought from abroad cut
limestone sills and architraves for the house that he planned. Drishane
was built with simple good proportions and clad in small, well-cut
weather slates. By his patient efforts Tom Somerville restored his
branch of the family to the ranks of landed gentry, a class out of which
they had dropped for five generations.

*Drishane House, County Cork. Photograph
by Boyle Somerville, taken in spring 1883.
Standing outside are Henry, Adelaide and
Aylmer Somerville. In the nineties households
like Drishane and Ross scraped along on
pension funds, windfalls and self-help.
Gladstone's series of Land Acts made him
very unpopular with the landlord class in
Ireland. One of the Acts, which absolved
tenants from paying arrears of rent while
doing nothing about the lenient landlords who
had allowed the rents to accumulate, gave rise
to a spate of anti-Gladstone jokes. Edith
recorded some in her diary, such as: 'Major
Lambert says he wishes Gladstone was so
deep in a certain place that the divil couldn't
see him without a telescope.' And there was a
mock telegram that read 'PARNELL ARRESTED.
GLADSTONE, STILL AT LARGE.' Gladstone was
known in England as the G.O.M. – the
Grand Old Man. To the Anglo-Irish he was
Gordon's Old Murderer. After the Land Acts
the gentry moved into the professions as
architects, lawyers, doctors, writers and artists,
gentry women confining themselves to the last
three categories. Gentility could be maintained
on a shoestring in Ireland. The Somervilles
had lost all their capital, and Drishane was
stripped by bailiffs, in 1811, when Thomas
Somerville III had stood as guarantor to a
relative whose business had failed.*

The haphazard and mixed fortune that was the Somervilles, encouraged in them adaptability. The Martins had no occasion to develop
such a quality. Unlike the Somervilles, the Martins, until the Famine,
had no reverses or great misfortunes to reduce the splendour of their
estate.

The Martins were one of the Tribes of Galway who acquired a
large part of Connemara in Elizabethan times. Violet Martin's ancestor,
Robert Martin, had set himself up at Ross, by Ross Lake on the
Oughterard to Galway road, by 1590. The chief Martin house was at
Ballynahinch; its estate extended over 200,000 acres. The family was
Royalist and Roman Catholic and skilfully avoided difficulties and
confiscations. They avoided Protestantism until Violet Martin's great-
grandfather changed his religion in order to marry that significantly
named Protestant, Elizabeth O'Hara, daughter of a native Irish family
turned Protestant. It was a love match in which he gave way.

Both Edith and Martin had the highest opinion of Irish use of
language and general intelligence, but Martin's feeling that at heart
'they' were all children, in need of firm control and guidance, led her
to fixed, Unionist views. It was not a particularly surprising stance for

a Martin of Ross, used to a paternalistic society for so many centuries. She felt that the country needed strong government, implemented by its top layer of landowners, and that the centre of government for the British Isles should be London. In comparison Edith was a positive home-ruler, as we shall see. She felt a capability for self-government would come, and would have concurred with Richard Lovell Edgeworth (father of the novelist, Maria) writing to Erasmus Darwin:

The people here are altogether better than in England. The higher classes far worse; the middling classes far inferior to yours,

Ross House, near Oughterard, Co. Galway, in photographs sent by Martin Ross to Edith Somerville. 'It is said that a man is never in love till he is in love with a plain woman; and in spite of draughts, of exhausting flights of stairs, of chimneys that are the despair of sweeps, it has held the affections of five generations of Martins' (Martin Ross, writing in Irish Memories).

very far indeed; but the peasants, though cruel, are generally very docile, and of the strongest power, both of body and mind.

A good government could undoubtedly make this a great country, because the raw material is so good and simple.

The Somervilles, for their class, were remarkably sympathetic to Nationalism, possibly because of their Scottishness. The high opinion of the local Irish people for the Somervilles pre-dates the time in 1858, the year of Edith's birth, when her grandfather hid two Fenians in Drishane after a 'disturbance' at Skibbereen, until they were able to get a boat and make for America and safety. O'Donovan Rossa, the Fenian leader, had a friendship with both Edith's father, Colonel Henry Somerville, and her grandfather, and wrote an embarrassingly eulogistic poem celebrating her father's safe return from the Crimea.

The Somervilles did not hold themselves apart from Catholics. Army and professional class connections overrode differences in religion. Best of all they knew the army family of McCarthy-Morrough at Inishbeg – the balls there are often described by Edith in her letters; in the same neighbourhood a Catholic branch of the O'Connell family were also friends of the Somervilles.

It is possible that local reverence for the Somerville family dates from an incident in the youth of Edith's grandfather. In 1823 a tithe war raged in the Castletownshend district. The Protestant clergy of the Established Church of Ireland were entitled by law to the tenth part of farming parishioners' income. Since most of the population was Roman Catholic, the tithes were not insisted upon. The Reverend Robert Morritt, the incumbent of Castlehaven parish in 1823, was avaricious, and by force claimed the tenth due to him. The resultant unrest came to a head in a battle on 23 June. The Reverend Morritt had called in police, and the farming people fought them. At a place called Traga-Leagaid there was a bloody mêlée. One policeman had been killed by a farmer, who cut him down with a scythe as he stood above him on a fence. The police shot dead two of the farmers.

Many of the farmers were tenants of Thomas Somerville and one of them rode to Drishane for his help. Thomas Somerville, twenty-five years old and recently married, mounted his horse and galloped to the battle. Country people, partly sheltered by field walls, were hurling rocks at the police, who lay on the ground, firing their guns at them. Tom Somerville rode between the two forces, shouting in Irish to the country people to be still and attend to him, and to the police that he was a magistrate and to cease firing. He released the men held by the police and calmed the opposing forces with assurances that he would solve the problem in court, at Skibbereen.

This incident clearly shows us that Thomas Somerville, Edith's grandfather, was absolutely confident of his command of spoken Irish, and that he would support his tenants against injustice. The battle was

The ruin of the O'Driscoll Castle from the landward side. It has since slipped into the sea.

A very early plate by Sir Joscelyn Coghill (c.1865) showing the old Castlehaven church and above it the Castle in which the Reverend Robert Morritt lived, and before him the Reverend Thomas Somerville. The Tithe War had its effect. Eventually, the Tithe Commutation Act of 1838 moved the burden of supporting the Protestant clergy from the peasants to the landowners. The Catholic/Protestant confrontation in Ireland came with the influx of Elizabethan English, the first after the Reformation of the English Church. Those who came to Ireland as Protestants were much less likely to be assimilated than those who came before the Reformation, like the Martins. The ousting of the topmost layer of native Catholic society by a new Protestant one is audible in the list of Rectors of Castlehaven church from 1403 to 1640: O'Driscoll, O'Callaghane, O'Driscoll, Cormac/Basse, Pratt, Stukely.

celebrated in a poem in Irish that became popular in the district. Entitled 'The Battle of Traga-Leagaid', it was rescued and recorded from three versions that were collated and translated for Edith by Douglas Hyde. It opens: 'Three years, eighteen hundred and twenty besides. So old was Christ the year the Battle was fought at the strand of the Boulders, at the Ocean south ...' After a description of the violence and deaths is the verse:

> Then came Captain Somerville, truly noble,
> And the priest, the *bunan*, great was their fame,
> They gave them freedom and relief,
> And they loosed them from the soldiers with pride.

Mrs Somerville, Edith's mother, and Mrs Martin, Martin's mother, were two of seventy first cousins, all grandchildren of Charles Kendal Bushe (1767-1843) and his wife, Nancy Crampton. Amongst these grandchildren, as C.L. Graves the critic remarked in his article 'Martin Ross': 'There was an unusually large proportion of women of the *maîtresse femme* type, charged with high explosive, handsome, vivid, commanding, and generous ...' Here is some indication why Edith and Martin – particularly Edith – grew up to be so independent. Edith was brought up by her father and grandfather as more than equal to her younger brothers:

> Every morning as the clock struck nine Grandpapa took his stand in front of 'the prayer table', and I beside him, holding his hand, with my father on the other side holding my left hand. It was a place of honour. I despised my brothers who stood with my mother at one side, facing the servants on the other.

Perhaps it was only army and navy fathers who brought up their daughters to be practical and expected them to become hardy and competent to manage – the same thing is noticeable in Scottish families, whose menfolk were often away on service. The upbringing of Edith and her sister Hildegarde may be a reflection of the necessity of leaving estate and household management in the hands of competent wives. There was no longer any money to employ the agents, estate managers and upper servants whose duties could be carried out by a wife.

The careers of Edith and Hildegarde Somerville give massive and detailed evidence of what women might do with their daily lives if competence was expected of them. Edith and Hildegarde introduced the breed of Friesian cattle to Cork and ran the first pedigree herd, as well as managing their farm. The pedigree herd was owned jointly by Edith, Hildegarde and Cameron, one of their brothers. A letter addressed to her 'Dear Partners', dated 17 June 1913, about the state of accounts, shows both the efforts made by Hildegarde and Edith to be competent cattle-dealers and Edith's astonishing vigour at the age of fifty-five:

> Dick, who had been rather struck by the Jones' Ayrshire Bull sale, laid down his cards when he heard of todays bargain, and said, 'By gash, you bet us all.' Before I leave the subject of the farm I may say that I cut one field of hay yesterday in blazing sun, east wind, and a high steady glass ... Do you realise that I have in one week sold five bulls of our own breeding? All due to Hildegarde's *male*volent influence on the herd. Your exhausted sister Edith.

Hildegarde introduced to Ireland the cultivation of violets for sale and ran a violet farm profitably. Indefatigable fund-raisers, the sisters raised money for endless good causes, from First World War ambulances, to kennels for the West Carbery Hunt hounds, to funding the first West Carbery District Nurse, who was stationed in Castletownshend.

At Ross the organization of the household and estate was more primitive, and Catholic and Protestant were still integrated. It was typical of Ross that the young Martins should have been educated, along with estate children, Catholics and Protestants together, by their own Aunt Marian and James Tucker, a former hedge schoolmaster. (A similar experiment, though more thought out on humanitarian and liberal grounds, was carried out by the Edgeworths at Edgeworthstown.) Tucker attached himself to Martin's Aunt Marian during the Famine and taught with her through it. He became indispensable to the Masters of Ross. Martin described him:

> He remained for many years, and filled many important posts. He taught us the three R's with rigour and perseverance, he wrote odes for our birthdays, he was controller-in-chief of the dairy; later on, when my father received the appointment of Auditor of Poor Law, under the Local Government Board, Tucker filled in the blue 'abstracts' of the Auditor's work in admirably neat columns.

Tucker was also an inspired actor, who electrified all of the schoolroom's theatrical productions. A loving portrait of him is given in *The Real Charlotte*, where he appears as Canavan, Sir Benjamin's aide.

The Martin houses at Ballynahinch and Ross were examples of the old Catholic Irish great house. Use of Irish was let slip along with Catholicism, but the Martins of Ross were Catholic until Martin's great-grandfather made the change to Protestantism on his marriage to Elizabeth O'Hara. His son married a Catholic, Martin's grandmother. Mass and spoken Irish were parts of Martin's upbringing, very different from Edith's. Such was the strength of the prevailing religion at Ross in Martin's childhood that she and all of her brothers and sisters had two baptisms – after their official Protestant baptisms they were taken by their wet-nurses to the priest; their parents knew and did not disapprove. At Ross, during Martin's grandmother's lifetime, the Angelus prayer-bell rang twice daily, at twelve and six. Familiarity with Irish Catholicism subtly pervades the writing of Somerville and Ross. The Somervilles who, on their flight from Scotland, had been High Church Episcopalians, took but half-heartedly to the lowness of the Church of Ireland worship, and in Edith's generation and that following, the temperament of the more thoughtful among them was to lead them to Anglo-Catholicism.

Owing to the poorness of the land, the Martin estates were not remunerative, and the lack of actual money, of any solid financial basis to the family holdings, was to prove disastrous during the Famine, when Ross was almost mortgaged out of existence. Martin describes Ross life well:

> Life at Ross was of the traditional Irish kind, with many retainers at low wages, which works out as a costly establishment with nothing to show for it. A sheep a week, and a cow a month

Martin sitting reading on the rocks at the edge of Ross Lake.

were supplied by the farm and assimilated by the household; it seemed as if, with the farm produce, the abundance of dairy cows, the packed turf house, the fallen timber ready to be cut up, the fruitful garden, the game, and the trout, there should have been affluence. But after all these followed the Saturday night labour bill, and the fact remains that, as many Irish landlords can testify, these free fruits of the earth are heavily paid for, that convenience is mistaken for economy, and that farming is, for the average gentleman, more an occupation than an income.

Two studies of boats in the harbour by Sir Joscelyn Coghill, c.1875.

The greatest of the Martins was 'Humanity Dick' (1754-1834). As an Irish M.P. he supported Catholic emancipation and succeeded in carrying the first modern legislation for protecting animals in 1822. He was a founder of the R.S.P.C.A. in 1824. Known in his homeland as the 'King of Connemara', proprietor of many thousands of acres and overlord of a large part of the Connemara population, he was thought quaint, outlandish and often laughable by the English Members of Parliament on account of his broad brogue. The Martins' notion of themselves as absolutely Irish is demonstrated in Martin's frequent anti-Saxon comments, and in this letter to Edith, where she is writing of a visit to a branch of the Morris family at Spiddal: 'It was a strange gathering of Galway people, O'Hara's, Lynches, Morrises and Martins and no brogues amongst them except the Morrises, and of course ourselves.'

After their vicissitudes in Scotland, the Somervilles were very small landlords indeed in Ireland, compared to such as the Martins. Army service seems to have provided the family with its sound financial basis, after the unique and enriching career of 'Tom the Merchant' was done. As a consequence the Famine seems little to have touched the family, who were often away on service, and whose tenants were few and well looked after. It was otherwise with the Martins, whose position as benevolent landlords, in some control of their lands and people, was ended by the Famine. At that time Martin's mother, father, grandfather and Aunt Marian were all at Ross dealing with the Famine. Aunt Marian was mistress of the household during the period. She was remarkable in that she caught famine fever, typhus, at the school she ran on the estate, and had drifted off into the trance state that preceded death, when her father, with furious confidence in her, bled her. She recovered, unlike her cousin, Thomas Martin of Ballynahinch; his house and estate were to fail to hold together through the Famine, and his remaining family removed to Canada, where they founded a new Ballynahinch.

At Ross the efforts to feed all the people who came to the house were herculean, and Martin's Aunt Marian, whose constitution was so remarkably strong, did all that humanly could be done. She and her brother wrote endlessly to London, pleading for aid, stressing the cata-

strophic proportions of the distress and death in the Ross neighbourhood. It is difficult for us to comprehend the attitude of such as Tre-
velyan in the English government to reports like those being sent to
London by the Martins.

Martin wrote of many incidents at Ross during the Famine, none
more awful than the story of the woman who had walked fifteen miles

> with a child in her arms and a child by her side, to get the relief
> that she heard was at Ross. Before she reached the house the child
> in her arms was dead; she carried it into the kitchen and sank on
> the flags. When my aunt spoke to her, she found that she had
> gone mad; reason had stopped in that whelming hour, like the
> watch of a drowned man.

The Famine brought to the fore a series of able Irishmen, practical,
eloquent and efficient Parliamentarians. These new practical National-
ists, so different from the old, fated romantics like Fitzgerald and Tone,
organized the Land League, boycotting and the withholding of rents,
and finished off the landlords who had somehow scraped through the
Famine, like the Martins. A consequence of the Act of Union, as Pitt
had hoped, was that Irish agriculture and trade had boomed because of
the demand for supplies during the Napoleonic wars. Profits made
during this period by fast-moving Irishmen set up a new class of
well-to-do farmers and middlemen ready to step into the shoes of the
landlords as they sold out and removed during or after the Famine.
The middleman had come into being when the great landlords had
removed to England at the Union, leaving their Irish estates in the
hands of agents. Some of these estates were not visited by their owners
from one generation to the next, and the profiteering instincts of the
agents and middlemen, combined with the complete lack of interest of
the absentee landlords, brought about the hugely over-populated estates, with tenants renting tiny patches of ground and cabins being
built in every available corner.

Land League tactics of withholding rents, of depositing a fraction in
the local bank as a token payment, were extremely effective. Robert
Martin, Martin's brother, received no rents from the Ross estates after
1879. The Coghills, Edith's relations who lived at nearby Glen Barrahane, were in deep difficulties from the early eighties. Edith entered in
her diary on 8 January 1882: 'Uncle Josc's tenants have paid up £300
and refuse to give more. The amount due is £1,600. Pleasing prospect
for Uncle Joscelyn until eviction forces the brutes to pay.' On 13
January in the same year Edith entered: 'Micky Collins was punished
for paying his rent by 2 of his sheep being killed last night by his
friends and neighbours.' The background knowledge of the land war
was used to effect later in *Naboth's Vineyard*.

Tenants could be evicted for non-payment of rent, but they were
protected from 'capricious' eviction. When they were evicted for

Glen Barrahane was a rambling conglomeration of extensions to what was once a simple house called Laputa, in honour of the visit to Castletownshend made by the gloomy Dean when he came to visit his friend the Reverend Thomas Somerville. It had a large schoolroom, studio and, most important, a large dark room, where Sir Joscelyn practised his photography and taught his nephews and nieces the art.

non-payment, the boycotting campaign ensured that no new tenant would take the vacated farm. Martin's description of the land war years at Ross, far less violent than at Castletownshend, as benevolent paternalism and the old ties of tenants to their once Catholic landlords were deep-rooted, strikes a very different note:

> The Disestablishment of the Irish Church came in 1869, a direct blow at Protestantism, and an equally direct tax upon landlords for the support of their Church, but of this revolution the tenants appeared to be unaware. In 1870 came Gladstone's Land Act, which, by a system of fines shielded the tenant to a great extent from 'capricious eviction'. As evictions, capricious or otherwise, did not occur at Ross, this section of the Act was not of epoch-making importance there; its other provision, by which tenants became proprietors of their own improvements, was also something of a superfluity. It was 1872 that brought the first cold plunge into Irish politics of the new kind.

In that year the Home Rule candidate, Captain Nolan, won a resounding victory over the Conservative Unionist candidate, Captain Trench, Captain Nolan taking 3,000 votes to Captain Trench's 600. The shock of this vote to Martin's father, who saw it as a betrayal by his tenants, caused him to be careless of his health. He caught pleurisy and died. The elections had been held in February; Martin's father died on 23 April. By that summer the house was shuttered and the Martins moved.

*Plate by Sir Joscelyn Coghill showing five
men of the Cork Militia, c.1860, coming up
Castletownshend hill.*

From the beginning of the nineteenth century, resident landlords
were emphatically against the subdivision of leases, and did everything
in their power to prevent it, seeing its dangers, but they failed. The
smaller resident landlords were in no way responsible for the over-
population crisis, nor were they guilty of charging high rents. In his
excellent and exhaustive study *The Land and People of Nineteenth Century Cork*, J.S. Donnelly shows that the Famine made resident landlords
extremely self-conscious and wary of raising rents.

A major point of Donnelly's thesis is that resident Cork landlords
were not rapacious bullies of a down-trodden peasantry, but that they
were merely outmoded, and no longer necessary. A new class of Irishman was ready to replace them, and the land war, utilizing the old
slogans against the rack-renting absentee and violence to property,
removed them.

Those landlords who insisted on staying had to be very sure of their
Irishness indeed, to sustain them through the lean times to come. In
letters and papers, one continually finds references to lack of money.
In order to make ends meet, Robert Martin took to journalism and
the theatre, and moved to London. He was frequently in Ireland for
charity concerts, where he would sing his hit songs. Now and then a
windfall would come his way – Martin writes to Edith in March 1887:
'I am pleased to say that Robert has the order for the Gaiety Autumn
Burlesque which will mean about £400.'

There are references to rents being withheld throughout the eighties in Edith's diaries; the Coghills were hit very hard by failure of rents, and the Somervilles' position was improved only after Aylmer's marriage to Emmie Sykes, who had £500 a year – hence the revival of hounds. Edith scrapes along, maintaining herself, and delighting in the odd gift of money from her godmother.

The Martins tried to live away from Ross, but in 1888 Mrs Martin and Martin returned as tenants, living in five rooms. Robert Martin joined the household with his wife and daughter, contributing £3 weekly to the carefully kept housekeeping fund. When Edith stayed there she insisted on contributing to the fund also. By June 1872, after the house had been closed and shuttered because of the death of Martin's father, rabbits would be seen running on the great steps before the main door of Ross. Since the house was built, in 1777, family, guests and petitioners had sat out after dinner and talked there until dark fell. This was a common great-house habit; Elizabeth Bowen records it happening at Bowenscourt. The Martins' disenchantment with their tenants, who had voted Nationalist in 1872, gave them a sad reluctance to trust and relate to their old tenant families, which is humanly understandable. It is as though they felt their 'people' had no more powers of memory than the rabbits on the front steps of Ross. Robert was to perturb and offend local feeling by refusing to be buried in the Martin family vault in Killanin, with attendant local mourning; he is buried, his epitaph 'Master Robert of Ross', in a plain grave at Oughterard, four miles away. He died in 1905. His only child, a daughter, Barbara Zavara, sold Ross out of the family in 1924 during the Troubles. The house was in very bad condition even at Robert's death, but is still standing today.

Clearly some landlords and tenants found the process of mutual rejection painful. Personal and family links over many generations were hard to jettison. The published and unpublished writings of Somerville and Ross, gentry as they were, are proof that they had a genuine relationship with the Irish that enabled them to appreciate, repeat and record Irish speech and wit.

CHAPTER 2

Edith When Young: Choosing a Profession

Of old, we are told, Freedom sat on the heights, well above the snow line, no doubt, and, even in 1884, she was disposed to turn a freezing eye and a cold shoulder on any young woman who had the temerity to climb in her direction.

From *Irish Memories*, 1917

Edith grew up, the eldest of eight, on terms of intimate familiarity with the children of her mother's brother, Sir Joscelyn Coghill. Living in houses whose grounds adjoined, the Coghill and Somerville children made close and lifelong bonds. Three of Edith's Coghill cousins were especially close to her.

Egerton Coghill was Edith's mentor as a painter. She followed him to his studio in Düsseldorf, and later, when he moved to Paris, she joined him there. He was of inestimable value to Edith in her fight to be allowed to study art abroad. In being the first male professional artist in the Coghill family, he was the same sort of sport as Edith amongst the Somervilles.

Egerton's brother Claude (Joe) was Edith's favourite dancing partner – with him Edith had an unusually close physical relationship. She cut his hair regularly, and he cut and dressed hers. Their dancing together was celebrated, and it was they who introduced and taught all the new dances to the neighbourhood.

Edith's constant companion and 'Twin' Ethel was the sister of Egerton and Claude. Ethel and Edith could have had some kind of literary career together had not Ethel's marriage in 1880 removed her to far-away County Waterford. Up to that time they had written plays together. Their literary efforts, and their locking themselves away from their families, who objected and wanted their company instead, pre-figure Edith's and Martin's later struggle to fight for their own working hours. Whenever Ethel and Edith escaped to write together, Edith noted in her diary, in one of her scrambled private words: 'We conflagrote.' Ten years later, with Martin, the expression would be 'we shockered', the verb being derived from the 'shilling shocker', as 'shilling light literature' was the market for which Edith and Martin at first wrote. Both 'conflagrote' and 'shockered' suggest indulgence in the

Edith photographed by Chancellor when she was a student at Alexandra College, aged seventeen.

forbidden. The disapproval of their families was a painful burden and
damper on literary ambition. Ethel Coghill's literary ambition did not
evaporate on marriage – as well as several children, she produced
several children's books, some of which Edith illustrated. *Clear as the
Noonday Sun* (London, 1893) was illustrated by Edith when she should
have been concentrating on *The Real Charlotte* – which, notwithstand-
ing this neglect, is Somerville and Ross's greatest novel.

Co-operation in artistic projects was clearly something that Somerville and Coghill children learned early and practised throughout their
lives. This was probably because such gentry families in Ireland were
often involved in public entertainments for good causes – the diaries
and letters mention dramas, public readings, orchestral concerts and
tableaux. All – down to the family dogs – took part and were thereby
conditioned. When Edith and Martin started writing together, they
employed Ethel as a critic, as they both valued her opinion, and she
received through the post at Lismore all the manuscripts of Somerville
and Ross's books, from the first chapters of *An Irish Cousin* onwards.

Biographers have paid very little attention to Edith's life as a young
woman before she met Martin, between her nineteenth year, when she
suffered an acute emotional crisis, and her twenty-eighth. And when
this crisis has been discussed – as for example by Maurice Collis, in his
Somerville and Ross: A Biography of 1968 – it has been misinterpreted.
According to Collis her crisis was adolescent and homosexual, caused
by the marriage of Ethel Coghill to James Penrose in 1880. He theorizes
that this left Edith psychologically undeveloped for the rest of her life,
searching for another female 'Twin'. It is a theory quite unsupported
by the evidence of source manuscripts. (The matter is discussed further
in Appendix 1.)

In *Irish Memories*, published in 1917, Edith was to describe 1886, the
year of her meeting with Martin, as 'the hinge of my life, the place
where my fate, and hers, turned over ...'; but far more critical for
Edith had been that other turning point in 1880, when she had rejected
marriage and turned herself into a self-supporting, single woman. On
the night of 30 November 1880, St Andrew's Day, she made in her
diary a black cross, signed her initials and wrote, 'I will paint. I will
also work.' Ethel Coghill married Jimmy Penrose on 30 December.
Edith played the organ and stayed up all the next night dancing at the
O'Donovans', coming home on the first of January. She had been
accustomed to the notion of Ethel's marriage for some months, and
although shocked when Ethel suddenly broke the news of her engagement, by September Edith was recording events in the engagement
with characteristic self-mockery: 'More talks of Ethel being married.
I mean to study the art of suicide practically, I rather incline to
chloro-form as being at once clean and picturesque if you only stiffened
yourself into a good attitude.'

Edith was notorious for a facetious gallows-humour in situations

*Sir Egerton Coghill (born 7 February 1853,
died 9 October 1921). He married
Hildegarde, sister of Edith Somerville, on 11
July 1893. Second son of Sir Joscelyn, he
chose engineering as his profession and studied
this as a Premium Apprentice at Erith
Engineering Works. When his elder brother
Nevill was killed in action 22 January 1879,
saving the colours of the South Wales
Borderers at the Zulu battle of Isandhlwana,
he became heir to the baronetcy. He then gave
up engineering for his great love, painting.
He succeeded his father as baronet in 1905.
(Picture by Boyle Somerville.)*

Egerton Coghill painting, with his fellow artist Baxter. Egerton's first studio was at Düsseldorf but later he moved to Paris, where he was a pupil of Bougereau at the Académie Julien in 1881–4. An accomplished painter, photographer and singer, he was quite without ambition. (Photograph by his father Joscelyn.) Egerton and Edith were the painters in residence of Castletownshend. They often sloped off together, through a barrage of cousinly chaff, laden with painting gear. Egerton's impulse to work was as strong as Edith's. Once, as they left yet another family party, Egerton muttered that the frivolities were meaningless – 'neither one thing or the other, like kissing your brother'. Religious observance of Sunday forbade painting on that day. On one very fine Sunday, Edith complained: 'It was Sunday and I couldn't paint. This thing will make a Jew of me. I can't stand it much longer.'

Edith, centre, and Egerton, right, in theatricals together.

where others kept a deathly hush, and even Martin was to find this
trying at times. This type of humour was well developed in Edith in
her late teens. In the month following Ethel's engagement in October
1880, her favourite dog died. Edith's diary entry is: 'Bones "the only
dog I ever loved" died – of my mother and the mange.'

Such self-mockery as her memo to study suicide 'practically' is a
sign that Edith had adjusted herself to Ethel's wedding and was able to
joke about it. It is no more serious than Edith later writing to Martin
of a coming charity bazaar:

> If it is not low to have a bazaar to build a church, I don't see
> why you should not have one to build kennels. It will be a fearful
> nuisance. Hildegarde and I stipulate for public funerals, the day
> after the bazaar. Novelty shall be led behind my bier with my
> brown boots on the saddle.

But in fact the year 1880 saw a far larger crisis in Edith's life than
Ethel's marriage. It had its origins in the Easter of 1878. At this period
in her life, her late teens, Edith was very feminine in appearance, dress
and preoccupations. A light-hearted girl, passionately fond of music
and dancing, at balls she had danced often until six in the morning.
She once danced a long-step mazurka down the long hill in Castletownshend to a waiting boat party. She was deeply involved with her
stays and with cinching her waist to a span of under twenty inches.
She had her ears pierced and wore a deal of jewellery. A photograph
of her in her seventeenth year shows Edith elaborately dressed and
coiffed, and wearing an array of jewellery that includes five rings. Her
letters dwell as much on feminine dress as do Martin's; she comments,
appalled, on a neighbour who had had her hair cut short and whom
she mistook for a man.

Edith was much in demand as a partner at dances. She was a
light-footed and elegant dancer and even men who were inarticulate
made the effort to ask her to dance with them. There is a hilarious
letter from Edith to Martin of December 1886 describing a shy boy
who stuck to Edith all night, unable to make conversation, but who
held her so tightly and close when they were dancing that Edith
thought she had the impression of his hot ear branded into her fore-
head.

She was attractive to men, and when she herself came to give her
deep, open-hearted affection to a man, her confidence (for she was
family top-dog and used to adoration and going her own way) was
badly shaken by a rejection. The experience was to alter her attitude
to men for the rest of her life. Hewitt Poole came to stay with his
uncle, Becher Fleming, at Newcourt, a house three miles west of
Skibbereen, in the spring of 1878. He was a cousin of Edith Somerville's: his great-grandmother was Judith Barbara Somerville, daughter
of Tom Somerville, the merchant. He gives a perfect example of how

Hewitt Poole in 1880.

*Hewitt Poole after his marriage to Mia
Jellett, 9 November 1880, when he was
established as a railway engineer. Hewitt was
persona non grata at Drishane after 1878,
and he never returned. This was awkward, as
his sister Lilla remained on friendly terms,
and his first cousin, also Hewitt Poole,
married Grace Somerville, daughter of Doctor
Jim, Edith's uncle. Hewitt and Edith
preserved silence on what happened between
them in 1878. On the Poole side Mia,
Hewitt's wife, believed that Hewitt had been
dismissed as an unsuitable match by Colonel
Somerville because of his poverty and lack of
prospects. Edith could never have brought
herself to cross her father, whom she adored,
and she told Hildegarde nothing then or later;
Hildegarde was a little girl in 1878, when
her sister was nineteen. The only trace of the
affair to survive on the Somerville side was
with Elizabeth, the daughter of Edith's stay-
at-home brother, Aylmer; Elizabeth was told
that Edith had experienced an unhappy affair
when young.*

a young man of no fortune, but good connections, could get on in Anglo-Ireland. He had a sketchy education, attending Bandon Grammar School no more than occasionally. He went on to study engineering at Trinity, Dublin; before his stay at Newcourt he had been rowing at Henley in a T.C.D. crew. He was a good-looking, well-built, accomplished all-rounder. He was a fine amateur watercolourist, particularly good at seascapes, a good rider and dancer, and an excellent shot. He and Edith were attracted to each other, and they sang, danced and walked 'circuitously' together.

Hewitt Poole, seated right, in his Trinity College Dublin crew at Henley Regatta, 1878.

In Dublin, studying at Trinity, Hewitt had seen a great deal of his cousin, Mia Jellett. He and Mia were double second cousins. The Jelletts objected to the possibility of a match between Hewitt and Mia on the grounds of their close relationship, and, probably a more weighty reason, on the grounds of Hewitt's lack of money. Mia's father, John Jellett, Professor of Natural Philosophy, was to be elected

Provost of Trinity in 1881. Mia was deeply in love with Hewitt, despite her family's objection, and when the news of Hewitt's flirtation with Edith reached her, she was overcome with jealousy. Hewitt became engaged to the determined Mia in 1879, and married her in 1880. Mia was never sure of the state of Hewitt's feelings during the period Easter to September in 1878, though she was to question him often. Hewitt always insisted that what had happened at Castletownshend 'meant nothing', but there are indications to the contrary.

Hewitt carefully kept Edith's invitation to a picnic at Lough Ine, done as a sketch; also tucked away in the Poole miscellanea was a carte-de-visite photograph of Edith that exists in no other collection of photographs. It was taken by Elliott and Fry in London when Edith was studying at the South Kensington School of Art in 1877. It must have been sentimentality that governed the saving of these mementos, as Hewitt would not know until ten or twelve years later that Edith would achieve fame as an author.

Edith's invitation to the Lough Ine picnic. On Monday 8 April 1878 it poured with rain and the picnic was called off. Hewitt sent Edith a consolatory poem. Further poems were exchanged. In her diary entry for the 19th she writes: 'A poem from Hewitt in answer to mine'.

During their flirtation, from 10 to 20 April 1878, Edith and Hewitt fooled about together and exchanged drawings and poems, and there is every indication that Mia Jellett was right to feel that it should be stopped before her own relationship with Hewitt was endangered. Even after their marriage, on 9 November 1880, Mia would question him on the depth of his previous feelings. As a railway engineer, Hewitt often travelled away from home, and some of his letters to Mia survive; he writes to Mia early in 1881 on the strength of his love for her: 'I suppose I need not tell *you*, who had a hold of my heart, and prevented anything else from going more than skin deep.'

After their flirtation in April, Edith and Hewitt did not see each other until September. In that month Hewitt was much in evidence at Drishane, staying the night twice. On 16 September, after an entertaining day, Edith and Hewitt went about visiting relations, then 'walked circuitously home'. Hewitt stayed overnight, and on the following day Edith enters: 'Hewitt went.' He never came to Drishane or Castletownshend again. Edith was careful to destroy or disguise any material relating to her personal feelings. Evidence of how gravely she was affected by the events of 1878 occurs in an intimate letter written to Martin Ross on 19 August 1888, which is quoted on page 41. In the 1930s, unthinking, she told Geraldine Cummins, her friend and first biographer, that at nineteen she was preoccupied with thoughts of death, and wrote a will stipulating that she was not to be buried in the family vault at Castlehaven, but to be cremated. This violently expressed wish caused a monumental row between Edith and her mother. From 1878 until 1882, the year in which Edith broke away from home to study art abroad, she had many heartbreaking rows with her mother on the subject of marriage and, more painfully, about how Edith was to support herself if she did not marry.

Edith allows no anguish to show in her diaries, though once, when the weddings of Ethel and Jim Penrose and Hewitt and Mia Jellett were almost upon her, in 1880, she wrote: 'What agony is my future position – I can only pray that I have strength of mind enough not to ...' (the entry is defaced and incomplete). An appended note to this entry for 12 June reads: 'This prayer has been intermittently granted.' Hewitt Poole was apparently the only man to whom Edith responded in a romantic way, but she herself enchanted men easily. Martin, later, was pleased to report to Edith the comments of the enchanted. Edith's earliest admirer was her cousin Herbert Greene.

At the back of Edith's diary for 1875, we find the addresses of the Anglo-Irish boys at English schools and universities to whom she wrote. They included Herbert at Harrow. Herbert had loved Edith from some date before he went up to Oxford. Sitting his entrance exams in the hall of Balliol, he completed his papers, then returned to his desk and wrote exultantly to Edith. He does not seem to have proposed to Edith until after her mishap with Hewitt Poole. That he did so frequently thereafter was common knowledge at Castletown-shend. We find Muriel Currey, a niece of Martin's, musing, in a note to her transcript of Edith's diaries at a date in the mid-nineties: 'Had Herbert given up trying to get Edith to marry him?'

Herbert and Edith rowing up river, c.1890.

Herbert Greene was a remarkable man, and Edith both admired his intelligence and was at times intimidated by it. His mother was Sylvia Coghill, sister of Adelaide, Edith's mother. A strong character, he became a Classics don at Magdalen, Oxford. He was ultra-conservative and after some years there he left for London, swearing that he would never look on Oxford again, because they had abolished compulsory Greek. When he discovered that, as an ex-don, he had dining rights at Magdalen once a year, he took to hiring a growler at Oxford station in which, with blinds pulled down, he would drive to the college in pursuit of his annual free dinner. He was known as 'The Grugger' to his pupils. He was one of the contributors to Liddell and Scott's Greek Lexicon, but despite this dry academic background he was capable, at about Christmas 1887, after years of refusals, of writing the following poem to Edith:

On a Picture: 'O'Donovan's Lake' by E. Œ. S.

So late, so late! how fast the hours are flying!
How soon the world, and we therewith, grown older,
Sink into shadow! Night winds breathing colder,
Their sad lament across the lake are sighing;
O'erhead the melancholy seabird crying
Sweeps westward, night rolls down the mountain's shoulder.
Scarce, should she come now, could mine eyes behold her,
Day dieth fast – and hope with day is dying.
O horror of great blackness grimly falling!
No moon shall cleave thy blinding folds asunder,
No star illuminate thy murky cope.
O thou that tarriest, hear my passionate calling!
But a brief space, no cry shall sound thereunder.
Still the light lingers, is there yet a hope?

Edith found it impossible to say 'No' outright to Herbert's proposals; normally direct and decisive, she contrived to be non-committal enough to keep Herbert in a state of hope until 1898. So that Edith, when Martin met her, had a faithful suitor who was publicly accepted by her parents as the 'right man'. Apart from this, Edith had the added interest of having suffered an unhappy affair. In the eighties she was often called upon to sing at parties. She sang either Nationalist songs or mournful songs of lost love. Her favourite one, which Martin came to love, was *Die Lotusblume* from Robert Franz's *Album of Lieder*:

The lotusflower repines before the glorious sun,
With sunken head and sadly
She waits till its journey be run . . .
She blooms and glows and glistens
And mutely gazes above; she sweepeth down drooping and
    trembling
With love and the grief of love,
With love and the grief of love.

This was closely followed in her affections by *Liebesglück*, by E. Geibel, which must have been peculiarly painful to Edith, who kept a stoic silence on the subject of Hewitt Poole for the rest of her life:

From far away the nightingale
Through all the valley
Her song was sending.

> We were silent we were silent
> To tell our bliss words would fail.
> The dearest thought
> Can ne'er be spoken,
> True love lies hidden in the breast . . .

From an unusually personal letter of Edith's to Martin, written on 19 August 1888, it appears that Martin was curious about Edith's disastrous nineteenth year – she had discovered that her sister Geraldine had met Edith in that year and had made inquiries. The letter also shows that Edith clearly thought, ten years after, that she had made a fool of herself:

> I am glad you have Geraldine. Give her my love, although I know I am not in the least the same woman that she thinks she met . . . Do not try and collate your edition with hers, it would not help you and I would rather you did not know how many parts of a fool I was. I daresay I am just as many now, but they are different parts. I should like to meet Geraldine again, but I would have a kind of envy and dread of that shadowy idiot of nineteen that was getting between her and me all the time. It would be a fine thing to be back there again, and to know better; but I suppose anyway, one would get there – i.e. into the wrong place – just the same? There are only a few people who know how to get just the best they can out of their time.

It may be that in confiding to Martin her pain and anguish from disappointed love Edith was able to distance herself from these feelings, which were clearly still alive in her in 1886, although deeply concealed. She was able to write a rondeau on the subject, now lost, which she sent to Martin in July 1888, which may indicate that she was released from her anguish. Martin treats the rondeau lightly and cleverly:

> I think the ideas of your first verse *awfully* good and pluckily put. The best lines in it in my opinion are the 2nd, 4th and 5th. I am not sure that the 6th explains itself easily, and the 3rd is too subservient to the rhyme exigency. It seemed to me also that 'plucked' might be better than 'picked', but I don't know. If I were you I should do this: make it a correct rondeau and re-write the second verse with some other misfortune than a thorn. That like many another true and beautiful simile has had its day I fear me, for instance 'My false love stole the rose and left the thorn with me'. But you put it very tenderly and well and I should preserve the 1st three lines of the second verse down to 'sunsets'.

Martin's comments here are among the first of such detailed and confidential exchanges on matters of expression, which was to become of vital interest to them both. They point forward to the letters exchanged when they were writing fiction in collaboration, which are full of such minutiae.

That the anguish through which she passed from 1878 to 1880 was to do with her *own* state of being married or single is shown by the way in which Edith recorded, and for the rest of her life clung to, a phrase from a countrywoman that she took down shortly after the year of weddings: 'I think I will never be married. I'd love to be an ould maid. A single life is airy.' She was still using this remark, with elaborations, in her article 'For Richer for Poorer' in 1933.

She could envisage an ideal marriage and, indeed, portrayed one in her account of her great-grandfather Charles Kendal Bushe and his wife Nancy Crampton in *An Incorruptible Irishman*; she knew how to define an ideal marriage for herself, refusing Herbert Greene's proposals for decades. She did not mean, in choosing 'a single life' for herself, that she had any notion of an ideal relationship between women, such as she had with Ethel Coghill, being a 'marriage'. Her lifelong relationship with Ethel shows us, in its continuation after 1880, that what gave Edith extreme anguish and a rigid commitment to work in November 1880 was the failure of another love, one that would have led her to marry.

Edith's personal feelings on marriage were violent. In novels, from *An Irish Cousin* (1889) to *Sarah's Youth* (1938), we find portrayed the conventions of marriage in the late nineteenth and early twentieth centuries, and the intelligent woman's reaction to them. In 'For Richer for Poorer', published in 1933, we find Edith still eloquent on the subject. In her youth and middle age she railed against the convention that parents had the absolute right to choose the most suitable husband for their daughter. Had Edith expressed the wish to marry, her mother and father, bound as much by their shortage of money as by convention, could not have allowed her to marry a poor man, however suitable he may have been otherwise. Hewitt Poole could not have been considered as a husband for Edith because of his poverty.

In 1886 Edith and Hewitt had a further series of encounters. Now married, with three children, Hewitt was an engineer on the Skibbereen to Baltimore railway extension. At a charity concert in the Town Hall they sang 'Friendship', Edith following up the duet with a solo: 'Bid Me Goodbye'. Later in the year Hewitt and some fellow engineers got up a hunt with Captain Beamish. This hunt was the pack described in Edith's letter to Martin on the Manch run (a celebrated run from Manch House, near the Bandon to Dunmanway road), later incorporated into *The Silver Fox*. Hewitt, hunting with Edith, offended her by some over-familiarity which, added to the anger and resentment she carried from their previous intimacy, hurt her again. Here Hewitt disappears from the diaries.

It is probable that, on the night of 16 September 1878, Hewitt Poole asked for the hand in marriage of Edith Somerville and was refused by

Edith Somerville photographed in Düsseldorf in 1882 when she was working in Egerton's studio there. This was the only photograph of Edith of which her mother approved. In all the rest, she declared, Edith looked 'a grinning idiot or a self-grave-digger'. Self-confidence was something that Adelaide Somerville took no pains to nurture in her daughter. When they were once sitting opposite each other at a dinner party, Edith became aware that her mother was looking daggers at her. As they left the table Adelaide told Edith that her appearance had made her long to sink under the table. Edith's hair was in disarray as usual. Her mother hissed: 'Your hair – it looks like a collection of filthy little furze bushes.'

her father on the grounds of his poverty. The character of Hewitt Poole, transparently clear in his surviving letters to his wife, makes it seem unlikely that he first flirted for fun with Edith and then became bored. More likely their marriage was forbidden by Colonel Somerville. Time and time again the novels of Somerville and Ross return to the romantic theme of an unrequited love, with a revival of feelings by a meeting between the erstwhile lovers some time after the break-up of their affair. We find the theme in *Naboth's Vineyard*, *The Real Charlotte*, *The Silver Fox* and even in short stories. 'High Tea at McKeowns', for example, gives the theme in its shortest form:

> ... when, some four or five years before, a subaltern of engineers, engaged on the Government survey of Ireland, had laid his career, plus fifty pounds per annum, and some impalpable expectations, at the feet of Muriel, the clearance effected by Sir Thomas had been that of Lieutenant Aubrey Hamilton. 'Is it marry one of my daughters to that penniless pup!' he had said to Lady Purcell, whose sympathies had, as usual, been on the side of the detrimental. 'Upon my honour, Lucy, you're a bigger fool than I thought you – and that's saying a good deal!'

This story is unusual in that Lieutenant Hamilton, who reappears in the course of the story, richer and promoted, actually recaptures Muriel. Most of the major novels leave this theme with a disastrous outcome. The most effectively described crisis of the heart is that of Francie, in *The Real Charlotte*, deserted by Hawkins for his rich heiress:

> The outflung emotion that had left her spent and humbled, came back in bitterness to her, as the tide gives back in a salt flood the fresh waters of a river, and her heart closed upon it, and bore the pain as best it might.

Always juxtaposed against the male characters who inspire sexual passion are men with whom the heroines have flirtatious friendships; sometimes the heroines marry the 'friend' rather than the 'lover', as Slaney Morris marries Major Bunbury. In *The Real Charlotte* Francie marries her old friend Roddie Lambert, who does not move her like Gerald Hawkins. Ulick Adare, of *Dan Russel the Fox*, is another example of a male friend with whom the heroine flirts. This type of man is no doubt based on Herbert Greene, who also influenced the character of Major Yeates, like him a Magdalen man, withdrawn from, yet still fascinated by, the country of his ancestors.

Hewitt married Mia just a few weeks before Ethel married Jimmy Penrose. Edith's immense strength of character and pride made of this rejection by one man, and the loss of her 'Twin' to another, a stumbling block. In an ordinary girl's life this might have been a passing mishap of adolescence, but for Edith it was a disaster that formed her into a singular woman. She did not think of marriage for herself after

this date. Even Mrs Somerville seems to have concurred with Edith
here eventually. At seventeen Edith had been given a coming-out ball
at Dunkettle, near Cork, the home of the Gubbins, who were old
friends of her parents, and up until her late twenties she seems to have
been considered marriageable by her mother. Mrs Somerville approved
of Edith's faithful suitor, Herbert Greene, and for many years must
have hoped, even as Herbert hoped.

The knowledge that Hewitt's lack of money prevented his acceptance as a suitor may have caused Edith, in a perverse reaction, to
develop her own resources and support herself financially. By the time
Martin appeared on the scene in 1886 Edith was doing well as an
illustrator, and in the previous year had produced *The Mark Twain
Birthday Book*. Having her own funds, she had begun her habit of
studying in Paris during the spring months. An unusual type of
woman, liberated and intent on a career, Edith was like nobody Martin
had met before.

*Dagnan-Bouveret, Edith's tutor at Colarossi's
in 1884. This was Edith's first term in Paris.*

It was to take two years for the idea of writing together to crystallize
in Edith's mind. She did not feel the immediate fixation that Martin
felt for her. Her fictionalized, not to say romanticized, account of their
instant recognition of each other in *Irish Memories* of 1917 is not borne
out by the letters. Edith was too busy to re-frame her life.

In the ladies' studio at Colarossi's,
February 1886.

CHAPTER 3

Martin Comes to Castletownshend

I think the final impulse towards the career of letters was given to us by a palmist. By her we were assured of much that we did, and even more that we did not aspire to (which included two husbands for me, and at least one for Martin); but in the former category was included 'literary success', and, with that we took heart and went forward.

From *Irish Memories*, 1917

Martin Ross was twenty-four in January 1886, when she came to visit her Castletownshend cousins. Her childhood and youth were lonely in that she rarely met companions of her own age. She was the last of Nanny Martin's children; her brothers and sisters were much older than she. When noticed in the family, she was treated as a pet. She was left very much to her own devices, read widely, and was trained as a pianist, rigorously, from an early age. Her father died when she was eleven – she made no sustaining connection with him. As we have seen, the Ross estate was left in dreadful disarray and debt. Mrs Martin, all other children having flown the nest, moved to Dublin, where she lived with Martin in a gloomy North Dublin house while Martin attended Alexandra College.

Although having the easy manner and address of the Martin family, Martin was reserved, and there is little evidence that anyone truly engaged her attention before she met her Castletownshend cousins. She and her mother passed their time in visiting the scattered members of the family, and Martin spasmodically occupied her mind in writing serious articles for newspapers and journals, a tradition amongst male members of the family. She was not a healthy young woman: she was subject to prostrating headaches, weakness and fainting fits. She did not eat properly, diet being a subject of no interest in her household. Martin's state of mind and health was of no concern – without exception her close relations dismissed her illnesses as 'imaginary'.

On meeting Edith Somerville, Martin, for the first time, experienced a strong voluntary attachment to another person: as her letters will show, Martin had the greatest difficulty in getting Edith's attention, for Edith Somerville, at twenty-eight, was a woman with a past, and a densely peopled and pre-occupied present.

'Standing at the top of the hill one looks down, almost directly, into the highest branches of two tall sycamores that are growing in the middle of the street, near the foot of the hill, set in a sort of giant flowerpot built of rough stones; they are always spoken of as "the two trees", and are the very heart and gossip-centre of the place' (Wheel-Tracks, 1923). Castletownshend photographed in the 1890s by Mrs Warren, wife of the Coastguard Officer.

Edith's sketches made at Pasteur's clinic in the Rue d'Ulm. She sketched patients as they waited in the street, like this study of a mother and child, and also inside the clinic, where she made this quick sketch of Pasteur (hunched over his desk) and an assistant making a list of inoculations. She had the great gift of being unobtrusive but pleasing.

When Edith Somerville went to Paris early in March 1886, it never entered her head that she would write a personal letter to Violet Martin. She did not give Martin her address. Completely absorbed by her studies at Colarossi's, the most significant work done by Edith that spring was a series of drawings that she made in Pasteur's clinic, a *coup* of which she was justly proud. She talked her way into Pasteur's presence, impressed him, and was allowed to make a study of him as well as his patients.

Determined to get all she could out of her Paris studies, Edith worked non-stop and barely had time to write to her mother. These letters were read publicly, and this was how Martin learned of Edith's doings while she was away in Paris. As soon as Edith had left, Martin wrote a long letter to her on 8 March; this was never answered, and nine weeks passed. Martin wrote again, barely suppressing an offended tone:

> My dear Edith, you know and you should blush to know that there is no reason in the world why I should write to you but there are people to whom it interests one to write irrespective of their bad qualities and behaviour – as I have heard each of your letters declaimed I have felt that I should like to make merry with you over many things therein but have been daunted by the thought of your many correspondents – you have one fatal fault, you are a 'popular girl' a sort that I have always abhorred – so bear in mind that theoretically you are in the highest degree offensive to me . . . if you were not such a popular girl I could say very nice things to you about coming home.

A silhouette of Charles Kendal Bushe by Édouard.

In the summer of 1886, after Edith's return from Paris, she and Martin started to assemble a collection of words peculiar to their families. This they titled *The Buddh Dictionary: A Dictionary of Words and Phrases in Past and Present Use among the Buddhs*. A Buddh is anyone descended from Edith's and Martin's great-grandfather, Charles Kendal Bushe, who, as Lord Chief Justice of Ireland, was a celebrated orator.

The great historian Lecky compared Charles Kendal Bushe's oratory with that of his fellows at the Irish Bar, Plunket and O'Connell: 'Bushe could address a jury with a persuasive charm that no rival could surpass, and certainly with a far purer taste than O'Connell ever displayed.' Like Richard Boyle Townshend of Castletownshend and John Townshend of Shepperton, Bushe voted against the Union with England. In the lists of members of the Irish Parliament who were approached by Castlereagh with bribes of money and titles to vote for the Union, entered by Bushe's name is the word 'incorruptible'. Bushe used his oratorical skill in his parliamentary speeches against the Union. Lecky quotes him in his *Leaders of Public Opinion in Ireland*:

> For centuries the British Parliament and nation kept you down, shackled your commerce and paralysed your exertions, despised your character and ridiculed your pretensions to any privileges, commercial or constitutional. She has never conceded a point to you which she could not avoid, nor granted a favour which was not reluctantly distilled. They have all been wrung from her like drops of blood, and you are not in possession of a single blessing (except those which you derived from God) that has not been either purchased or extorted by the virtue of your own Parliament from the illiberality of England.

After Grattan's death it was Bushe and Plunket who carried on the fight for Catholic emancipation. Edith was to write a remarkable book about Bushe, *An Incorruptible Irishman*, that gives many verbatim passages of his wit. He was, as might be expected of an orator who could speak impromptu in Parliament for more than two hours and hold his audience spellbound, a raconteur of great skill; his nick-name was 'silver-tongued Bushe'. Martin's mother spent part of her childhood at Kilmurry, in Co. Kilkenny, with Bushe and his enchanting wife Nancy Crampton. Martin, too, inherited from her mother adulation for this great man: she wrote that all who had known him 'made a fetish of his memory'.

The Buddh Dictionary celebrates the cult of the 'silver-tongue'. Edith Somerville referred to Buddh language as: 'the froth on the surface of some hundred years of the conversation of a clan of violent, inventive, Anglo-Irish people, who, generation after generation, found themselves faced with situations in which the English language failed to provide sufficient intensity, and they either snatched at alternatives from other tongues or invented them'.

Pages 50–53: *Illustrations from* The Buddh Dictionary

Absquatulate *was an intensely expressive word and much used, as at Castletownshend there were numbers of short-tempered adults and children. The preceding entry, 'arsaces', reinforces this point. Girl children were encouraged in that time-consuming and silent occupation, embroidery.*

The word **flangey** *was often applied to hats. Edith, more so than Martin, was a hat-fancier. Her favourite summer hat in the eighties was a cartwheel straw, a yard across, trimmed as the inspiration took her. Although her country hats were of the staid county-lady type, made by Heath in London, for special occasions Edith made special hats. At her niece, Katharine Coghill's, wedding in 1944, when she was eighty-six, she appeared, late and sensational, in a home-made hat, which she had swathed in green and on top perched an entire stuffed seagull.*

Grawby. *Neither Edith nor Martin particularly enjoyed the company of children. With a few exceptions, they kept their distance from them, perhaps not expecting much in the conversation line. In Castletownshend the children occupied a world remote from the adults, it seems at the adults' express desire, if the great number of words in this dictionary relating to their undesirability are serious and not chaffing.*

Edith's Studio, the **Purlieu,** *was where she spent her working life as an artist and illustrator. She was trained to professional standard in the studios of Colarossi and Délécluse. In the Paris studios it was strictly forbidden to sketch fellow students and tutors; concentration on the model was all. Edith developed a remarkable talent for rapid, sidelong sketching, of which this sketch of a fellow student is a good example. She also managed to sketch, sideways, without being caught, her tutor, Dagnan-Bouveret. This skill was to stand her in good stead in her later life, when she seems, in the to and fro of conversation, to have taken sketches at the same time as taking down speech.*

Receipt. *Relatives of the Somervilles, Coghills and Townshends were spread all over Ireland, and a lot of time was spent visiting. Extensive visiting might take a member of the family away for a month or so. Punctilious letters of thanks were written immediately on return. Edith often records in her diary the sending of a 'receipt'. Almost as inevitable as the writing of receipts was the writing to Lost Property Offices to regain luggage. Many adventures befell Edith and Martin as a result of parting company with baggage. Edith learned to travel light.*

Sassoferrara. *This sketch by Edith of her uncle, Kendal Coghill, is unusual in showing his face relaxed and tranquil. He was a very excitable and flamboyant personality and a good example of a 'Coghelian' conversationalist. Edith wrote of him in Wheel-Tracks: 'It is, indeed, hard to say which was the warmer, the Colonel's heart, or what he liked to call his "Little Tem". One might rely on both with confidence; but the hot temper was temporary, and the generous heart stood fast ... The language of everyday was too tame and hackneyed for his needs. If he sent an invitation to dinner the guest was asked "to gnaw an enemy", or "to expand a waistcoat". All girls were "sweet flowers", all males were "mere man-things". The Colonel once drove his car at speed into a group of nephews and dogs, mistaking the accelerator for the brake; the nephews escaped, but he killed one dog and injured another. He was unrepentant, roaring: "Dam' cur! Dam' cur! No harm to have one less in the place!"' As a matter of course there would be at least one 'sassoferrara' daily for the Colonel, as for his sister Adelaide Somerville, Edith's mother.*

The diverse origins of gentry families in Ireland, a rag-bag covered by the umbrella term *Anglo*-Irish, is shown by the fact that, of the families listed by Edith and Martin as users of Buddh words at Castletownshend, half did not have English origins. The Somervilles, Martins and Plunkets were Anglo-Norman families to whom England had been the merest staging-post, for one or two generations, in the near millennium of their family histories. The Coghills had a middle European descent by the marriage of Hester Coghill to Colonel Tobias

Cramer, who took the name of Coghill in the absence of male Coghill heirs. The Somerville family, based in the Scottish lowlands from 1180 to 1690, contributed some Lallans words to the Buddh language. The Greenes, a wealthy family fond of travel abroad, and the Chavasses, cousins of Edith who later lived at Seafield in Castletownshend, and once a Catholic Savoyard family, contributed foreign words.

In the summer of 1886 Herbert Greene was present on his usual summer vacation from Oxford; accepted by Edith's parents as their future son-in-law, he was blissfully unaware of any serious consequence to result from his light-hearted participation with *the girls* on their comical dictionary. There is a strong possibility that the dictionary was a deliberate parody of a serious academic lexicon, the solemn Herbert's lifelong work. They both enjoyed chaffing Herbert, and Martin was not above savage cuts at his pedantry, from which she suffered badly. 'What is Herbert writing these days, apart from errata?' she once asked Edith in a letter.

Unlike any society Martin had previously known, Castletownshend was peopled with volatile, theatrically humorous characters overflowing with physical energy that they expended on subjects as diverse as mesmerism, photography, opera and archaeology. All of this was new and startling to Martin, but before the year was out she had succumbed to the charms of Castletownshend for ever. A selection of words from the dictionary, as yet unpublished, with their definitions, will give an idea of the society in which she found herself in 1886:

Absquatulate v.i. Generally used in the imperative tense as a command to children to remove their superfluous presence. 2. To retire. (Deriv. Ab. from; squat, to sit to crouch. O.C.)

A-pers prep. après. Expression used as a reminder that the conversation is not fit for the ears of the domestic. (Fr.)

Baste, a gradual n. A slow horse.

Blaut v.i. and n. Violently to express immoderate fury.

Bosom-salad n. A vegetable structure, used for the purposes of concealment and decoration. (Deriv. Gr.)

Contraptious adj. which designates the ingenious employment of the wrong thing in the right place. (O.C.)

Crampton dash n. The extravagant imagery employed by the Buddh in excited narration. (Deriv. O.B.)

Dawny adj. Term in the Buddh pharmacopoeia expressive of a vague feebleness.

Doldromizer n. One having a foolish and stupefied demeanor. (Deriv. O.B.)

Dwam n. A heavy and half unconscious state resembling coma. (Deriv. O.C.)

Dwawmy adj. A term in the Buddh pharmacopoeia descriptive of dull and lethargic languor. (Deriv. O.C.)

Feelim A Buddh perversion. That which is found in old chests and coughers.

Flangey adj. applied to an unwieldy and incoherent arrangement of dress or headgear. (Deriv. Flange, a raised edge or flank, thence, anything which projects. Mar.)

Flop n. A lavish and unreserved depositing of the affections upon one whose reciprocity is wholly superfluous (for the most part a feminine practice) (Deriv. Mod.B.)

Gommawn n. masc. or fem. A common idiot.

Grawby n. fem. A raw, unformed child; generally a species of agile restless outlaw, the terror of the well-doing and the scourge of the domestic. (Deriv. possibly, Grub, an unfinished immature creature. O.Buddh.)

Gub n. A vague pursuing horror, the embodiment of the terror of darkness. By the superstitious it is conceived capable of inflicting unimaginable injuries. The person enduring this pursuit is said to be *gubbed*. (Deriv. Mod.B.)

Hah-me-dear! int. A triumphal cry expressive of the unworthy exultation of the Buddh over a fallen foe. (Deriv. O.C.)

Hamp n. An adored one of either sex, whose special attribute is to stimulate the adorer to unusual feats of strength or skill. (Gr.)

Hifle v.i. Denoting the energetic progress of one who has some definite object in view. (Deriv. Mar.)

Hightum n. The Sunday frock. (O.C. Hightum, Tightum and Scrub, degrees of comparison or caparison.)

Hurlo-thrumbo n. A large, unwieldy old-fashioned conveyance.

Lively Sarah n. Sal volatile. (Facetious translation.)

Medear n. Method of address – seldom implying affection. (Deriv. Buddh.)

Moy n. The unstamped envelope. (Deriv. O.C. literally 'me'. First comes me coit, then comes me petticoit, then comes me polly-doodles, and then comes moy.)

Purlieu n. A receptacle for rubbish, literary, artistic, bestial and human.

Receipt, the stamped n. The letter of polite thanks which the punctilious guest is expected to write to his late host as soon as possible after the termination of the visit. (Deriv. O.C.)

Sassoferrara n. Burst of violent abuse. A blowing-up. (Deriv. O.C.)

Schumack n. Generic name for all composers of the class of music to which the epithet drim and drew is applied. (Deriv. Compound of the names Schumann and Bach. Mrs Somerville.)

Scoops, the mother of n. Term in hymnology, applied to melodies which are dear to vocalists of the portamento school.

Shay n. The onus or responsibility entailed by bossing any show. (Deriv. possibly from the Fr. 'chez'. at home – the consequent mental wear and tear.)

Sheba n. Any new and prized possession which is calculated to excite hopeless envy in those to whom it is displayed. (Deriv. Queen Sheba's despairing resentment at the sight of King Solomon's high-class furniture. Rev. J. Bushe.)

Sink n. Either Drishane or Glen Barrahane. Varies with the person employing the term. (Deriv. the well-known capabilities possessed by these establishments for absorbing and assimilating property other than their own. Mod. B.)

Stirk n. A sudden fit of mulish and irrational obstinacy. (Deriv. O.B.)

Suburbs n. All places save those inhabited by Buddhs. (Deriv. Mrs Somerville.)

Suburbans n. All persons who are not Buddhs.

Turbulence n. A domestic disturbance. (Deriv. Col. Coghill.)

Turf boats n. Good useful boots (see Wogans). (Deriv. resemblance of the objects in question.)

Wave, the n. A phenomenon known only in Castletownshend, where, during the summer season, idle multitudes throng from house to house overwhelming or absorbing all with whom they come into contact. (Deriv. Col. Coghill.)

White-eye n. A significant and chilling glance calculated to awake the fatuous to a sense of their folly.

Wogans n. Boots (see Turf boats). (Deriv. name of maker.)

Abbreviations: O.B. = Old Buddh. O.C. = Old Coghill. Fr. = French.
Gr. = Greene. Mar. = Martin. Mod.B. = Modern Buddh. Som. = Somerville.

Theatricals in the shrubbery at Glen Barrahane. Here Claude Coghill, Egerton's younger brother and Edith's favourite dancing partner, holds his daughter Hebe upside down. Violet Coghill and Willy Plunket look on. Violet was adored by the Castletownshend young. She was a doctor, and Hebe followed her example.

Right: Sorcerer group at Bolton Hall in 1885. Edith is second from the left.

A fancy dress group, Glen Barrahane, August 1891. Edith stands (third from the right) between Ethel Coghill and Martin. Herbert, looking rather bored and out of place, is the standing, bearded man on the left. Edith and Ethel called each other 'Twin' as they were born within the same fortnight. On her birthday each year Edith crowned herself with a circlet of May blossom, perhaps because of the wondrous effect this had on her mother, who was deeply superstitious.

Many of the words in the dictionary are to be found in the Somerville and Coghill family letters. Commonly used was the splendidly expressive 'blate, blaut or blort' – Martin used it often after coming into the Drishane circle. Edith, writing to Martin at Ross, described an attempt by six of the Drishane family to leave, in a hurry, to catch a train in order to get the Bristol boat. It was discovered that there was only one car for six people, and Edith was heavily laden with artist's gear. Mrs Somerville flew into a rage:

> 'Oh I loathe and detest artists of all breeds and generations!'
> Papa with an ashen face said he wouldn't go at all. Mother kept
> up a steady flow of blort. Hildegarde, Mr Hodgson and I laughed
> until we couldn't stand. Boyle alone kept his head and despatched
> Jeremiah for Hurley's car.

Mrs Somerville's word 'Schumacks' was enlarged upon in Edith's memoir *Wheel-Tracks*:

> Cameron and I discovered a passion for playing duets –
> preferably at sight, which combined the thrills of novelty and
> difficulty – and we spent our pocket money on the classics,
> arranged for four hands, and our time in thumping them, at full
> speed, on the old Erard. My mother, rooted and bound in the
> schools of Rossini and Italian Opera, and Victorian drawing-room
> 'Pieces', detested impartially all our duets, denouncing them to us
> as 'Your Schumacks!' a term of comprehensive hatred and
> contempt, in which the names of Schumann, Schubert and Bach
> were all involved, and were – as it were – massed for convenience
> in execration.

Hildegarde, Lady Coghill, dressed as Cleopatra, c.1900. Paddy, her eldest son, attends her. Dr Violet Coghill, sister-in-law of Hildegarde, was an enthusiastic inoculator of infants and has been at work on Paddy's left arm. Hildegarde did much to dissolve Martin's shyness. Inhibited and physically restrained when she came to Castletownshend, she soon joined in the theatricals. In the picture on page 61 she is dressed in a tablecloth, which Hildegarde had arranged on her as a toga.

The Buddh Dictionary also lists phrases, the most frequently used of these being 'The pigs are out'. The definition of this phrase is: 'By this is conveyed the fact that some person is in a dangerous state of irritation or that there has been a general blowing up by those in authority (deriv. "The pigs are out and running through the pratie garden" – author unknown – from which comes the idea of aggressiveness and destructive onslaught. O.B.).' The phrase would most frequently have been applied to the fits of temper of Kendal Coghill (who referred, when calm, to his 'Little Tem.'), those of his sister Adelaide, Edith Somerville's mother, and Edith herself. Edith's mother was an extraordinarily volatile woman who deliberately engineered situations in which the pigs invariably got out. Here Edith writes to Martin about Hildegarde and herself escorting their mother back from church. Their mother insisted on walking through the garden of Glen Barrahane back to Drishane, despite the fact that it had been leased by people she did not like and did not wish to see. They crawled through the shrubbery by the house, Edith and Hildegarde getting hysterical with laughter as their mother berated them in a louder and louder voice for making so much noise: 'Hildegarde finally tumbled flat over a small fuchsia bush, driving it into the earth like a tin-tack, and nearly giving mother a fit of apoplexy from the combined effects of rage, terror and laughter.'

The dictionary gives examples of humour peculiar to Martin, Edith and Herbert when they were compiling it. Edith and Martin enjoyed a more subtle and quirky humour than Herbert. Edith wrote in *Irish Memories* of Martin's sense of humour:

Sir Joscelyn Coghill and his brother Kendal dressed as babies for a ball in August 1887. Kendal was an Indian Mutiny veteran, spiritualist and sailor. His brother, also a noted yachtsman, was the first secretary, and later President, of the Photographic Society of Ireland, founded in 1854, and a founder member of the Society for Psychical Research, founded 1882.

Wherever she was, if a thing amused her she had to laugh. I can see her in such a case, the unpredictable thing that was to touch the spot, said or done, with streaming tears, helpless, almost agonised, much as one has seen a child writhe in the tortured ecstasy of being tickled. The large conventional jest had little power over her; it was the trivial, subtle absurdity, the inversion of the expected, the sublimity getting a little above itself and failing to realise it had taken that fatal step over the border; these were the things that felled her, and laid her, wherever she might be, in ruins.

Martin enters, under Herbert's 'large, conventional jest', the definition of 'Liffé is a trifflé' which we find Edith using in a letter to Hildegarde when she and Martin were trying to write *The Real Charlotte*. They were maddened by visitors taking up their time, and one of the worst offenders was Herbert, commandeering them at all hours of the day. Herbert in his lordly way assumed, even until 1898, that he would eventually marry Edith. Edith concealed from Herbert the eruptions of fury he caused in her, but revealed them to Hildegarde:

Martin and Jimmy Penrose dressed as Greeks
for the same ball as the Coghill babies.
Jimmy was married to Edith's 'Twin' Ethel
Coghill. He was a delightful, witty man, a
great favourite with both Martin and Edith.
They dedicated A Patrick's Day Hunt *to*
him: 'To J.E.P. Professor of Embroidery, and
collector of Irish Point.'

Herbert is a great trial. He haunts the Lout Hole to smoke and read and is incessant in his demands that we go out in the boat with him – He also has formed an unreasonable hatred to the grass court, which he calls a swamp (it is in *admirable* order) and sulked all day yesterday because we had a sort of tennis function and played on it – 'liffé is no trifflé' here at present.

In becoming an habitué of Castletownshend, Martin had a great deal of adjustment to make in herself. She had to come to terms with expressive, high-spirited people who were openly affectionate, and who showed interest in and concern towards her. She herself having had a neglected childhood – her mother was a balmily benign but unconcerned woman – Adelaide Somerville's intense relationship with

all her children, particularly with her eldest child, Edith, came as a revelation to her.

A domineering, possessive woman who almost consumed her children, Adelaide was difficult to live with. Of all her children only Edith and Boyle fought free of her. When Martin came to Castletownshend the battle was in full swing between Mother and Edith. *The Buddh Dictionary* gives laconic entries relating to Adelaide. 'Medear' was often used, and unlovingly, by Mrs Somerville, and indeed many of the entries under 'M' make one wonder what it can have been like to engage in argument, or even to converse, with Edith's mother. There are comments on her mother in Edith's diary, too: 'Mother in bed with a fiendish cold, brought on by boasting.' Even in the daily running of Drishane there were opportunities for explosions: 'Mother's denunciations of beeswax as a floorpolish are worthy of the most vituperative of minor prophets.'

The Buddh Dictionary, the first work in collaboration between Somerville and Ross, is the work of young and frivolous writers, but it shows their relish of language, their determination to put down verbatim happy flights of speech. The dictionary definitions show their skill already at capturing phonetics and pronunciation – they would later use this skill cleverly to place their characters in minute gradations of social class – but on finishing the dictionary Martin and Edith were still going along on their distinct paths, Edith as a painter and illustrator and Martin as a serious journalist. On 27 March 1887 Martin composed a letter to Edith, away again in Paris, including an account of a mishap with a large harrier at Ross. She remarked 'the whole thing would make a nice little story'. She wrote it to amuse Edith (which it did –

A group photograph in August 1894. Mrs Somerville, centre left, with walking stick, looks benignly at Herbert, Edith's faithful suitor, of whom she approved. Herbert Greene is often beside Edith in group photographs. Similarly magnetized was her favourite nephew, Desmond, here sitting between Edith and Herbert. The dreadful Maria poses centre front.

she cried with laughter). It was her first expression of a type of humour that would flower in the R.M. stories, and it issued from Martin in a response to Edith.

In 1887 Edith again left early in March for Paris. It still did not occur to her to write private letters to Martin. In the first letter she wrote to Martin from Paris, on which she forgot to put her own address, she asks Martin to read it aloud to Edith's cousin Minnie, in order to save writing the same sort of general news twice. But Edith had decided that Martin should visit her in Paris, if Nannie Martin could be persuaded to allow her daughter to experience bohemian art student life.

Martin found Edith's ways exasperating:

> What makes you so awfully clever? Who but a person with a really great mind would have thought of writing from Paris and giving no address? ... As I took occasion to remark to Herbert this morning I believe your address to be Rue de l'Enfer, Quartier Latin ... Friday morning – I still continue to write in the belief that sometime or other I shall find out where you are.

Martin did get to Paris, and did not like it. Her response to the city, and Edith's society, was muted. She recoiled from the hard life of the art students, their poor food, cramped accommodation and long work-ing hours. She did not enjoy the company of Edith's fellow students – many of them American – and she was quiet and reserved during her stay. She apologized to Edith for her reserve in a letter sent from Portsmouth at the end of May, when she was visiting her sister Edith Dawson:

> I must say an artist's trade seems the pleasantest all round especially when it gives an opening to your cousin to come and improve her mind in Paris. I think I was a sort of dumb dog over there and assumed a sort of aristocratic languor all the time – so it seems on reflection – but I was inwardly full of enthusiasm and pleasure – so don't make any mistakes about that.

During the summer at Castletownshend, when Edith was absorbed in painting a landscape for Herbert, Martin responded enthusiastically when Edith suggested that they might collaborate together on a novel. The family, Adelaide and Herbert to the fore, decided that this was one of the best jokes of the summer and a period of suffering began for Martin and Edith. It did not end until the family was brought face to face with bound volumes of *An Irish Cousin*, published by Richard Bentley in his autumn list of 1889.

CHAPTER 4

Two Styles into One:
An Irish Cousin

I think the two Shockers have a very strange belief in each other, joined to a critical faculty – added to which writing together is – to me at least – one of the greatest pleasures I have. To write with you doubles the triumph and enjoyment having first halved the trouble and anxiety.

Martin to Edith, from Ross, 16 September 1889

Because the family derided their efforts and took a perverse delight in preventing them from writing, the production of *An Irish Cousin* was hard work, and hard work carried out furtively. Neither Edith nor Martin had attempted a full-length book before, but both had published short pieces. Their styles were quite individual. We can read work by Somerville and Ross that was published before they began writing together. During the eighties and nineties a wide range of flourishing magazines and journals kept up a demand for articles by talented amateurs. Martin's articles tended to serious political comment, as she was more openly disturbed by the predicament of Ireland than Edith, who worked at the light relief of cartoon-strips and comic stories.

We can appreciate Edith's eye for physical detail and broad humour in 'Mrs Maloney's Amateur Theatricals', published in *Home Chimes* on 9 May 1885; here she described Mrs Maloney, whose company is giving a performance of *Macbeth* in a small Cork town.

> . . . To see Mrs Maloney move down the main street in a sort of quiet *andante sostenuto* was in itself a musical education. She was habitually clad in a harmony of black and crimson, through which a long gold chain meandered like the theme of a fugue. A *nocturne* in black and gold bedecked her stately head (I say *nocturne* advisedly, for it certainly looked as if she slept in it), and she carried, as an insignia of office, a formidable looking roll of music.

We can see Martin's capacity for abstraction and moralizing and her impressionistic descriptive power in an article like her 'Cheops in Connemara' (*The World*, 16 October 1889); this is an account of a visit to a newly built National School, solitary in a vast tract of bog, where

Edith and Martin at work in the Studio.
(Photograph by Hildegarde.)

Martin heard the children recite, incongruously, the king-lists of Ancient Egypt.

> Education is a fine word; a word charged with respectable
> associations. Whether pronounced as here written, or in its other
> varieties of ejjication or eddication, its weightiness is felt to be
> very great, even if it is variously comprehended; indeed it has in
> this respect a position somewhat more assured than religion.
> Coupled with the word national, it has been much and skilfully
> bandied about the pages of reviews, with a sound as of the
> heaviest artillery, wonderfully in contrast to the docile lispings or
> tearful whinings of the daily task, whose present or future purport
> is what all this noise is about.

The merging of their styles was, on the whole, a lasting success.
Only once did a reviewer make a sharp comment that makes us realize
what adroit adaptation to each other Somerville and Ross made in
combining their styles. Writing of the R.M. story 'Harringtons' the
reviewer remarked that he was put in mind of the outcome of a
collision between a funny story on a bicycle and a ghost story on a
train. The child of Ross and the child of Drishane had different con-
ditioning. The intellectual tone of the two houses was very different.
Literary taste in Drishane was in general robust and Dickensian –
discussions flared into loud arguments and often worse, full-blown
family rows. The Somervilles were omnivorous and speedy readers.
The Heavenly Twins by Sarah Grand (1893) was eagerly consumed.
Edith entered in her diary: 'All here reading Heavenly Twins – much
controversy.' The book deals with venereal disease, sex-role exchange
between sister and brother, and women's rights – subjects not mentioned at Ross. To be in Drishane drawing room after dinner and be
part of such free discussion was new to Martin and must have been, at
first, shocking.

At Ross on the other hand there was a quiet appreciation of the
Classics, Shakespeare, Milton, Scott and lyric poetry; it was a stu-
diously bookish house where reading was a private occupation. In the
peace and calm of Ross, Martin received a letter from Edith sent from
Drishane on 15 January 1891:

> Improbable though it may seem I am going to try to write to
> you after dinner. The family are immersed in their books, and
> you may judge of my devotion to your interests when I tell you
> that I have plucked myself from the depths of a new American
> novel to write to you ... (now they are all talking *and talking of
> books*, so you may imagine the row) ⋀⋀⋀⋀ this
> expresses my feelings of fury, I can hardly think.

Edith managed to stagger distractedly through another page of letter
but had to stop:

I am finishing in bed at 11.30; after a fiery argument; the Chimp on one hand, and Mother and I on the other re Richard Jefferies. I was longing for you to be there, though you would have been deafened. Mother and I, from totally different points of view, held the same opinion, while the Chimp talked rot about Nature. I made him produce *The Elegy*, and read to him some of our champion bits of twaddle, however he was as undefeated at the end of the row as we were, and poor Hildegarde nearly mad with fury as she was trying to finish a very interesting, pathetic and religious novel called 'Gloria' (translated from Spanish) and couldn't get forrad with it for the clanging of the heronry.

Things were much quieter at Ross. Most nights, after dinner, Martin and Mama sat alone by the fire. In an undated fragment of a letter to Edith written after dinner Martin included a description of her mother as she sat beside her:

Mama is very delightful in her reading of 'the face of the waters' – she turns a page, and in turning becomes apparently overwhelmed by the greatness of the world, lays the book in her lap and casts a gaze of passionate abstraction on the ceiling – she resumes the book, on the far page, skipping one completely. She is suddenly fascinated – glues her nose to the next turn over, reads two pages like the wind – then the fragrance of the pine (that Mat has hewn for the fire) becomes too much for her – and empress-like meditation falls upon her. It may end in sleep as sudden as everything else – but she is enjoying herself and the book very much.

Just before Edith and Martin began to write their 'Shocker', as it was disparagingly termed by the family, Martin had her hand read by a palmist. She preserved the reading at the back of her diary, with her own comments. The reading gives an uncanny insight into her constitution – she is physically weak and lacking in stamina after periods of prostration, yet about to be galvanized into writing a fine novel. Martin's careful preservation of this reading, and her comments on it, would seem to indicate that she was in some agreement with the analysis.

Monday, October 3rd 1887
Line of affection shows great warmth of affection – extreme fidelity but not much passion. Will have many friends and will be trusted by both men and women [Martin comments at the side 'interesting – scarcely human'] . . . is proud – naturally low spirited rather than high. Delights in theatres. Tragedy more especially. Has large reverence. A good deal of superstition – a little credulity. An immense amount of conscientiousness. A tendency to bother about trifles. Likes her own way. Delight in

planning and organising – but very often fails to carry out her plans. A little apt to take her colouring from her surroundings, is sensitive and sympathetic – is a most delightful companion on account of a certain amount of adaptability . . . Great deal of tact. Is more of an idealist than a realist, not enough brain power or physical strength to carry out her aspirations – ought to make money by her own exertions. Is given to castle-building and dreaming. Is irritable, not excitable. Has a great dislike to hurting other people's feelings.

It is subject for amazement that two minds so perfectly fitted to each other, and genetically related, should have been housed in bodies whose individual styles were so very different. Edith had difficulty, like the Old Loony of Lyne, in being 'all there at a time'; ceaselessly, multifariously, active, she seems to have found peaceful repose impossible, even in her childhood. Constance Bushe, one of her Coghill cousins, determined to draw a portrait of small Edith, had eventually to draw her asleep, by candlelight. It tells us much of Edith's strength that she woke, because of the candlelight near her eyes, and calmly realizing it was Constance, slept again.

Two studies of Edith Somerville by Constance Bushe. When Edith was a small child in 1862–4, between her fourth and sixth years, her mother was distracted first by the birth of Cameron in 1860, then by the birth of Joscelyn, a sickly child, who died at the age of two in 1864. Boyle was born in 1863. Adelaide Somerville preferred her male children and frankly flirted with them, but with her daughters, particularly her eldest and most original child, she was awkward and cruelly thoughtless. Edith spent a great deal of time, to the extent of having a bed there, in the Bushe Rectory, where Constance gave her care and guidance in drawing and painting. The distance between Edith and her mother never lessened, but they were mutually fascinated and could not do without each other's company despite their frequent rows.

The forbidding face of Constance Bushe, of whom Edith wrote: 'Constance was one of the elect in whom is felt to be ... genius ... it lighted her eyes; one felt it in the richness of her laugh, and knew it in the comprehension of her sympathy. Her face, fragile and delicate as it was, none the less brought to mind, in the strong characterization of the features, the stern profile of Savonarola, but etherialized, and in an instant transformed to sweetness by her smile.'

Her adult taste in clothes was influenced by what was tough, practicable and hard-wearing. She tended to fling on what came to hand, carelessly. Once, having mislaid her habit coat, Edith took off for a day's hunting in Ethel Coghill's coat. Edith was full-breasted and largely made. Ethel was not. Undeterred and thoughtless, Edith rushed off. She came back half a day later with warped ribs and congested lungs, in agony, but having ridden her hunt. She liked dressing for dinner and being grand for short periods, preferring dark reds or greens in heavy velvets for her evening dresses.

Most memories of Edith come to us from people who were young when she was middle-aged or older, when she had lost her bodily suppleness and speed. But her contemporary, Maurice Townshend, of the Castle, recorded her extraordinary walk. She had a springing, jaunty walk, often placing her hands on her hips. She gestured a lot, and also had the mannerism, which she kept to the end of her life, of tossing her head and turning it to one side during converse. Edith presented the figure of a person of intense physical energy, with a chaffing, jibbing speed of mental response that illuminated her face and changed its aspect. Both concealed deep shyness and reserve, but in different ways: Edith with extrovert humour and bonhommie, Martin with sympathetic charm.

Photographs of Edith, though momentarily neat and tidy, mostly fail to capture her charm. Her mother mourned over the 'self-grave-digger' that Edith seemed deliberately to aim at the camera. One or two photographs capture her relaxed or amused. Hildegarde caught her completely at ease in a photograph that shows Edith's uncontrollable hair, complicit in her general waywardness. It was long and bound up at the back as was all ladies' hair at that time; but it was cloudy, straying, and a bane to Edith at all times.

Edith, writing to Martin of a hunt where her horse had taken her at speed through a thorn brake, wrote: 'All my hair was dragged down and I was nearly mad.' There is much of Edith in that emancipated lady horse-coper, Miss Bobby Bennett, of the R.M. stories. Trapped in an awkward situation with Major Yeates when all her hair had been unpinned in the heat of the chase, she exclaimed: 'I declare to goodness I wish I was bald!'

Martin revelled in grand dress, and the trappings of ladydom. She had presence, grandeur, a patrician bearing. Smooth, calm, graceful movements were bred into her from birth; pleasantness and good manners in attending to people of all ranks, gentle voice and demeanour were ingrained. She had a fineness of bone, hair and skin that impressed all who saw her. Despite what was in fact an odd, eccentric face she utterly charmed both men and women by force of habit. Edith, when she did charm, charmed by unusual force of personality.

We see the contrast between the two in this diary entry, made by Edith when she was in London working at life-drawing on 28 April

Left: *A Somerville family group, c.1890. Edith sits at her mother's right. Her face shows the self-grave-digger look, an expression Adelaide brought on in Edith by a 'blort' of domination over her. From the left: Hugh, Edith, Cameron, Adelaide, Aylmer, Hildegarde, Henry.*

Below: *Hildegarde's study of Edith, 1894.*

1893: 'Hot studio. Woman. Did better and Mr Loudon told me so. First commendation on record – my record at least. Martin flaunted down in green silk attire and had tea in the dirt with the studio ladies.'

Edith always worked at speed, tossing off mounds of paper in sketch and note. She evolved a sort of compost-heap system of creativity, surrounded, in her studio, by maturing heaps of material. Martin worked slowly and neatly. She tended to know where things were, once done. Not for nothing did Edith appear in *The Buddh Dictionary* as 'The Queen of Filth', and not for nothing was she known affectionately to her cousin Fanny Currey by the name of 'Slummy'.

We can track the two personalities in their manuscripts, Edith forging on, covering reams as fast and heedless as talk; then Martin comes with spidery, hatching deletions, minuscule insertions, long lines leading to a space in the margin where she re-writes a paragraph.

Detail from a group photograph of 1890 showing Edith and Martin in 'hightum, tightum and scrub'. Edith is top left, Martin top centre.

Edith and Martin had some difficulty in fixing upon a trade name for their literary firm. At first, because Adelaide Somerville objected so strongly to her daughter's profession and to the family name being used for 'trading' purposes, Edith agreed to hide her identity under the name of an ancestor – Geilles Herring. But after a few painful instances of being referred to as a Grilled Herring, she changed to Viva Graham (which name the second edition of *An Irish Cousin* bears instead of Somerville) and finally, by the time of their second novel, *Naboth's Vineyard*, she overcame her mother's opposition and used her own E. Œ. Somerville.

Martin had much less trouble in arriving at her pen name. Being Violet Florence Martin of Ross she was pleased to use her own surname as her Christian name, as she was very proud of her family. There was nothing at all unusual in women using their surnames as their familiar

names. Edith's friends in the Paris studios give us some extraordinary
examples: Fräulein von Poncet was known as 'Ponce', Miss Kincardine
O'Neill as 'Kinkie' – the problem of duplication of Christian names
encouraged such adjustments. In Castletownshend there were already
two well-established Violets before Martin's arrival. Martin's own favourite sister Edith (Dawson) is called Edith throughout her papers;
Edith Somerville, as a signal of Martin's esteem for her, features as
'E.Œ.S.'.

In a letter written after the publication of *An Irish Cousin* in 1889,
Edith refuses to write with Martin again if it is going to kill her. A fit
of exhaustion had caused Martin to collapse after the book's comple-
tion. For Edith writing was only one of a number of possible ways of
making a living – she could have lived by her art, and developed these
talents rather than her literary ones. But for Martin writing with Edith
was her fulfilment. Without Edith she would not have been able to
sustain the creation of a full-length novel. She would not have flowered
so profusely, though she would surely have enjoyed a temporary vogue
as a superb writer of short 'pieces'.

Many of Martin's letters show that without Edith she was incapable
of long-sustained effort. Her frequent neuralgic headaches and collapses
were followed by long periods of inertia and her creativity was always
in flux. She never learnt Edith's clever system of rotation of activities,
so that no moment lay fallow:

> The headache was bad, this morning it is lying in wait
> somewhat stretching mesmeric claws at me but not grabbing so
> far and I have the most romantic delicate fatigue, and inability to
> get up so here I stay.

Tired of trying to organize Ross, Martin fell into a depression in
the middle of August 1889:

> At present I think of nothing but the atrocities of bad servants
> and the knaveishness of hangers-on and I feel a profound and
> paralysing depression on these subjects. I feel tired of the whole
> show and find the machinery of life more trouble than it is worth.

The combination of Edith's generosity and tendency to exalt Martin
after her death, with what Ethel Smyth called her 'almost insane
diffidence', has obscured the fact that Edith was the major partner in
their writing together. Fortunately many passages in Martin's letters to
Edith survive to show that Edith, in her published memories of their
work, diminished her own part. As an instance of Edith's blithe re-
writing of history we have her description, in *Irish Memories*, of the
writing of their first book, *An Irish Cousin*, where she claims that the
inspiration to write the novel came from a visit that they made *together*
to the old Townshend house, Whitehall. Here is Martin's letter to

Edith of 21 August 1889, just after the book's publication and its warm reception by most critics:

> I seem to remember very much the first beginnings of the Shocker just now – when I was humping over the Dumpy [i.e. huddled at the studio stove] and you were mucking with paints at the window you told me of the old maniacs face at the window over the Whitehall door – and remember you were the person who suggested we should try to write together a shocker or a story of sorts on that foundation – and you also were the person who lifted us through the first chapters – but no matter – we little thought that I, at Ross, should take *The World* with a view to seeing my own writing in it, and should see the Shocker in large type heading Bentley's list therein.

Again, in *Irish Memories*, Edith had a shortage of material relating to 1886: the working partnership did not begin until the summer of 1887, but Edith wished to idealize. She 'borrowed' a sentence of Martin's and applied it to 1886. The result was: '... in those August nights ... when, as Martin has said, "Land and sea lay in rapt accord, and the breast of the brimming tide was laid to the breast of the cliff, with a low and broken voice of joy."' Edith pirated this sentence from an essay of Martin's about Aran published in 1906 in *Some Irish Yesterdays*. Edith could not have foreseen that Maurice Collis, accepting Martin's words as relating to Castletownshend and 1886 instead of Aran many years later, would comment: 'In these words Martin gave utterance to the intensity of their dawning love.'

Martin was perfectly honest with Edith about her own deficiencies; it is Edith who has edited them away from the general reader. After a particularly good review of *An Irish Cousin*, Martin writes to Edith: 'You *shall* write another story with me or without me it would be too bad to let go such an opening as we now have, and I am not man enough for a story by myself.' Working hell-for-leather on a series of articles for a set date, Martin writes, in 1891: 'It you didn't insist on my co-operation I shouldn't be surprised at you writing the whole set in the fortnight but if you are dependent on me then the chances are not good.'

Martin, before her meeting with Edith, had developed a wordy, over-wrought, Carlylean style that Edith was not in the least shy of criticizing. Martin learnt much from Edith's pithy, smooth style; her adaptation of it lifted her into the realms of superlative writing. That Martin absorbed a great deal from Edith is as apparent as her absorbing the characteristics of Edith's handwriting, so that their hands were to become, at times, difficult to tell apart. Here is Edith criticizing the style of one of Martin's newspaper articles, sent for approval when finished:

What struck me when I read it first was a certain tightness, and want of ideas being expanded – It read too strong. Like over-strong tea. It felt a little crowded and compressed in style, and *perhaps* now and then – (that *I* should say it to you) – a superfluously ingenious adjective – entirely expressive and well applied but still its very ingenuity tending to load the sense and task the readers strength of appreciation.

Again Edith finds a splendid way to phrase her objection to a single sentence that Martin had written: 'The sentence seems to me thick and awkward.' Here is a key to Edith's writing system: she read out loud, and felt the sound of her sentences – she never wrote a 'thick' sentence. The writing style of the R.M. stories, speeding the reader on at break-neck pace, is a tribute to Edith's pared-down, streamlined sense of what fits a particular place in a sentence. In her later writing, where Edith, writing alone, produces embarrassing, purple, romantic passages, we may be fairly sure that this is the result of her not reading aloud, of no longer speaking the sentences, as she and Martin did, before writing them down.

Edith seems to have thought, quite seriously, that her writing was a very poor relation of Martin's, a workaday thing. Here she writes of changes she is making in some passages that Martin had sent down from Ross: 'I think the latter is very good and if I water it down here and there where the going strikes me as being rather heavy I hope you won't mind. I shan't improve it, but I shall make it more meet for the intellect of fools.'

If the *Experiences of an Irish R.M.* give us the perfect stamp of Edith's mind, *The Real Charlotte* and *The Silver Fox* give us Martin's; in writing they could lose themselves in each other, and do not seem to have been conscious at the time of who was leading. Pressed often in her later life to explain how two people could write together, Edith is recorded (in the interview with a reporter from *The Minute* in 1895) as saying, breezily, that it was just like paint – there was yellow and there was blue, and if you mixed them together, there was green. She said that their separate blue and yellow styles were distinct, but the green was a style also and more than the two styles apart.

First editions of Somerville and Ross books, given to or bought by relations, tend to have lists on the flyleaves, or bookmarks, identifying the fictional characters with their models. At Drishane, Glen Barra-hane, Ross and the Castle, the inhabitants would pounce on new books and race through them, identifying features and traits of character.

In a passage in *Irish Memories*, Edith gives some idea of how their fictional characters were assembled: 'We sat on the sandhills ... and talked, until we had talked Major Sinclair Yeates, R.M., and Flurry Knox into existence. *Great Uncle MacCarthy's Ghost* and the adventure of the stolen foxes followed, as it were, of necessity.'

A photograph taken to illustrate the Minute *interview.*

Edith and Martin claimed to have drawn only three human characters direct from life, Lady Dysart from Edith's mother, Charlotte Mullen from Emily Herbert and Slipper from 'Pack', a local man. But
many more of their characters mingle quite recognizable portions of
people known to the Castletownshend and Ross circles. They made
their characters rather as Martin said she made use of leftovers: 'Sent
to heaven in a curry, as in a chariot of fire.'

Mrs Somerville hotly objected to Willy, of *An Irish Cousin*, as
merely a 'vulgar Aylmer', Aylmer being her favourite, spoilt, son. The
diaries and letters, particularly Edith's to Hildegarde, are crammed
with raw, uninhibited characters, later to reappear, curried, as it were,
and preserved in immortal stories. Martin's awareness of the real-life

grounding of their fiction is shown clearly in this letter of 18 May
1889, which again uses a cooking metaphor: 'Let us take Carbery and
grind its bones to make our bread – Cut, my dear! It would be new
life to me to cut it – and we will serve it up to the spectator so that its
mother wouldn't know it!' Relatives who felt uneasy at encountering
themselves in some fiction of Edith's and Martin's had good reason. In
a letter of 20 May 1889, Martin writes to Edith: 'We now regard all
our most cherished relatives through (or shall we say athwart) a web
of sensationalism and countings of foolscap.'

Although Edith had published a few comic prose pieces before
meeting Martin, her connections in London journalism were on the
graphic and illustrative side. Her own 'special conquest', as Martin
called him, was Mr Williamson, a sub-editor on *Black and White* who
placed many of Edith's comic-strip stories. Edith's contacts, though
useful to her as an illustrator, were of no use when Edith and Martin
put their first novel before the public in 1889.

The Martin family commanded a network of excellent literary connections built up by Martin's father and her brother Robert, who, as
we have seen, was a celebrated song-writer and journalist. His best-
known song was called *Ballyhooley* – a name that Robert used to sign
his articles. When *An Irish Cousin* received its first reviews, opening
paragraphs invariably mentioned that Miss Martin was the sister of the
celebrated Ballyhooley, Robert Martin; Somerville and Ross slipped
into public notice on his coat-tails. Foremost among the Martin literary
connections, from Edith and Martin's point of view, was Edmund
Yates (1831–94), who was a novelist writing 'shilling shockers' until
becoming a full-time journalist. His best-selling novel was *Broken to
Harness: A Novel of English Domestic Life* (1864). He was acting editor
of *Temple Bar*, working with Mary Braddon, the author of the best-
selling sensational novel *Lady Audley's Secret*. In 1874 Yates founded
The World: A Journal for Men and Women, on the staff of which were
Miss Braddon, Mrs Lynn Linton and Wilkie Collins. He was keen on
employing women, and Edith and Martin were fortunate to find
favour with him at the outset of their career.

Martin began to write for *The World* in 1888. The journal paid
well, and both Edith and Martin appreciated Yates's good financial
terms and his help in reviewing *An Irish Cousin*. In the spring of 1888
Edith was scraping around for funds as usual and wrote to Martin: 'I
am trying to heap up riches to go to Paris . . . will you come with me?
Now that you have got your fangs into Edmund perhaps you will be
able to manage it.'

Financial solvency for them both depended on publicity – and publicity was what Martin, string-puller supreme, gave to the partnership.
She fixed reviews of *An Irish Cousin* in all the major papers. Her aim
was business-like and mercenary – in a letter of 4 September 1889 she
discusses with Edith a rather low offer made by a publisher:

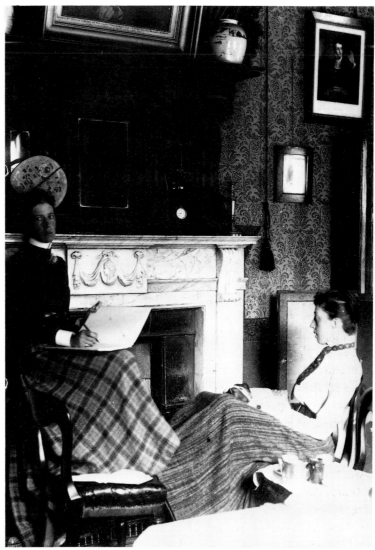

Edith and Martin working in the dining room, Drishane, May 1894. Egerton, at the camera, slipped a plate in when he was setting up his tripod, or dismantling it, and took an unposed photograph (above) as well as a posed one. The unposed photograph is unusual in showing Martin with pince-nez; Edith has tossed her head and blurred the image of her face. Dot has moved to her rightful place. Martin has put her feet up. In the eighties and nineties Edith favoured an artist's floppy tied bow at the neck in soft wide ribbon. Martin more often wore ties, as she is doing here. Edith is wearing a Victorian patent form of detachable cuff and collar which, daily changed, gave an erroneous impression of entire cleanliness in clothing.

I send you back Mr Langbridge's letter. I think a little more money might be skirmished out of him ... If he would say £20 down, it would be well worth it. I should not seem too keen about it, as it is certainly not a brilliant offer. Those two extra fivers seem remote. At the same time we might be very glad even of the £15 by the time we got it – I know *I* should – and I should much enjoy writing with you if it could be managed. A few more high class reviews might make him raise his price.

An Irish Cousin had just received a very laudatory review in the *Athenaeum*, followed by others in the *Spectator*, *The Times*, the *Observer* and the *Saturday Review*. As their reputation rose, so did their rates of pay.

Edith and Martin in Paris in 1894, recuperating after The Real Charlotte. *Edith treated herself to a course of study at Délécluse's academy, and both revised their wardrobes.*

Martin's letters reveal exactly how the reviews of *An Irish Cousin* were precipitated. On 21 August Martin wrote to Edith: 'I am afraid this is a baddish time for books to come out, but we must make up for that by energy. What about Egerton's man on the *Saturday Review*? I incensed Edith about Willie Wilde and Desart (*Daily Telegraph*) and must concoct a discreet line to Edmund Yates.' Her next letter of the 24th has: 'Molly Helps has been very kind about it [*An Irish Cousin*] – and said at once that she would write to Charlie Graves, who reviews the light literature for the *Spectator*, to give us a good word. Furthermore she said that she would recommend an article of mine to the Editor of the *Spectator* – who is a personal friend of hers.' The efficacy of this type of connection was impressive: Molly Helps contacted Charlie Graves in mid-August and he obtained the book for himself. His review in the *Spectator* appeared on 14 September!

Martin had a sales representative's grasp of the more mundane outlets of the book trade. The same letter, of the 24th, mentions her efforts to have *An Irish Cousin* stocked by the Free Libraries that had been endowed by Andrew Carnegie, the Scots/American philanthropist:

> I said in a letter to Robert that I relied on Carnegie – I said well – today I heard from him 'we subscribe tomorrow and will ask him for your book, which we feel satisfied must be good'. We will also recommend Eason and Son to get it, and have ordered a copy for ourselves from Messrs Hodges and Smith. Katie [Martin's sister] and I have always agreed that we would rather marry Carnegie than anyone we know. Were we not right? I shall send

him six advertisement leaflets . . . I wrote the best letter I could to Edmund Yates today – indeed I write letters all the time . . . I should make Aylmer ask for it at every underground station if I were you.

Had Martin not been related to such an influential circle it is likely that their career would have died at birth. On all sides cousins rallied to spread the 'good word'. On 28 August Martin wrote: 'Mama had a most kind letter from Gregory. He has much literary influence – or rather many literary friends, and so has Augusta – he says they will both do their best for it.' At this stage the Gregorys' house, Coole Park, had not been taken by the Irish Celtic Renaissance, and literary taste there had not yet narrowed to the heroic past.

Martin's aptitude as an agent made up for a severe deficiency in Edith, who had no talent at all for financial matters and taking advantage. The excellent reception of *An Irish Cousin* was due to Martin's efforts, as Edith acknowledged, and indeed Martin stated: 'You will agree that I have done some work among the editors and made them toe the mark in style.'

They were established as writers, and their second novel, *Naboth's Vineyard*, of 1891, was as well received as their first. Reviewers praised their rendering of dialogue and their pictorial gifts. Capitalizing on this, Somerville and Ross contracted to make a series of tours for the *Lady's Pictorial*, beginning with *Through Connemara in a Governess Cart*, of 1892, for, unlike novels, journalism could provide them with a certain income.

The sextoness's mother. A quick drawing from a photograph. Edith was grateful for photography as an extension to her art. She incorporated it and used it freely as a source.

The drawings on this and the next two pages illustrate a riding tour through Wales, described in Beggars on Horseback (1895), with an ascent of Snowdon, on foot and with a native guide: 'The ascent began as seductively as the first step towards a great crime.' It rained a lot and they had to buy umbrellas to keep dry while riding. Edith thought of another solution: in a general store in Bethesda she was captivated by the tarpaulin cloaks that the quarrymen wore and was about to purchase one under Martin's horrified gaze (nothing more unfashionable could be imagined) when Edith decided that the crackling sound of the stiff cloak might startle the horses and desisted.

Left: *Two line drawings showing the 'Tommies', their hack hired horses, en route.*

Right: *Martin with a newly bought Welsh umbrella.*

Far left: *The ascent of Snowdon begins.*

Above: *Riding through the rain.*

1 *The Reverend Paley Dabble disapproves of Chiromancy and buys a book on the subject that he may the more effectively denounce its fallacious tenets.*

2 *He feels bound to study the work conscientiously, and cannot help being struck by the fact that his hand coincides with the definition of 'The Psychic Hand' (the Psychic Hand is described as characterising only the highest order of human being).*

3 *He begins to think there is something in it; and his original disapproval is converted to enthusiastic belief as he discovers clearly marked on the Line of the Heart evidence of a deep and lasting passion.*

4 *He applies himself to the science with all the enthusiasm of a Neophyte. (N.B. - But we may suspect an ulterior motive.)*

5 *The ulterior motive.*

6 *He takes the earliest opportunity of going to see Her, with a view to utilising his recently acquired knowledge.*

CHAPTER 5

'I Will Work':
Edith as an Illustrator

I was making drawings for the *Graphic* in those days, and was in the habit of impounding my young friends as models. My then Studio – better known as 'The Purlieu', because my mother, inveighing against its extreme disorder, had compared it to 'the revolting purlieu of some disgusting town' – (I have said she did not spare emphasis) – was a meeting place for the unemployed, I may say the unemployable, even although I could occasionally wring a pose from one of them.

Edith, writing of the late eighties in *Irish Memories*, 1917

We are fortunate in the amount of visual record that remains of the heyday of Somerville and Ross, the nineties and the early years of this century. Those specially made skirts of Edith's, with the deep, baggy pockets littered with sugar for the horses and biscuits for the dogs, held also the little flat notebooks, one for sketches, one for speech, that she used automatically throughout her life. Her speed as a recorder of speech and of scene and character was worthy of a crack Victorian reporter. Thousands of her drawings are extant, and many of her paintings. A lot of her work was scattered over County Cork via jumble sales, to which she would contribute drawings and paintings on request.

Opposite, below and overleaf:
'Chiromancy and Its Consequences', from the Graphic, *8 January 1887, with Martin as a model.*

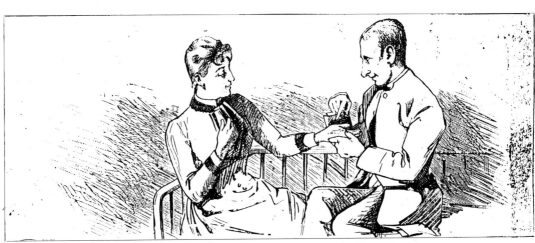

7 *With a throb of delicious certainty he finds in her hand a line he hardly dares to expect – 'Union with a Clergyman'.*

There are also photographs. Sir Joscelyn Coghill was the first photographer in County Cork, and his son Egerton was also a gifted photographer; more surprisingly, so was Martin Ross. Martin's eyesight was very bad, but she had an uncanny sense of visual design and composition. We are lucky that so many of the photographs have survived, as the indoor games were violent and destructive. A card game called 'Animal Grab' resulted in broken furniture, and Edith's diary entry reads: 'Lotty [later Mrs George Bernard Shaw] and Hewitt and I played "grab" after dinner, am still quivering from the effects.' So it is with horror one reads: 'Boyle and I have invented a lovely new game called "go-old-photograph book". It is played by 2 or 4 persons and consists in catching the leaf of an album on your fingers and fist in various ways.'

Edith worked hard at her art, and we may trace to her this sentence given to Christopher Dysart in *The Real Charlotte*:

> Half the people in the world were clever nowadays he said to
> himself with indolent irritation, but genius was another affair; and
> having torn up his latest efforts in water colour and verse, he
> bought a camera, and betook himself to the more attainable
> perfection of photography.

Edith's professionalism was absolute, even in her teens, when she began to sell her drawings to a card manufacturer called Page. Her

8 *Shall he lose any time in pointing out to her the obvious method of fulfilling her destiny?*

9 *No! With the eloquence of conviction he unfolds to her the decrees of Fate. But when he implores her to join her line of life with his, he is met by the horrid intelligence that, though correct in the main, his divinations have failed in one important particular. She is already engaged to –*

10 *His Rector.*

lettering, binding designs and illustrations for the Somerville and Ross books, marked up in pale blue pencil, are meticulously presented and finished.

She was often irritated by the imperfections of her work; Ethel Smyth noticed this even in the 1920s, when Edith was in her sixties. Edith comments in her diary in 1883, when she was painting a commissioned work: 'It looks like a feeble copy of a feeble copyist of Du Maurier.' Edith had a thorough training, and was well versed in the techniques of critical appreciation. She began her studies at the South Kensington School in 1877, at eighteen; she later studied at Düsseldorf, where her cousin Egerton had a studio, and at Colarossi's Studio in Paris. Edith admired the work of Egerton Coghill, and that of her cousin Rose Barton, but the painter she felt closest to was a now forgotten Royal Academician called Priestman. In a letter to Geraldine Cummins, Edith wrote that Priestman was 'the only painter to put on paint as I did'. She particularly admired his landscapes. 'I was always attracted to his paintings at the Academy – we never met.' Edith's successful landscapes are vigorously painted, with bold broad brushstrokes. She told Geraldine Cummins: 'I was taught in Paris that it was the first impression that mattered – paint rapidly so as to keep it fresh.'

Her training abroad stood her in good stead through her life. In Düsseldorf and Paris, where her tutors were Dagnan-Bouveret and Collin, she absorbed *pleinairism* and the use of a certain range of colours and a system of broad brushwork in underpainting from which she did not depart. Her dedication and self-absorption when studying art in her twenties were so extreme that she happily lived a daily life that Martin found appalling, and in some ways disgusting, when she tried to share Edith's life on visits to Paris. As Edith could stay longer in Paris the further she stretched her money, she lived as cheaply as possible. The hurried, poor meals, the fried potatoes bought from street sellers and eaten *en route*, the cramped, airless quarters and the foul coffee all revolted Martin. Installed at their easels by eight in the morning, students worked through to evening classes with a few short breaks. Martin could not understand their self-absorption and complete lack of interest in the outside world. For many of these students, particularly the women, like Sarah Purser (who was to become one of Dublin's most successful artists), the studio days in Paris were hard-won and lived through in a state near poverty, in order to gain a training that would fit them as drawing and painting teachers, 'Paris trained', and enable them to earn their livings and independence. Edith wrote:

> Colarossi's never took 'a day off'. Weekdays, Sundays, and holy days, the studios were open, and there were élèves at work. Impossible to imagine what has become of them, all those strange half-sophisticated savages, diligently polishing their single weapon, to which all else had been sacrificed.

All the Reverend Paley Dabble's original approval of the Black Art reasserts its sway. culminating Act of Repudiation.

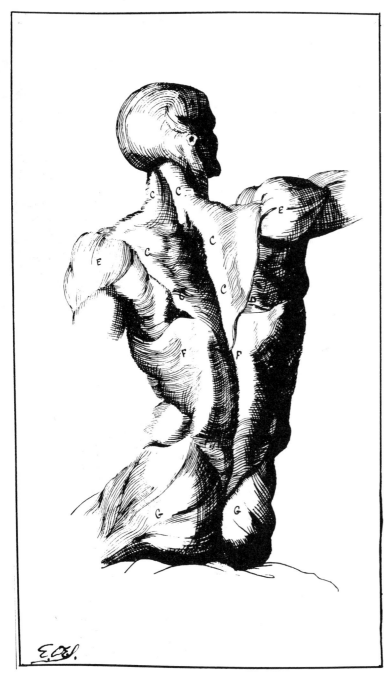

At the South Kensington School of Art, Edith was trained to draw from casts and did not respond to the general lifelessness of tuition there. When she began to work with Egerton abroad her horizons enlarged. 'There . . . I made my first dash into drawing from life, under the guidance of M. Gabriel Nicolet, then himself a student . . .' As part of their anatomical studies, art students, as well as drawing from life, used medical text books that showed écorché figures with the musculature exposed. This plate shows Edith's meticulous copy of a plate by Jean Cousin, which she made in Düsseldorf in the spring of 1881. Long familiarity with the study of nudes and of posing well made Edith an excellent study herself. Neither Edith or Hildegarde was affected by the prudery of false modesty, something that afflicted many women in their society, and both were unembarrassed by nudity.

Opposite: *Three paintings by Edith.*

Top: *An early student work, much influenced by the vogue for peasant realism amongst her tutors, called 'Gathering the Harvest' (c.1885).*

Right: *A religious procession, probably painted in Brittany when Edith was on a holiday with Cameron at Saint Jacut in 1891. She exhibited a beach scene, 'La Plage, Saint Jacut de la Mer', at the Royal Hibernian Academy in that same year.*

Far right: *Up the river at Rineen. A detail showing Edith's brushwork.*

When Martin returned to Ross she relied on Edith's advice on redecoration and repairs. In June 1888 she writes to Edith: 'I must do as much as I can but I am ignorant – I wish you were here to show me – can you tell me of anything that can take two old coats of paint off the stairs?' Edith's colour sense was excellent and subtle, Martin's was abominable. Painting Ross inside in 1892 she composed a colour

scheme: 'Persian red (baths, boxes, turf boxes, my face and clothes), pea green and turquoise blue'. Edith's remarks on Martin's 'refinement in dress' in *Irish Memories* do not dwell on Martin's sense of colour. Here is Edith on the subject in a letter to Martin on 3 June 1890: 'As for that foul brimstone and brickdust shirt – if you *like* to look a pale, muddy, putrid heliotrope, you will wear it – that's all.'

Edith's taste is responsible for the choice of the best Irish craftsmen to carry out commissions for the Somervilles at Castletownshend. Seamus Murphy, on one of his first commissions, made the memorial seat for Boyle Somerville at the gates of Drishane. Edith had it made 'for the use of the people of the village'. Harry Clarke, Ireland's most remarkable stained glass artist, made the memorial windows for Kendal Coghill, Egerton Coghill, and Henry and Adelaide Somerville. He stayed with Edith at Drishane when working on this commission, and though he was an intensely shy man, Edith liked him as much as his work. St Barrahane Church is not typically Protestant. High Church Anglo-Catholic influence is in restrained evidence beside the astounding blaze of Clarke's windows. Jem Barlow, the medium, claimed that at a service one Sunday in St Barrahane's the spirit figure of Aunt Sydney appeared, caught sight of the Clarke windows, started, then exclaimed 'Romish!' and dissolved.

As a painter Edith seems always to have stayed within range of classification as 'Brittany School'. Her naturalism, good brushwork, and unusual choice of subject impressed the art critic of the *Daily Telegraph* in November 1887, whereas the pure impressionism of her cousin, Egerton Coghill, a finer painter, did not appeal to him at all:

Edith painting out of doors. (Photograph by Martin Ross.)

'Retrospect'. This painting, five feet by three and a half feet and made in 1887, is one of Edith's biggest. The model is Mary Norris, who was very much at ease with Edith. Her diary says: 'Went to work early – madly interesting . . . thundering good model – she never stirs.' We find village people in Edith's sketchbooks and paintings who escaped being recorded by camera. Sir Joscelyn and his clattering equipment frightened off models, who found Edith more engaging.

Winter Exhibition at the Dudley Gallery . . . quite one of the most vigorous and masterly pictures in the collection is Miss Edith Somerville's 'Retrospect' (80). An old woman sits opposite a glass, pausing from her sewing to look at her own reflection. There are introduced accessories of a battered candlestick, a couple of buttons, and the odds and ends of a poor old seamstress's workshop. The balance of the low tones, and the vigour and decision shown in the handling are rare and remarkable qualities to find in a lady's work . . . if minute wonders find no favour in the visitor's eyes, he may retreat to the other side of the room and wonder at a dashing 'Impression' (40), by Egerton Coghill. Seen close, the white light on the water is 'lumped on' as with a trowel, and is unintelligible; but a long, a very long focal distance will explain the idea.

The uneven quality of Edith's work is not surprising when we remember the fraught conditions under which she worked. Some of her drawings for book and magazine illustrations were 'finished' while a messenger waited at Drishane door to ride to Skibbereen to catch the train, and post, to London, for a publication deadline. Many of her sketches, jotted down in her pocket books, were notes made by the wayside and not with complete concentration. When she *was* concen-

trating Edith's work has a lovely, clean, accuracy, as we see in her
quick sketches of geese, notoriously un-still subjects, or in her more
careful studies of Kendal Coghill and his nephew, Egerton.

Sketchbook studies of geese, probably for 'The Goosegirl', a large canvas painted in 1888.

A sketch by artificial lighting of Egerton Coghill made on 5 November 1885. Egerton and Edith were such keen workers that they rigged up a 'night-school' for themselves at Glen Barrahane and drew each other when a relative could not be impounded. We are not told how they lit the Studio for the winter months – they may have used lights from the theatricals, a version of Tilley paraffin lamps.

On remarkably little money Edith acquired a thorough training as an illustrative artist, and her range of techniques, the various modes of presentation of drawings to blockmakers, was very wide and professional. They are crisply good to look at even now, after years of wear, after having been shunted from one heap to another, one house to another, one country to another, and back again. Technically outstanding is the study of two women's heads from side and back view, an illustration for a travel book.

Edith preferred to draw characterful things, even unlovely things; she studied such subjects with intent care. She seems to have been irritated by, and had no patience with, the conventional subject. Trying to draw a baby, she gives up – 'Too pretty'. Absolutely characteristic is the situation she found herself in at the West Kensington School of Art, at nineteen. In a studio full of art students drawing plaster casts of foliage and standard subjects, Edith, having rooted about, had found for herself a plaster foot, a large, 'knubbly' foot, and set to work. A Mama, with daughter in tow, visited the studio and made a progress around the drawing boards, eventually arriving at Edith. She was aghast: 'A NAKED foot, my dear!' and swept off.

Edith's delight in the unlovely, never to leave her, resulted in many of her drawings being re-drawn by slick graphic artists, or even rejected outright. Edith records, with absolute scorn, that one editor refused a drawing as being 'too realistic'. In her scrapbooks we find her re-writing the titles of articles and stories where such tinkering with her work has taken place. There is: '*The Bagman's Pony* by Martin Ross, with illustrations "stolen" by J. Finnemore from sketches by Miss E. Œ. Somerville' in the issue of *Black and White* for 11 June 1892. In the same magazine's Christmas number of 1893, we find the story '*Matchbox* by E. Œ. Somerville with "no" illustrations by the author, and Hal Hunt'.

As an illustrator, Edith had a happy ability to use models of any sort, combined with imaginary backgrounds, to produce illustrations purporting to be realistic life sketches. Mrs Somerville, Hildegarde and Martin appeared in the most improbable guises. Hildegarde's back, with the addition of a chowrie, once featured in an illustration as a Paris tram-horse's hindquarters; needing a savage, Edith stripped her brother Boyle to his underpants and added a few details to suit the requirements; Boyle, as it was winter and the studio cold, got a bad chill. It was Martin who posed, in various contorted positions, for the comic-strip Miss Neruda Jones.

Edith had no qualms about using illustrative stand-ins and substitutes. One of the funniest must be the appearance of the Drishane servant, Whoolley, as a Copenhagen market woman. In 1894 Edith was at Drishane, Martin at Ross, and Edith was working on the illustrations to the Danish tour. Edith remarks that she was drawing 'with complete insincerity' from local models. A diary entry gives:

'Impounded mother to pose as the Hofjagermesterinde, and Mary Ann Whoolley as a Copenhagen market woman.'

Whoolley peers at us suspiciously, the right-hand woman of a pair, from page 108 of *Stray-Aways*. She was the servant who once came into a room to stoke the fire when, for some reason, the subject of conversation was woollen combinations. Whoolley whipped her skirt over her head, proudly, to demonstrate that she wore no such things, or indeed anything instead. This is an indication of how easygoing Castletownshend households seem to have been, quite happy with any amount of eccentricity in their servants. Geraldine Cummins noted, in the 1930s, that Edith chose her servants not for such estimable qualities as good cooking, cleanly habits or thoroughness, but simply for their conversational powers.

The most improbable illustrative stand-in of all must surely be the appearance of Herbert Greene, Oxford don, reactionary and Edith's suitor, as the model for the recruit on the cover of *The Kerry Recruit*, an old Irish song of the Crimean War. Edith's system of smoothly fitting together bits and pieces from different sources to make an illus-

Three wash drawings from In the State of Denmark, *published as a serial in the* Ladies' Pictorial, *1893.*

Above left: *Edith and Martin in a railway waiting room.*

Above: *On the way to Denmark, Martin became accidentally separated from Edith, whose wash drawing shows an impression of Martin adrift in Hamburg.*

'A second half-hour was spent in the endeavour to find out in a phrasebook the Danish for "bread and butter", a thing which riper knowledge has shown us does not exist in Denmark in the readymade slice.'

tration was not unlike the system Edith and Martin were to use in their writing. They maintained a mountain of fragments, verbatim speech, landscape descriptions and character sketches, and sifted and shaped this into their prose.

Edith's determination to get some kind of rapid visual memorandum from which she could work later led her to use a Kodak. We find 'Kodaking' as a verb in the diaries. She used the camera in situations where there was no time to sketch, or where the situation made sketching impossible. In the Aran Islands in 1895 Edith found that the inhabitants fled at the sight of a sketchbook, fearing the 'evil eye'; so Edith sent a telegram to Hildegarde to send Kodak post haste. A series of Kodak 'snaps' taken by Edith at Rea Races on 26 March 1894 shows us how quick and good was her eye for composition. These photographs remind us of the subject matter of some of Jack Yeats's paintings and record the artist's real-life sources.

The Somervilles and Coghills were adept photographers, and their albums show how able Boyle, Hildegarde, Egerton and other members of their circle were. They printed and developed their own photo-

Four Kodaks by Edith from Rea Races, March 1894. These were visual notes which she worked up later into illustrations by patchwork. We can find small elements from sketchbook and photograph incorporated into book illustrations.

graphs, the many colours and tones of which – cyan blues, magenta pinks, a range of sepias – are a result of the home mixing of chemicals and the varying tints of the early chloro-bromide papers. Affected by dampness and other afflictions, the images have faded, some beyond recall, including a few historically fascinating prints like a photograph of the lady students of the Académie Délécluse (1894) with Edith seated on the ground.

The interest that some of these photographers had in types of Irish face is quite evident. Splendid portraits survive. The popular image of the Irish in the Victorian press, studied in depth by Lewis Curtis in his book *Apes and Angels*, was of a clothed ape-person. The popular notion of the Irish as a lesser race, much closer to the apes than the English, survived well into the 1900s. Sydney Czira, an Irishwoman and member of Maude Gonne's Inghinidhe na h-Eireann, in New York raising funds after the Rising of 1916, discovered a British propaganda film,

distributed as a riotous comedy, showing the Easter Rising with the Irish Volunteers played by actors made up as apes. She persuaded the authorities to ban the film.

The many Irish faces recorded on film, or by Edith's sketches, are certainly of recognizable Irish types, mostly unknown to the English reader. Though Edith did not baulk at the ugliness of a Judy from Menlo, or of certain tramps, she was a connoisseur of the fine Irish face. She described herself as 'an amateur of beggars' and spent an extraordinary amount of time in converse with them, taking down their stories or drawing them. Some of the most magnificent faces she recorded were those of beggars.

Edith was ever ready to take up her pen in support of the arts and her eloquent clarity must have revitalized many a flagging cause. In 1945, at the age of eighty-seven, we find her writing to the *Cork Examiner* suggesting the setting-up of an Arts Centre:

Sir Joscelyn at the helm of his yacht Gyneth. *On his right Cameron, on his left Egerton and Hildegarde, c.1890. Edith used this as a set scene for her illustration 'There was a long, almost imperceptible swell' to 'The House of Fahy' in the* Badminton Magazine *of July 1899.*

A government subsidy, extending over a considerable period of years, is a need implicit in a scheme such as this, with provision for well-salaried, thoroughly cultivated custodians for the different interests Dramatic, Musical, Artistic and Out Door, selected on a basis of intelligence and culture exclusive of Sex.

Edith was fortunate in growing up with a model of an independent artistic single woman in her cousin, Constance Bushe, 'one who has ever been my patron Saint in Art, that cousin who preferred reverie to Shakespeare'. We find reflections of Constance's character in Edith, in her rituals and disdain for appearance. At Drishane the afternoon tea ritual was presided over magisterially by Edith; the arrangement of flowers about the house, an art she had learned from Constance, was sacred to Edith, and from Constance came a happy inspiration in dress to make the special occasion. At her niece Katharine Coghill's wedding, in 1944, Edith marked the event with a hat. The bride recalls: 'Heaven knows how she contrived it but she certainly must have trimmed it herself. It was basically a straw hat, I think, lavishly trimmed with emerald satin, on the top of which appeared to perch a seagull. I remember it with joy and gratitude.' Certain of the Somerville children were able to wear unusual clothes unselfconsciously and gracefully. When Boyle Somerville returned from service in Japan, he brought Japanese robes with him for his sisters. Vivid memories of Hildegarde and Edith drifting about in the grounds in their robes after dinner remain with those who saw them.

A study of Edith by Hildegarde (left) and a study of Hildegarde by Edith. Swimming down at the Dutchman's Cove early one morning Edith and Hildegarde took a plate camera with them and photographed each other. Hildegarde submitted these prints to a French publisher who was compiling a volume of photographic nude studies for studio use. It is not known if this book was ever published – so far it has not been traced. Edith, being ten years older than Hildegarde, suffered a stricter regime of tightly laced stays, and this shows in her figure. As old ladies they were proud of these beautiful prints, both as photographic work and as reminders of what they once were, fine figures of women.

Adelaide Somerville, an accomplished pianist, trained her children, it seems almost from birth, as thorough musicians. Two of her sons, Cameron and Jack, were successive Commandants of the Army School of Music at Kneller Hall. Edith was the organist at St Barrahane's from 1875 until 1945. Her contralto voice was first professionally trained in Düsseldorf, in 1881, when she was studying art in her cousin Egerton's studio there, and later in Paris. She returned from Düsseldorf laden with Mendelssohn cantatas, which still grace her organ loft. The organ case has pinned to it programmes of benefit concerts like the recital on 29 August 1923. There were three organ pieces by Edith, four selections of violin pieces by Nevill Coghill and three pieces by the choir, the most intriguing being number 10: 'Hymn – "It were my Soul's desire". The Choir (with intervening passages by Dame Ethel Smyth).'

Edith's dramatic use of facial expression, her carrying contralto voice and her impressive appearance made her a natural choice for the Gilbert and Sullivan operas then coming into fashion. Edith's first big success was as Little Buttercup, the bumboat woman in *Pinafore*, which was

first performed at the Opéra Comique, London, in May 1878. Edith
took part in a performance in Yorkshire in 1884; in 1886 she had to
refuse the offer of the part of the Queen of the Fairies in *Iolanthe* as she
was due to spend part of that year studying in Paris. Anyone hoping
to understand what Edith Somerville was like must remember her
tearing into her solo as Little Buttercup, 'When I was young and
charming I practised baby farming', or the vigour of her duet with her
husband-to-be Captain Corcoran, 'O, bliss! O, rapture!' From her
Pinafore days come three exclamations that she used from then on,
straight-faced: 'My amazement, my surprise!', 'Hor-ror' and 'O, bliss!
O, rapture!'. These look rather odd in the diary entries if one does not
understand their significance to a generation that thrived on Gilbert
and Sullivan.

Similarly, there is much intricate detail in the works of Somerville
and Ross that relates to dancing. For example, an instance from *The
Real Charlotte*, after Francie and Hawkins leave the room in search of
teaspoons at Charlotte's tea party:

> Francie and Hawkins re-entered the drawing room, the latter
> endeavouring, not unsuccessfully, to play the bones with four of
> Charlotte's best electro-plated teaspoons, while his brown boots
> moved in the furtive rhythm of an imaginary breakdown.

The splendour of the last phrase is enhanced when we realize that a
breakdown was a dance, then very popular, of a riotous, violent nature,
usually danced in the small hours when the elders were in bed.

Edith and her cousin Joe (Claude) Coghill were the best dancers,
and teachers of dance, in Castletownshend. It was with Joe that Edith
danced the difficult long-step mazurka down the village hill, with no
musical accompaniment to guide them, only the muttered, breathless,
breakneck triple-time of the mazurka.

When Edith met Martin she had already experienced ten years of
art and music training and practice - periods of study abroad with all
the rigours of professors and life classes. She had acquired a working
knowledge of French and German, appeared in leading roles in theatrical and opera productions, and was an all-round musical performer,
instigator and participator. Martin saw Edith at that time as a travelled
and talented cosmopolitan, and though Edith laughed at the idea, we
can see the basis for Martin's feeling. In Martin's second letter to Edith
in Paris in 1886, when Edith was studying yet again (quoted on page
48), we see Martin's curious response to Edith's popularity, her status
as a character and as a ruling personality of Castletownshend. Edith
was an almost theatrically emphatic public personage, in comparison
with Martin, who did not like limelight.

When the Martin party arrived for their stay in Castletownshend in
January 1886, Edith must have seemed slightly overwhelming. Not

Two line drawings for A Patrick's Day
Hunt.

Emmie and Cameron playing cards. A wash drawing, summer 1895.

many days after their arrival Edith, short of amusement, had dressed and made up as a witch and visited various houses, including that in which the Martins were staying, frightening them out of their wits. At first Edith was very taken with the features of Nanny Martin, Martin's mother. When she had finished making a drawing of her, she turned to Martin, whose portrait she painted after completing one of her brother Aylmer in the uniform of Methuen's Horse. Her energy and ability to work in trying circumstances as well as her insistence on using feminine forms of speech wherever possible are well shown in this entry for 30 January 1886: 'Deadly cold. Miss Helps and Violet came and sat in the Purlieu all morning – as also did many others – howsoever I pursued the peaceful alto of my way and did up 3 or 4 studio drawings.'

Edith at work in the Studio. (Photograph by S. Lester.)

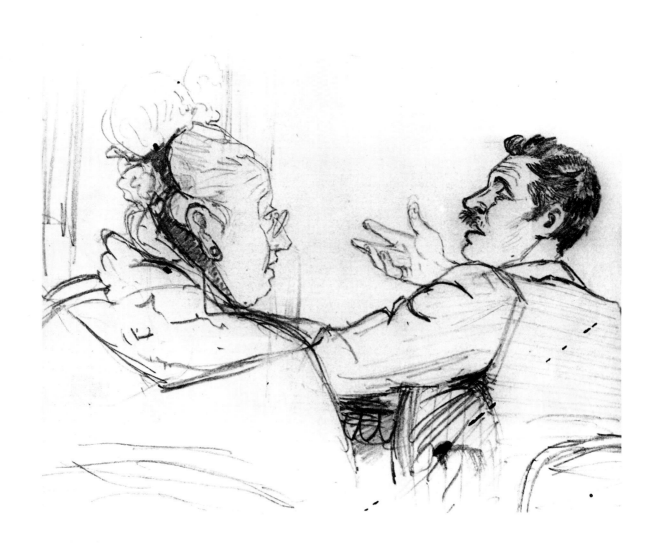

CHAPTER 6

The Persistent Eavesdroppers

Martin Ross and I, though very indifferent diarists, had one good habit among many bad ones, and that was a habit of persistent eavesdropping and of recording its spoils. It is one of Ireland's charms that the agreeability of her people is not at all disconcerted by publicity. The tactful eavesdropper may, as likely as not, be easily accepted as one of the party, gathered in by a gay and roving eye. Even if direct invitation be not extended, there is no hushing of voices, no closing in of the circle. There is something imperial about this indifference.

From *Wheel-Tracks*, 1923

Reviewers and appreciative readers like Yeats and Lady Gregory realized that Somerville and Ross portrayed Irish speech and manners with an exactness and skill of observation that were peculiarly their own. They made no attempt to dramatize or poeticize Irish speech, unlike the Literary Revival writers, but wove into their work direct reported speech. Their humour in dialogue, at its subtlest, captured the flippant Irish habit of putting a comic mask over the serious and painful subject. The gentry class to which Somerville and Ross belonged had become past-masters at holding on to their gravity, facial and otherwise, in precarious situations. Juxtaposing the comic and serious, to put on a brave face and resolutely see the funny side of life, was perhaps a reflex response to this.

The lurching from comedy to catastrophe was something that Edith and Martin were used to observing and describing. The diaries, particularly Edith's, show us how life in Ireland in the later part of the nineteenth century was for the Anglo-Irish a compound of summer-vacation entertainments, balls and jollity amid agrarian unrest and violence that ground on through the years. Edith includes laconic entries on violence alongside accounts like these:

In the evening the boys came up and we had a most lovely hop, opened the conservatory for cooling purposes, as there are such nice draughts there, one gets cool awfully quickly although the lamps never can keep lighted.

Conversation piece. An Edith Somerville sketch.

Breakfasted at Salter's Hotel to start by the 8.30 train. Waited
at Drimoleague for an hour ... proceeded to Skib, in state and a
cattle-truck.

Two horrible outrages near here. At Murryboolahan they cut
off a horse's tail and ears and at Ballydehob they cut off a man's
ears, sparing, however, his tail. Carved a good deal. Horrid slow
work at that sandalwood.

Met Annie Townshend of Whitehall, she has received a letter
from the League, telling her she will be shot.

... a poor old man of 85 was shot in the face between Schull
and Skib. He was mistaken for his son, George Swanton, a J.P.,
one of his eyes has been shot away and they fear he won't
recover.

The speech recorded by Edith and Martin was not all gained by
eavesdropping, but in conversation also. Country people talked to
them, reassured by their manners, their easy, interested voices and the
thick soles of their boots. Martin, writing of the difference between
Irish and English speech, wrote:

One might safely say that this bare, still country carries an
amount of genuine conversation to the square mile that the
crowded vicinity of Tunbridge Wells could never rival. It has
been so for centuries, and all the while Connemara has remained
bare and still, scarcely stirring, hardly even aware of the marching
life of England.

Genuine conversation, the inspired use of words, this was always for
Edith and Martin what marked the difference between English in England and English in Ireland. How grateful we must be that they recorded it so perfectly in use, as now even Ireland is infected with the
dead prefabrications of slang. In 1910, in response to Dr P. W. Joyce's
book *English As We Speak It in Ireland*, they wrote an essay called 'The
Anglo-Irish Language' in which they said:

Ireland has two languages: one of them is her own by
birthright; the second of them is believed to be English, which is a
fallacy; it is a fabric built by Irish architects with English bricks,
quite unlike anything of English construction ... it is a tongue,
pliant and subtle, expressing with every breath the mind of its
makers.

Both Edith and Martin had phenomenal memories. Martin could
recite the Psalms from memory and, hampered by her sight, also had
a highly developed aural memory. She would come back from conversation with Rickeen, a Ross tenant and former groom, with vast

tracts of converse locked in her memory, walk into the house and repeat them to Edith, who would write them down, or she would write them down herself. Edith could memorize in this way too, but not to such an extent, and to collect local stories she evolved a system of recording that Claude Chavasse saw her use on a visit to his parish at Altar. With a notebook in her lap and pen in hand, she would look at, and encourage, the talker, without looking at her hand and notebook as she wrote. This is an example of Edith's ability to do two things at once. Reciting and reading aloud, a pleasant feature of evenings at home, explain both their highly developed memory and the complex punctuation used with great skill by Edith and Martin. Nineteenth-century punctuation was an aid to reading aloud, which gives an added appreciation of writing skills.

One of Edith Somerville's pocket books.

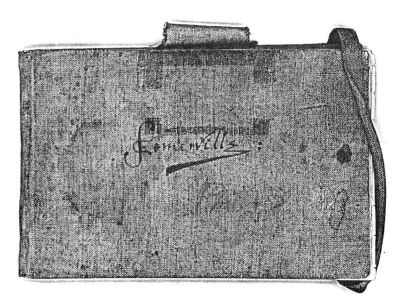

Edith and Martin held themselves apart from the Irish Literary Revival, thinking its use of dialect artificial, though admiring some aspects of its literature. Yet the books of Somerville and Ross, in their use of direct recorded speech, were of interest to Irish Revival writers, and their influence has yet to be studied properly. In 1911, Lady Gregory said: 'I was the first to write in the Irish dialect – that is, the English of Gaelic thinking people. I wrote in it before Synge did. He said he was amazed to find in my *Cuchulain of Muirthemne* his desired dialect.'

She was wrong in claiming to be the first in this field – *Cuchulain* was published only in 1902. Long before the 'dialect' literature of Revival writers began to appear, Somerville and Ross had been publishing novels based on recorded dialect. Their second novel, *Naboth's Vineyard*, published in 1891, has a cast of characters from the native

Irish middle and peasant classes. Edith and Martin visited Aran in 1895, before Synge went there, and Martin wrote the fine essay 'An Outpost of Ireland' about Aran. They were both familiar from childhood with Irish-thinking but English-speaking minds. Martin's Ross district was in the heart of the Connemara *Gaeltacht*, Edith's an area of West Cork where Irish was receding. Short stories written by Martin have dialect more complex than anything found either in stories on which they collaborated or in those by Edith alone.

Lady Gregory was closely interested in her cousin Martin's work, sending appreciations of the novels as they appeared. She read the R.M. stories to Yeats, to his huge amusement. The bizarre humour, thought processes and exact dialect of these stories, peculiarly Irish, had an influence in Ireland itself. It is wrong to assume that the R.M. stories were popular only with English-oriented gentry who wanted stage Irishry. They contain no stereotypes, only characters drawn from life who often speak with words taken down as they were spoken.

Lady Gregory sent her own books, and those of her colleagues in the Irish Revival, to Martin for her much valued comments and acute criticism. Here, in 1905, Martin gives a characteristically careful critical appreciation of Synge's *Well of the Saints*:

Photograph of the sexton from Buttevant by Sir Joscelyn Coghill, an instance of a model who posed for artist and photographer.

February 20, '05
Dear Augusta
I have held my hand about thanking you for the *Well of the Saints*, until I had read, marked and inwardly digested it. Of course I recognise the skill of the idea, or rather, the skill in presenting such an idea, and I should like to have seen it acted – and realised its charm more completely. Personally I do not like it nearly as well as *Riders to the Sea*. There is not that powerfully sustained interest and onward carrying progression, to *my* taste. This is cast in a form so simple as to be at times too simple as far as mere reading goes. I suppose the dialect is of the nature of a literal translation of Irish, but it seems to me to lack fire and spontaneity – you know, and no one better, what the power of repartee and argument is among such as these. It is inimitable in my opinion, I mean that no one who is not one of them themselves can invent it – and it is so much a part of themselves that to present them without it makes an artificial and unreal picture . . . what I felt throughout was a monotony of idiom, suggesting a poverty of material and a tameness in retort suggesting some timorous clinging to an ideal. I know I am touching on the fringe of large questions here – such as the choice of the ideal or the real – I am not at all qualified to lay down the law on either, but my instinct is for the real. Sometimes, of course, Mr Synge hits the living note, but sometimes he seems to me to move stiffly, and not with strength.

*The sexton from Buttevant. As a pair of
confirmed 'brogueaneers' Edith and Martin
put a high value on their conversations with
beggars, which they recorded: 'I may as well
acknowledge at once that Martin and I have
ever adored and encouraged beggars, however
venal, and have seldom lost an opportunity of
enjoying their conversation . . .' Edith carried
two notebooks, one for sketch and one for
speech. At Castletownshend she made studies
of a beggar who had once been a sexton at
Buttevant, and some of these she kept framed
on her walls. Illustrated here is a study from
a sketchbook. She published her first
conversation with him in* Wheel
Tracks:

*'An old man was one day announced as
wishing to speak to me. (I have yet to meet
the Irish servant who will shield an employer
in the case of a beggar.) I found him leaning
on his stick, a haggard, gentle old fellow,
with the tremor of palsy on him, clad in a
long and ragged black coat. He curtseyed low
to me. I asked him his history. Curtseying
again, he replied rolling each period with a
skilled propriety: "I was a sexton in the town
of Buttevant, my Lady of Honour! But I lost
my hearing, child and the ladies of the place,
Ladies of Honour, like yourself, my child,
and Colonel's Ladies, they frowned upon me,
aweenoch, upon me that fretted them with
my mistakes by reason of my infirmity, and I
lost my situation in the Church o'Buttevant!"
He paused and I uttered responsive and
sympathetic sounds. "I'm going the roads ever
since, my dear," he resumed: "If thrippence
would take me to the Lord in Heaven, I
couldn't give it!"*

*'It is a journey that is usually accomplished
without payment, but I gave him a viaticum,
and he wished that God might have the Gate
of Heaven open before me; which is as much
as one can expect for a shilling.'*

Martin and Edith writing together have been described as 'poet and painter' writing in unison. Martin's more abstract and thoughtful prose possibly developed as compensation for her impressionistic eyesight; Edith's acute sight and sensitivity to colour and detail lead her to specialize in scenery and landscape. Wordsworth's description of rowing across a lake pursued by a huge and mountainous shadow – which leads him to ponder on the force of nature and its possible malignancy to man – is well known, and it is interesting to compare Martin's attempt, in prose, to describe the same force. She had gone into an underground chamber at Cloonabinnia, in 1889:

> The air was dead and cold; the sense of suspended weight, of indifference to the human creature, was oppressive. At length the opening became feasible only for a lizard or an eel, and after that for the water, moving in unimaginable stealth through the veins of the rock. We turned and worked back towards the daylight, lost to us for some minutes; the darkness seemed desirous to keep us, and created a childish horror of its dominion. Then the sane, firm radiance of outer day was born, the trodden grass, and the grey January sky; it seemed a new heaven and a new earth.

Edith, in contrast, is aware of texture and colour, the mutation of shapes. Here she describes a landscape:

> In the second or third mile the face of the country changed. The blue lake that had lain in the distance like a long slab of *lapis lazuli*, was within two fields of them now, moving drowsily in and out of the rocks, and over the coarse gravel of its shore. The

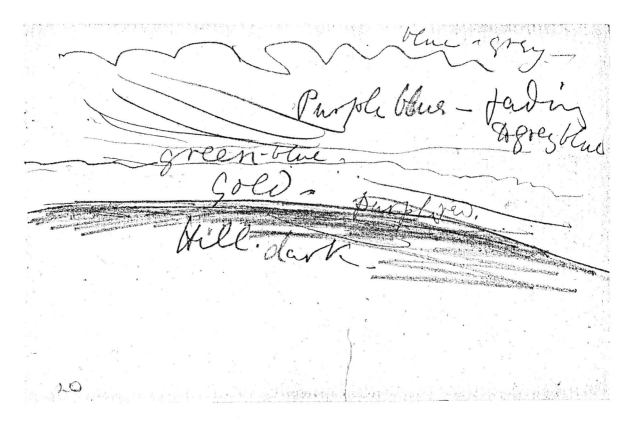

*A notebook page on which Edith has quickly
jotted down a landscape shape and written in
the colours.*

trees had dwindled to ragged hazel and thorn bushes; the fat cows
of the comfortable farms round Lismoyle were replaced by lean,
dishevelled goats, and shelves and flags of grey limestone began to
contest the right of the soil with the thin grass and the wiry
brushwood. We have said grey limestone, but that hard worked
adjective cannot at all express the cold, pure blueness that these
boulders take, under the sky of summer. Some word must yet be
coined in which neither blue nor lilac shall have the supremacy,
and in which the steely blue purple of a pigeon's breast shall not
be forgotten. The rock was everywhere. Even the hazels were at
last squeezed out of existence, and inland, over the slowly swelling
hills, it lay like the pavement of some giant city, that had been
jarred from its symmetry by an earthquake.

Martin's exquisite, understated, contorted humour was happily occupied in dealing with the queries sent to the letter columns of periodicals, letters that asked for explanation of humour, dialect, things puz-
zling to the English mind, mostly from the hugely popular R.M.
series. Here is Martin, in splendid form, answering a query in the
Spectator. The writer wanted to know why Flurry Knox refused 'to be
seen dead at a pig-fair' in certain articles of attire:

I have never given a necktie to a male friend, or even enemy;

but a necktie was once given to me. I showed it to a person whose opinion on such matters I revere. He said at once 'I would not be seen dead in it at a pig-fair.' The matter of the tie ended there; to use the valuable expression of the wife of the male friend (in connection with a toy that might possibly prove injurious to her young) I 'gradually threw it away'. That was my first experience of the pig-fair trope, and I have never ceased to find comfort in it nor ever questioned its completeness. I am aware that nothing, presumably, will matter to me when I am dead, yet, casting my mind forward, I do not wish the beholder of my remains, casting his eye backward, to be scandalised by my taste in ties, or other accompaniments, while I was alive. I do not myself greatly care about being alive at a pig-fair, neither is it an advantage, socially or otherwise, to be dead there. Yet this odium might be enhanced, could even be transcended, in the eye of the beholder, by the infamy of my necktie. To this point I have treated the beholder as a person able to appreciate the discredit, not only of my necktie, but also of being dead at a pig-fair. There remains, however, and in a highly intensive manner, the pig-fair itself. We trust and believe the pig-jobber is critical about pigs; but we do not expect from him fastidiousness in artistic and social affairs. He will not, we hope, realise the discredit of being dead at a pig-fair, but there can be neckties at which he will draw the line. Considering, therefore, the disapprobation of the pig-jobber, joined to that of the other beholders, and finding that fore-knowledge of the callousness of death could not allay my sense of these ignominies, I gradually threw away the necktie.

(The 'male friend' and his wife are Egerton and Hildegarde.)

This is a good example of Martin's thoughtful, arabesque humour, polished and measured. Although both Martin and Edith gloried in heavy-handed puns (Martin brightly suggested *From Cork to Claret* as the title for their book on the French grape harvest) Edith's humour has a swiftness, like spoken retort, that in comparison with Martin's is less literary and self-conscious. Here is Edith writing to Martin at Ross on 23 April 1887. Edith is trying to persuade Martin's mother to approve of a plan that will give herself and Martin an uninterrupted session of writing together at Ross, and she writes to Martin's mother 'a letter which combines the subtlety of a diplomatic note with the pathos of little Nell's death-bed scene in Thackeray's beautiful novel "The Mill on the Floss"'. Edith has not thought about this joke – it speeds out in her usual dashing penmanship. This difference between them, of speed of response, of carefulness in writing, can be seen in their early handwriting. Martin's is small, slow, a consciously assembled set of marks, sometimes difficult to read. Edith, in writing as in so many other physical capabilities, had her mechanism set fast – she

raced in her writing as she raced in thought. Yet it was Edith who had
the clear legible hand from which the typesetting of their books was
done. We can only wonder at Edith's patience. Martin could be wilful
and lazy. She enjoyed being in bed, and wrote much in bed. Edith
chaffs her, in the early letters, as 'lazy slut'.

Edith described Martin's giving of her time to the restoration of
Ross as 'setting a razor to cut down trees', but Martin's own diary
entries on her maintenance work at Ross are eccentric interludes in the
low-key rote of weather, ill-health, socializing, reading and writing.
On 19 March 1895 she writes: 'Wettish windy day. Very bilious. Went
out and slashed trees in the rain with my new slasher. Up to the post
later.' Dreamy though her accounts may have been of long walks over
the bogs, with fine description of scenery, Martin was often actually
out with the purpose of collecting firewood, always in short supply,
or shooting something edible. When Edith was at Ross, both she and
Martin would go out shooting. Martin's prospects of shooting anything, with her pince-nez precarious on the bridge of her nose, must
have been poor.

It is generally agreed that Edith supplied the power and mass of raw
material, and that Martin controlled the finish and form of their work.
Edith's energies bore up Martin through long periods of physical illness. The early letters show Edith worrying over Martin, her 'Dear
Child', like an omni-competent elder sister, concerned over Martin's
diet, her well-being, physical and mental.

The overall effect of their writing is emphatic and entrancing;
their reputation was once popular and high, and they are regaining
popularity as the stigma of Anglo-Irish landlordism wears off and the
curious are prepared to read a page or two. Reputable critics were
wholehearted in their praise for the R.M. and *The Real Charlotte*.
Writers whose style would not suggest a sympathy with the likes of
Somerville and Ross, but who carefully recorded their appreciation,
include Arnold Bennett, who wrote in his autobiography:

> *The Silver Fox*, by Somerville and Ross, is within its limits, a
> perfect novel. The style exhibits a meticulous care not surpassed
> by that of Henry James. It actually repays a technical analysis. It is
> as carefully worded as good verse. There is reason for every
> comma, and the place of every preposition and conjunction. All
> prose which pretends to be artistic should be as meticulous as this.
> Yet in fact the quality is almost unknown. Except in Henry James
> and Pater I know of no modern prose of which it can be said that
> the choice and position of every word and stop has been the
> subject of separate consideration.

Stephen Gwynn and Frank O'Connor had very high opinions of
The Real Charlotte, Stephen Gwynn describing it as 'probably the most
powerful novel of Irish life ever written'. The popularity of this book

Mary Peter, a servant. The standard of wit and humour in the conversation of servants at Ross and Castletownshend was high. Edith and Martin took down astonishing outbursts of speech, like this response by a job-cook when a complaint was made to her about the lack of hot water in the bathroom. Edith wrote: 'When reproached she replied, with a heat that she had been unable to impart to the water: "And how would there be hot wather, with that misfortunate owld boiler perishing out there in the scullery? Sure, didn't I hear the Major screaming in his bath! Frozen alive in it he was! And as for that ould scullery!" she continued, " That's the mountainy place altogether! I declare to God, Ma'am, if you had hair on your legs you'd see it waving with the wind that there is from all them owld doors that's in it! I has four pairs o'stockings on me this minyute, and I couldn't feel me toes no more than if I had wooden legs"' '.

in England (it appeared in the Oxford University Press World's Classics in 1948) is reflected in a letter to Geraldine Cummins from Lord David Cecil: '*The Real Charlotte* is a masterpiece; one of the very few novels of the first rank that has appeared in England this century.' Released in March 1948, the World's Classics edition went out of print in two months, the only title in the series to have done this. It has been re-published since.

Their popularity can also be judged from the speed with which critics wrote obituary articles for Martin after her unexpected death on 21 December, a Tuesday, 1915. Katherine Tynan's moving tribute, called 'Exit, the Spirit of Laughter', was published on 30 December, and the tribute of E.V. Lucas, the English writer and critic, who had been their enthusiastic publicizer and popularizer, appeared under the

title 'The Two Ladies' in the *Spectator* of 1 January 1916. Many appreciations were to follow, up to the substantial biographical article by
C.L. Graves in *The National Review* in 1918, but Katherine Tynan's
obituary notice is the most interesting. It is very intimate as an appreciation of Martin, and very ill informed as to the nature of Edith's
capacities:

> Just at the time we needed her most Violet Martin is dead. It is
> a poignant thought that we shall have no successor to *In Mr
> Knox's Country*. I do not know how much part Miss Somerville
> had in the books beyond the illustrations, but, in any case, the
> collaboration is at an end. That most pleasant and happy page of
> Irish literature is turned down. If there is a muse of laughter, she
> sits with her head bowed to her knees, weeping.
>
> England knows the two Irish cousins mainly as humorists. They
> are humorists of the finest sort of humour which hurts no one and
> leaves no bitter taste in the mouth ... In a sense the humour of
> these writers did them wrong, for it obscured their qualities ...
> We needed this sane sweet spirit in these bitter days.

It seems to have occurred to no one at all that Edith would carry
on writing. The delight of critics in 1917, when Edith published *Irish
Memories*, still a joy to read, was tempered with the sadness that the
book was the celebration of the end of Somerville and Ross:

> It is sad to look on the title-page of *Irish Memories*, and
> sorrowful to realize that it is the last on which we shall see the
> joyous names of E. Œ. Somerville and Martin Ross coupled
> together ... Death has divided these two ladies whom no critic
> poring over their books could separate.

We might wonder what this particular critic thought of the further
fourteen books that were to issue under the joyous, still coupled names.

Although it was not until 1932 that Trinity College honoured
Somerville and Ross with honorary degrees, with Martin as it were *in
absentia* at the ceremony, Lady Gregory and Yeats had been well aware
in the first years of the century that Somerville and Ross were authors
of note. In 1904 they tried to persuade Edith and Martin to write a
play for the Abbey Theatre. Martin wrote to Edith at Drishane:

> I must tell you that Augusta was here yesterday and was
> rampant that I should write a play for the Abbey Street Theatre
> ... apparently they want what they are good enough to call a
> Shoneen play – I suppose that means middle class vulgarity ... It
> seems to me that they want now to rope in the upper classes and
> drop politics ... Augusta was enraptured when I divulged the fact
> that you had faint aspirations towards a play ... 'A week at Coole
> would do it – We could give you all the hints necessary for stage
> effects etc. ... the characters and plot picked from your books ...

I will look through them at once . . .' I gave no further encouragement of any sort and said we were full up.

Any subject taken too seriously caused Edith and Martin to break up into helpless laughter and facetiousness. The Abbey Theatre plays had this effect on Martin. Yeats and Lady Gregory would have been surprised to read this letter of Martin's to Edith:

> I must tell you of the Irish Play to which I went on Friday night . . . I thought Diarmud and Grania a strange mixture of saga and modern French situations, George Moore and Yeats were palpable throughout. Biblical terms were not shrunk from to describe the progress of the emotions of Grania who was excessively French in her loves. In the first act she is on the verge of an enforced marriage to Finn . . . she states her reasons for objecting to this and finally deludes Finn's friend Diarmud into falling in love with her and taking her away from the marriage feast à la Young Lochinvar. The next act is some time afterwards and the really novel position is that she has become tired of Diarmud – I give George Moore some credit for that – Never was anything like her ecstasies of love for him in the first act – she then falls in love with Finn which she might have done in the beginning and saved the writing of the play – and the curtain is Diarmud's discovery of them in howlts and his resolve to go and hunt an enchanted boar which a family witch (a stout lady in a grey tea gown and a conversational English accent) has prophesied is to be the death of him. Diarmud is carried in to make dying speeches to Finn and Grania and to be carried off to a funeral march with Grania striking attitudes all over the place . . . if this is the lofty purity of the Irish drama I am mystified . . . I saw Maud Gonne at the Play and thought her looks terrific . . . Yeats was with her in a box all the time except when he was with Augusta . . . I never looked his way and I daresay the Irish Literary Revival was quite disastrously unaware of my presence in the shades at the back.

The subject that gave Edith and Martin the greatest fund of amusement was class. Snobbery they found fascinating, and Edith and Martin brought their own wit and humour to bear on the Irish and Anglo-Irish passion for genealogy – they had both had a thorough training from birth. Even to understand the network of their own relations was a stiff task. Genealogy, with its attendant manias and snobberies, continually surfaces both in their memoirs and their fiction. In England it took three generations for a tradesman's children to mutate into gentlemen, but in Ireland a man could experience this mutation in his own lifetime. To buy a coat of arms from an obliging Herald signified that a man had arrived at 'gentleman' status. Family trees of child-like fantasy were the delight of the newly arrived.

In their passion for genealogy Edith and her brother Boyle kept track of Somervilles all over the world. An example not only of Somerville female stamina, but of how far the Anglo-Irish adventured from home, is Mrs Jonas Morris Townshend. Born in 1799, she fell in love with her cousin Jonas, of the Point House, Castletownshend and he persuaded her to run away with him to Australia. Boyle, then a lieutenant in the British navy on Hydrographic Surveying Service in Australia and the Western Pacific, determined to find his great-aunt Mary. He wrote to Edith from his ship, H.M.S. Dart, docked in Sydney: 'She lived with him in the then almost trackless bush, ninety miles from Sydney, and had several children. She is now eighty-seven years of age and a most delightful old lady.' Boyle took his camera with him, and having found her, photographed her. She died two years later, in 1894.

Mrs Annie Townshend of Whitehall, a real-life ancestress of old Mrs Knox, of the R.M. stories, in her usual ragged disarray, was one day climbing into a first-class railway carriage when she was stopped and challenged by a gaudily and expensively dressed lady, an *arriviste*. Mrs Townshend threatened to recite their respective genealogies on the station platform, before an interested gathering. The *arriviste* faded away and Mrs Townshend of Whitehall proceeded.

For many families in Ireland in the 1800s, both Irish and Anglo-Irish, genealogical trees were articles of faith, fictions based on the flimsiest evidence. Irish families had lost their descents through disuse

Coats of arms at the foot of the staircase in the Castle.

and lack of interest, and many Anglo-Irish families cloaked their humble origins in grandiosity in the pages of *Burke's Landed Gentry of Ireland*. Sir Bernard Burke presided over a golden age of easy gentility for Anglo-Irish families and was lax in pressing for proper proofs of descent. A galloping mould of appliqué heraldic devices got a grip of Victorian country houses.

Victorian do-it-yourself periodicals featured armorial bearings applied to every conceivable kind of surface, one article even going so far as to demonstrate how to mould and cast your own armorial fireback. There is throughout the happy assumption that the reader of course has armorial bearings of his own. A charming note of doubt is struck in an article that advises enthusiasts on how to construct a heraldic frieze, involving some thirty shields, right round their drawing room. Should they experience difficulty in drawing up thirty blazons of one's own connections, it is suggested that some shields might be 'sentimental rather than genealogical'. A man might blazon emblems relating to the professions in his family, or the emblem of his town, until, by hook or by crook, he had achieved the full, stunning, heraldic display.

The tumultuous ostentation and snobbery of Victorian Ireland, passionately concerned with its genealogies, was chronicled, mercilessly and minutely, by Somerville and Ross. The subtlety of their use of genealogy to place their characters in the social order of their novels is as marked as their use of pronunciation and phrasing to the same end. Here is Charlotte Mullen protesting the purity of her blood to Christopher Dysart in *The Real Charlotte*:

'I'm no relation of the Fitzpatrick's, thank God! My father's
brother married a Butler, and Francie's grandmother was a Butler
too –'

'It's very intricate,' murmured Christopher; 'it sounds as if she
ought to have been a parlour-maid.'

'And that's the only connection I am of the Fitzpatrick's,'
continued Miss Mullen at lightning speed, oblivious of
interruption; 'but Francie takes after her mother's family and her
grandmother's family, and your poor father would tell you if he
was able, that the Butlers of Tally Ho were as well known in
their time as the Dysarts of Bruff.'

'I'm sure he would,' said Christopher feebly, thinking as he
spoke that his conversations with his father had been wont to treat
of more stirring and personal topics than the bygone glories of the
Butlers.

'Yes, indeed, as good a family as any in the county. People
laugh at me and say I'm mad about family and pedigree; but I
declare to goodness, Mr Dysart, I think the French are right when
they say, "bong song ne poo mongtir," and there's nothing like
good blood after all.'

Less of a caricature, and more affecting, is Julia Duffy, whose mother
had been a dairymaid, in the same story, trying to impress the senile
Sir Benjamin Dysart with her family status:

'Sir Benjamin,' began Julia again, 'I know your memory's
failing you, but you might remember that after the death of my
father, Hubert Duffy' – Julia felt all the Protestant and aristocratic
associations of the name as she said it – 'you made a promise to
me in your office that I should never be disturbed in my holding
of the land.'

'Devil so ugly a man as Hubert Duffy I ever saw,' said Sir
Benjamin, with a startling flight of memory; 'and you're his
daughter, are you? Begad, the dairymaid didn't distinguish
herself!'

'Yes, I am his daughter, Sir Benjamin,' replied Julia, catching at
this flattering recognition. 'I and my family have always lived on
your estate, and my grandfather has often had the honour of
entertaining you and the rest of the gentry, when they came
foxhunting through Gurthnamuckla . . .'

Their tour-de-force on family vicissitudes was *The Big House of
Inver*, which concerned the Prendeville family, 'one of those minor
dynasties that, in Ireland, have risen, and ruled, and have at last crashed
in ruins'. The name of Prendeville mutates, as it descends through the
social orders, from Prendeville, to Prendy, to Pindy, just as Isabella,
the favoured Christian name for the first-born girl, mutated from

Isabella, to Ishbel, to Shibby. The portrait of Shibby Pindy, a latter-day embodiment of Lady Isabella Prendeville, is as powerful as that of Charlotte Mullen in *The Real Charlotte*.

The story of the Prendevilles is loosely based on the family of St George of Tyrone House, whose real-life history is less believable than Somerville and Ross's account of the Prendevilles. There is an extra-ordinary mausoleum in memory of the St George lady on whom Somerville and Ross modelled their Lady Isabella. It is visible from the windows of the house front. It has cast iron doors and window tracery and belongs to the meat-safe type of design popular in Scotland in the days of body-snatching.

When John Betjeman was working in Dublin at the beginning of the last war he took a tour in the West of Ireland. Meandering down to the Burren from Galway he came upon the St George mausoleum. Seeking to describe the fate of this Anglo-Irish family on its 'home' ground he uses the word 'extinguished':

> There in pinnacled protection
> One extinguished family waits
> A Church of Ireland resurrection
> By the broken, rusty gates.
> Sheepswool, straw and droppings cover
> Graves of spinster, rake and lover,
> Whose fantastic mausoleum
> Sings its own seablown Te Deum,
> In and out the slipping slates.

It was because they were proud representatives of their names that Somerville and Ross were able to write so well of family houses. Readers of *The Big House of Inver* can appreciate the will of Shibby Pindy that her house should survive with its family, the two meaning-less if separated.

During the period when it was uncertain whether the Somervilles could afford to keep on living in Drishane, Edith wrote a letter to Hildegarde that reveals how bitterly hard was Edith's fight to keep the house, and how it would most certainly have been out of Somerville hands by 1910 had it not been for her strength of will:

> Cameron, having ordered the green-house, promising to pay £40 down, and the rest at Christmas, departed, telling Strawson that Miss Somerville would give further orders. Accordingly I made all sorts of plans and arrangements, got the old house down, and ordered the new one. Then came a letter from S. asking for the £40 promised, before beginning work. I sent his letter to Aylmer. After a week another letter from John Strawson, again demanding the money. I wired to Aylmer (who is still

Study by Sir Joscelyn Coghill of Norry, a servant.

Castletownshend schoolchildren photographed by Mrs Warren at the National School in 1892.

recuperating his overworked constitution at Lahinch) and heard this morning that he 'hasn't a penny at the bank', and Cameron had taken the £50 to India! You may faintly imagine my lawful rage – I had, of the two, dissuaded the job. I had said, and I was right, that fifteen shillings worth of timber would have held the old house up for a long time, but Aylmer himself suggested using Collins' fine and Cameron eagerly agreed. Now the old house is swept, everything will die, and 'what to say to Strawson I cannot cannot tell' – the longer I live the less opinion I have of men's business capacity. With but few exceptions, they are impulsive and untrustworthy and *dishonest* – in our family anyhow.

Adapting one's manners and very name for class-conscious reasons was common, but the soft speech also affected slurred forms of names. The tendency to soft contractions was strong, and accounts for many strange-sounding place names like Castle Matress, originally Castle Matrix, which was odd enough. And what is one to make of the sensibilities of the Irish family with the glorious and euphonious name of O Maoilbhearaigh, meaning 'descendant of a devotee of St Barry', Englishing themselves to O'Mulberry?

It is worth remembering that Maria Edgeworth's pioneering novel of Irish social realism, *Castle Rackrent*, is actually a study in depth of an Irish aristocratic family. Sir Tallyhoo Rackrent, having died without male heirs, was succeeded by his cousin-german Sir Patrick O'Shaughlin, who complied with the condition that his family change its name to Rackrent. The Irish aristocracy performed multiple contortions in order to hold on to their lands. Remarkable families, like the Butlers of Kilcash, even held on, surreptitiously, to their Catholicism. Instances of intermarriage between upper-class Anglo-Irish and upper-class Irish were not rare, nor were cases like the O'Shaughlin/Rackrent metamorphosis.

Martin had an eye for the human contortions consequent upon acute class-consciousness, an area where Edith's happy bonhommie made her less observant. Here Martin writes to Edith of some local girls:

> The Parks told me strange tales of the Morris girls who live at
> Corran, they fly up when afternoon visitors come and put on
> evening dresses, low necks and short sleeves and come down
> cracking with paint ... to someone who wanted their horse taken
> round they said that they would send for the groom but that they
> did not know where the stable was.

Occasionally Martin lets slip a comment that is self-revealing, as this hilarious aside in a letter to Edith shows: 'I somehow like the Morgans, they are passing kind, though they *do* call Skib. "town",' or this, about a Mr Burke O'Flaherty, lately returned from abroad, where he bred ostriches: 'He was surprisingly interesting about his ostriches and knew Olive Schreiner's sisters. It was typical of him and Oughterard that he

Rapid sketch, two inches across, of countrywomen talking.

was not aware that Olive Schreiner had written a book.' Schreiner was the author of *The Story of an African Farm*.

Miss Hope-Drummond, of *The Real Charlotte*, in a puzzled reflection, said 'Irish society is so intolerably mixed'; it is this unique mixture that contributes to the amazing oddity of the society recorded by Somerville and Ross. As social historians, their subject matter could not have been a richer, or more neglected, field. Stephen Gwynn and Martin Ross, in one of the many series of letters they exchanged, discussed the difficulties caused by the inability of the Irish Nationalists to accept that some of the old Anglo-Irish class could be, by choice and passionate commitment, part of a new and independent Ireland. Class-consciousness was ineradicable and is still thriving in the Ireland of today. Stephen Gwynn ruefully wrote to Martin: 'Caste is at the bottom of nine-tenths of our trouble. A Catholic Bishop said to me "Drink did a lot of harm in Ireland, but not half as much as gentility."'

The reputation of Somerville and Ross in Ireland may well have been harmed by their gentility. A review of *The Real Charlotte* by T.P. O'Connor in an English weekly, castigating the authors as 'shoneens' – middle-class apers of all things English – seems to have blasted their reputation in Ireland for years. Their scrapbooks, meticulously kept, contain no Irish reviews until the appearance of *Some Experiences of an Irish R.M.* in 1899 – the book that gave them the irremovable label of 'comic writers'. New Ireland has never claimed Somerville and Ross as her own. They have been curiously unregarded in their own country – perhaps because they flourished at a time when their class was rejected and ousted and perhaps, too, for laughing when they shouldn't have.

"**E** came from **E**ngland, and wanted no guide.
Now he's larning the lie o' the bogs,
From inside!"

R. S.

"**R** is for **R**iver.
Young Reilly kept cool.
If ye give him fair warning
Young Reilly's no fool.

And **S** was the **S**axon
That gave him the warning.
I'm thinkin' he'll hardly be dhry
Before morning."

CHAPTER 7

Hunting: The World of the Irish R.M.

We were told of a lady who classified friends from acquaintances by finding out if they had read and appreciated *The Real Charlotte* or no, and who now was unable to conceive how she had ever existed without the assistance of certain quotations from *The R.M.* Perhaps one of the most pleasant of these tales was one of a man who said 'First I read it at full speed, because I couldn't stop, and then I read it *very* slowly, chewing every word; and then I read it a third time, dwelling on the bits I liked best; and then, and *not* till then, thank Heaven! I was told it was written by two women!'

First reactions to the *Irish R.M.*, from *Irish Memories*, 1917

Hunting was the chief recreation of the countryside. As well as being a pest control, fox-hunting kept the hunters in trim for the serious tasks of shooting, fishing and the killing of edible game. In the households of the Anglo-Irish living in remote areas, the food was often appallingly bad. Salmon, trout, hare and duck were a welcomed addition to the diet. In winter the Flemings of Newcourt had 'an eternal diet of salt meat. In the autumn, some fat sheep and bullocks were killed and cut up, and the joints put into barrels of brine. The only variety of food for the dinner table was an occasional rabbit or hare, or wild duck. If the cabbage failed, a seaweed was used as vegetable.'

Hunting was a masculine pastime. Although its enjoyments surpassed all other available country pursuits, so did its dangers. Women, tied to yearly childbearing or to presenting themselves as daintily feminine in the marriage market, did not hunt as a rule until the mid nineteenth century. Hunting attracted those with high spirits and energy, the unmarriageable, widows and viragos. Liberated women took to lawn tennis, hunting and bicycling, as enthusiastic evangelists.

Propriety decreed that women who hunted should ride side-saddle, adding yet another danger to an already dangerous sport. They were dragged and killed by their skirts, entrammelled in the saddle. Worst of all, their bodies were distorted by the unnatural seat: they were twisted sideways, with their right legs jammed and numbed, for up to eight hours a day. Edith Somerville's right leg was damaged and

Two illustrations from Slipper's A.B.C. of Fox Hunting.

troublesome, giving her great pain, from her late fifties onwards. She
began riding at four.

The strength needed to maintain upright carriage, balance and control of the horse put immense strain on the leg muscles. Edith writes
to Martin after the great, physically arduous, Manch run: 'I am a bit
stiff today and very sore under my right knee from a vile garter that
I put on to keep my stocking from slipping and rubbing having cut
into my leg from being too tight when the muscle contracted for
jumping.' A rider riding astride basically stands in the stirrups when
the horse is at the gallop, or braces the legs in equilibrium for the
rising trot, but the rider riding side-saddle has nothing but balance to
maintain her in concert with the horse. She cannot utilize fully her
own weight and gravity – hands and balance are the main controls.

Edith was an outstanding rider; she spent so much of her life on
horseback that it is surprising that she 'flourished about' until her
mid-fifties before being crippled by her right leg. Her grandfather
seems to have determined that Edith would be a rider. He wrapped
her up in a rug and put her on the back of a cob

> no older than myself. Grandpapa then, at my earnest entreaty, left
> the cob to my sole guidance, a proceeding that moved my mother
> (not unnaturally, I think) to such shrieks of remonstrance that she
> frightened the cob into galloping off with me across the croquet
> ground into the shrubbery. Why the small circular bundle that I
> must have been remained on the cob's back I shall never know,
> but what happened was equally improbable and that was that we
> galloped into the ropes of the swing. One of these caught the cob
> round his neck, and in a moment he was rolling on his off-side
> and I, in my enveloping rug, was rolling in the ferns beside him.

In the next year of her life, her fifth, she was given a bay pony
called Gift, with a small, old side-saddle: 'In this I rode daily, and
somehow escaped deformity, although my father's adjurations to "keep
the left shoulder up" resulted in its being a little higher than the other.'

Martin's death in December 1915 is thought to have been caused
by a hunting fall in November of 1898, a displacement in her back
causing the slow growth of a brain tumour. She had often damaged
her back, and been bed-ridden, by falling down the notoriously irre-
gular backstairs at Ross. One has only to look at the happy, vague face
of Martin riding Confidence, having just cleared some poles, to wonder how she hunted at all with her bad sight. Edith wrote in *Irish
Memories*:

> Before I knew how extravagantly short-sighted she was, I did
> not appreciate the pluck that permitted her to accept any sort of a
> mount, and to face any sort of a fence, blindfold, and that inspired
> her out hunting to charge whatever came in her way with no

Martin riding Confidence.

more knowledge of what was to happen than Marcus Curtius had when he leaped into the gulf.

Martin rode on any horse that was offered, quite unconcerned; her fragility and slightness belied her strength of nerve when in good health. She usually had a lead from Edith and was close behind her when the accident happened:

> Martin rode Dervish at a fixed pole into the seven acre field; he took it with his knees and fell right over it, pitching Martin in the mud and apparently falling on her. Mr Purdon and I picked her up. Thought her dead. When recovered found her shoulder was bruised but no bones broken, and only a few small cuts on her face.

Edith's relief here in the diary entry was to leave her in the following weeks when Martin could not walk without excruciating pain and spent weeks prostrate and in low spirits.

When Martin eventually hunted again, in 1909, she was cautious, and seems to have suffered bad loss of nerve. A sentence from a letter

Martin, c.1900, after her hunting fall with Dervish. She suffered prolonged bouts of invalidism after this accident in November 1898.

that describes a Lissard meet, when Edith was away in 1894, gives us an idea of her spirit; she had managed without a lead from Edith for some time, galloping along with the rest of the field, when she suddenly realized that she was alone. She was guided by boys on hedgerows cheering her on: 'I flew on awfully bewildered, but vaguely feeling direction.'

Edith schooled her own horses. From 1895, a year after the publication of *The Real Charlotte*, Edith was an intermittent horse-coper. She needed to make money by buying untried hunters, schooling them and selling them, as all too clearly income from writing was very little and insufficient. Martin writes, astonishingly, in 1889, of an offer from a publisher: 'I do not think that £15 is enough for 170 pages.' At this stage they were earning single guineas for articles. £7 and ten shillings each for an entire book seems preposterously little. Edith could earn more than four times that amount by schooling a single hunter.

As a result, Edith rode to hounds on any horse that happened to be

Above: *Edith on Slavey, one of the hunters she schooled and sold at a profit.*

Right: *Edith on Bridget, her favourite. Edith bought Bridget at a horse fair in Bantry, and when her owner led the mare, skittish and ramping, to Edith he apologetically remarked that the mare would be as quiet as a chicken for Edith to ride. There followed the Somervillean aside: 'Wouldn't you be looking at her for a long time before you thought of a chicken?' (Photograph by Elliott and Fry, 1905.)*

in hand; but folk memory in the Skibbereen area recalls her on her 'white horse', Bridget. Edith wrote of Bridget in *Irish Memories*:

> Among horses, Bridget leads, the rest nowhere. Her father was a thoroughbred horse, her mother a Bantry mountain pony. She herself was very little over 15 hands one inch, and she succeeded in combining the cunning and goat-like activity of the spindle side of the house with all the heroic qualities of her father's family. 'She has a plain head', said a rival horse-coper, who had been so unfortunate as not to have seen her before I did, 'but that suits the rest of her!' I suppose it was a plain head, but anyone who had sat behind it, and seen its ears prick at sight of a coming 'lep' would not think much of its plainness. I hunted her for ten seasons, and she never gave me a fall that was not strictly necessary. Since her retirement from the hunt stables she has acted as nursery governess to a succession of rising riders, and at the age of seventeen she carried Martin for a season, and thought little, with that

featherweight, of keeping where both of them loved to be, at the
'top of the Hunt'.

The West Carbery Hunt would take the field wherever foxes had
been making depredation. Edith kept a great mound of letters from
country people asking her to bring the hounds to kill foxes. Meets
were arranged often on the basis of letters like these:

> Dear Miss, just a few lines to let you know the fox is making a
> great set on me I am beggard with him he have 8 hens and 2
> ducks carried and I badly in want of them. Excuse me for making
> so stiff I remain your truly Mrs Cotter.

And another:

> I thought I had the house well fastened but he scrope under the
> door . . . every wet night always we finds his foot marks around
> the fowl house we found them in the fields around partly eaten
> and wasn't it a terrible loss to any poor young woman . . . when
> ye will come the way here after, we will do all in our power for
> ye to help ye to catch him.

*West Carbery Hounds. A meet at Drishane
in April 1892. Aylmer and Edith, Martin
and Hildegarde, facing the camera, from left.*

Running a pack of hounds required a great deal of money, time and energy. Edith was always short of money, but she justified the expense of her pack, the West Carbery Hounds, by the employment it gave to the huntsmen, kennelmen, copers, farriers and vets, and by the entertainment and spectacle it gave to the local people. Irish town dwellers, who have forgotten their roots, suppose hunting to have been the elitist sport of the detestable landlords only. A hunt could not operate without the support and appreciation of all classes in the countryside through which it operated. Farmers, even small ones, rode out with the West Carbery. We see them in photographs, wearing their working clothes, gaiters and bowlers, riding hairy horses. Men and boys, following the hunt on foot, swarmed all over the country-side, taking vantage points and giving leads to the riders and huntsmen. A meet at Skibbereen was a big event, to be dressed up for and revelled in by all. Ireland has become urbanized and sophisticated in a very short time. The judgement that hunting was a sport for landlords only is rarely endorsed by country people. Those who might disagree would find attendance at a meet of the present-day West Carbery Hunt illu-minating. The great yearly occasions of Irish country life were inti-mately tied to the local hunts and their races, for example the Fairy-house Races, which were the Easter Monday races of the Ward Hunt, and those of the Kildare Hunt at Punchestown.

The mixed composition of the population of West Carbery may explain the happy relationship, in general, between it and the West Carbery Hunt and its Masters. Bandon, Clonakilty and Skibbereen had been strong Protestant settlements, and this Protestant strain may ex-plain the overall lack of violent anti-landlordism. Although National-ists were there, and known well to the Somervilles, the prevailing feeling of a majority seems to have resulted in a reverence for the time-honoured system as it was. Martin wrote to Edith in 1894, apro-pos of Aylmer's success with all and sundry as Master:

> I really don't see or hear of any other part of Ireland where the farmers are so friendly and the rebel paper will back up the gentlemen in improvements and in sport. I see that one day the Skibbereen district will be a fifth province in Ireland – refusing to receive home rule, and governed by Aylmer, under a special warrant from the Queen.

A number of Castletownshend features and peculiarities are legacies of the redoubtable Madam Townshend, who flourished, which is per-haps too mild a verb, in the first half of the nineteenth century; she was Edith's great-grandmother. What is now called 'Madam's Bower' at the Castle, an extraordinary wild garden with a centre-piece that combines a Norman motte with a Gothic folly and New Grange burial mound, is a monument to her taste and will-power. She wanted to have a large stone incorporated in her 'Bower', decided that one of the

Edith in hunting habit aged thirty-nine.
(Photograph by Elliott and Fry, 1897.)

'Five Fingers', the Stone Age alignment above Castletownshend,
would do perfectly, and had one dragged to the 'Bower'. She does not
seem to have liked it on arrival, as it languishes, unused, well away
from the centre of the garden. This is why one sees, on the ridge, only
three fingers as one drives down to Castletownshend, the fourth being
recumbent and the fifth a hostage.

Another of her achievements was to introduce deer into the Castletownshend woods. Faced with a plan to put a public road down the
Rineen River, which could have only passed one way out to the
village, directly in front of the Castle windows, Madam discovered
that no public road could pass through a deer forest and hastily im-

Edith in hunting habit in 1905,
aged forty-six.

ported some from the Bantry estate. Deer forests needed to be walled, and as a result the workmen involved in the building of the Catholic church, a discreet mile or so away from Castletownshend proper, were set to more important work, the building of Madam's wall. The deer multiplied, and provided the occasion of a 'Cry havoc!' in a hunt that Martin rode during one of Edith's absences. The letter that Martin wrote to Edith describing this hunt is one of the most perfect, time-stopping evocations of Castletownshend in her letters:

> The hounds had a noble time in the wood. They started a deer
> at the back of the lakes and flew *shrieking* down by the foxes' den.

We took our stand at the turn of the road where one looks up to
the arch and there you may say we saw fun. In ten minutes about
a dozen bucks and does were on foot, flying towards the arch
(some of them) flying back below us, round again past the foxes'
den and so on. It was lovely to see Rantipole [a hound] screaming
all alone about a hundred yards behind a buck, Negress once was
fifteen yards only from another, and the row was delicious; with
the echoes, and the young leaves and the sunshine all very
condusive [Martin's spelling – a Buddh word]. After about half an
hour Aylmer called them off, and nine couple came wonderfully
quickly, partly I think because they were quite done. They just
flopped into the lake and swam and looked very nice. When after
tea Hildegarde and I went forth and played a round of golf there
were still hounds yelling in the woods, and Patsy Sheehan was
winding his horn until it was twilight. Your mother is below the
window gardening. She is dressed in black velvet bodice, long
train and no hat or gloves – she snuffles audibly as she goes. Her
face is pink. That which she works at is round the corner, so I
cannot say what it is, but she goes to and forth with a dripping
water-can regardless of the fact that it is blazing noon – It *is* a
day. You know well the hazy glitter and misty blue of the
harbour, and the sparkle of every leaf that has a sparkle in it, the
red anemones in the garden, the crows, the gulls and transcending
gulls your mother's shrieks to Hildegarde as she approaches from
Glen Barrahane and photography.

Few writers have been so in sympathy with the animal world. They
had wanted to write the first dog novel and projected a gothic adventure entitled *Kennelworth*. It was never completed, as they felt the
public might not be ready for it; how they would have delighted in
Virginia Woolf's *Flush*. Both Edith and Martin enjoyed communicating in animal noises with their animals, and they were unnervingly
realistic mimics. They commanded a wide range of human and animal
voices. Here is a fictionalized version in *Mount Music* of Edith's mim-
icry of an English huntsman who was with the West Carbery when
she was a girl (Christian Talbot Lowry – the novel's heroine – is in the
kennels, surrounded by eagerly affectionate hounds):

> Dearest things! apostrophised Christian, 'I feel like Nero – I
> wish you only had one lovely head, so that I might kiss you all at
> once!'
> 'Rot!' said Larry, who was leaning against the wall facing her,
> and saying: 'Down, you brute!' at intervals, to hounds, who,
> having failed to force their way to Christian, were directing their
> attention to him, to the detriment of his greyflannel trousers. 'And
> look at your dress from their filthy paws!'
> 'Good Gawd, Mr Larry Sir! Don't say paws! 'Ounds 'ave *feet*,'

Hildegarde and Percy Aylmer with Egerton's water spaniel Pastel, the model for Maria in the R.M. stories and perhaps one of the highest developments of dog personification in fiction.

responded Christian, whose imitation of Cottingham was no less accurate now than it had been some eight years earlier; 'and I don't care a pin for this old skirt anyway.'

Edith's intentness upon aural as well as pictorial realism in her writing led her in 1916 to make this prophecy:

> For anyone who knew the perfection of Martin's rendering of the tones of West Galway, of the gestures, the pauses, that give the life of a story, the words lying dead on the page are only a pain. Perhaps, someday, portable and bindable phonography will be as much a part of a book as its pictures are.

Edith recorded a few of the occasions on which Martin imitated animal sounds, like this bizarre situation:

> We were in London, and stayed at the Bolton Studios, that strange, elongated habitation, that is like nothing so much as a corridor train in a nightmare. There, one night, Martin got ill, and I had to summon, post haste, the nearest doctor. He came, and was an Irishman, and was as clever as Irish doctors often are, and as unconventional. He is dead now, so I may mention that

The West Carbery Foxhounds, Drishane, 1908. Mike Hurley is on Edith's left.

when, in the awful, echoing corridor, at dead of night, the delicate subject of his fee was broached, we discovered that there was an unprocurable sixpence between us. He eyed me and said, 'I'll toss ye for the sixpence!' 'Done!' called Martin, feebly, from within. The doctor and I tossed, double or quits, sudden death. I won. And there came a faint cock-crow from the inner chamber.

Martin's party-piece, brought forward to enliven quiet dinner parties, was to produce the cry of her terrier when its tail had been shut in a door. When they were staying in Oxford, as guests of Herbert Greene, who was then Dean of Magdalen, he took them through the Bodleian Library. In an upper room Edith became aware that Martin's attention was riveted by a large brass ventilator grille. Suddenly she whipped it open and sent down the ventilator shaft and through the walls of the Bodleian the agonized cry of a terrier with its tail stuck in a door. In *Irish Memories* Edith passes over this *outré* exhibition quickly:

> I have often wondered what the grave students in that home of learning can have thought of the unearthly cry from the heavens, Sirius, as it were, in mortal agony. We were not permitted to wait for a sequel. Our host, with blanched face, hurried us away.

Although Edith described Herbert as 'a man with whom it seemed unwise to trifle', Martin apparently felt differently. Her attitude to Herbert was not friendly.

The Somervilles differed from other Castletownshend families in their relative impecuniousness. There were many children to be brought up

Edith on Quinine at a meet of the Galway Blazers at Athenry, Martin Ross standing in the foreground.

on little money. Hence Edith's determination to earn her own living and not be a drain on her parents' income. This is why we find her and Martin, similarly short of money, active and thinking of work when all about them were wasting their time. They spent a large proportion of their earnings on the upkeep of their family houses, and it was they who were to take responsibility for the maintenance and care of the houses, rather than their brothers. In 1892 we find Martin, who kept minute accounts of her spending – unlike Edith, who gave away more than she cared to remember – writing to Edith from Ross: 'To get the kitchen chimney cleaned, the pump mended and the kitchen thoroughly cleaned and whitewashed cost me close on a pound.' At this stage in their career, they were paid, on average, one guinea for an article. Martin, writing without Edith's stimulation, could take weeks to write an article.

Edith often tried to persuade Martin to adventure on a trip, which they could then write up and so recoup the money spent; Edith refused to be prevented from doing something she wanted to do 'for want of a little tin'. Martin, much more realistic about financial matters, prevented Edith from spending money which she did not have in letters like this one of 31 August 1889, concerning a proposal to sell to Thomas Cook, the tour operator, the idea of a guide book about touring in Connemara:

> Now as to Cook. It would be charming – but I haven't the money – what with the saddle, the piano, each three pounds, and another three pounds towards helping that unhappy Lucy [a widowed friend] to India (we are doing it amongst us) you can see what is left of Bentley [Richard Bentley, their publisher] – even if I gave up the saddle there wouldn't be enough.

It was always Hildegarde who was in charge when Edith was away. When Edith was in Paris in January 1900, she wrote to Hildegarde a letter that shows her constant care for the house:

> I am thankful to hear that you are hiring Joanna to clean Drishane. Martin says that that is the way Ross rotted to pieces, only having men in to light fires and open windows, and letting filth accumulate. I think Joanna should go up regularly every day for two or three hours and take the rooms in succession – beginning with the *book rooms* out of wh. all the books should be taken by companies and warmed and dried and dusted . . . it is only a false economy to let valuable things go to decay.

In order to maintain their houses, and thus their family status, Edith and Martin managed a double life, as sociable country ladies and as professional writers. Conditions for writing were much better at Ross than at Drishane. Martin, who was either very busy at Ross or prostrate in bed, found the excessive socializing of Castletownshend a new, and sometimes trying, experience. Phrases from her letters reflect this: 'Castletownshend inertia has me in its grip', 'the business-like waste of time'. Tennis was played *ad nauseam*. An indicator of how closely Castletownshend was linked to London is that no sooner had lawn tennis been invented than the game appeared in Castletownshend, and lawns were levelled. But by 1887 Martin was writing to Edith: 'Katie tells me that tennis is a very old-fashioned game now at Castle T. Said I not well that you were both effete and spasmodic. No healthy moderate interests – all is at fever heat, with nauseated reaction.'

Edith, too, was exasperated by the demands made upon her by her fellows, who were intent upon nothing but light entertainment:

> To attempt anything serious or demanding steady work is just simply impossible here, and I feel sickened of even trying – we are all so tied together – whatever is done must be done by everyone in the whole place and as the majority prefer wasting their time that is the prevalent amusement.

That Edith and Martin stuck to their work and achieved as much as they did is staggering when one realizes how much of Edith's time, after her mother's death, was taken up by the organization of household, farm, workers and animals, even when it was not vacation time and Castletownshend was free from guests. A note from Martin to Hildegarde that has survived in the Coghill family papers gives us some idea of Edith's daily work load: 'Edith would write to you too, only that she is packing a big box of your own – and has had her usual day of kennels, farm, then Dairy books, letters, and now the Ban Oosal and Miss O'Donovan and the organisers to tea.'

When Edith did write to Hildegarde during the crowded summers, she wrote of the crammed timetable, as in this letter of 27 July 1913:

> What with farm and getting this house ready for the Aylmers, and hounds, and choir, and Sassiety (tea parties innumerable, both small and great) – and Constance Bushe's protegees coming to be cared for, I begin to feel that the stationmastership at Clapham junction would be a pleasant lounge.

Somehow the writing was fitted in. There was no timetable: writing time was snatched at propitious moments.

It was Martin who insisted that Edith carry on as Master of the West Carbery Hunt for as long as possible. Business-like, she realized that humorous hunting stories were to make them more money than their serious novels. In 1887 a sub-editor with the *London Illustrated News* had said to Martin, as he responded gloomily to stories of Irish life: 'We have had an overdose of Ireland.' Martin saw that their hunting stories, with their practical and lifelike detail and uproarious humour, were marketable in a way that serious studies of Irish life

A game of doubles. Edith, foreground, and
partner versus Hildegarde and partner.

were not, and that Edith's position as M.F.H. gave them status and authority.

Hunting, then, for Edith and Martin was a joyful combination of business and pleasure. The thrills of free-range steeplechasing, the speed and spontaneous action, far outweighed the significance of a kill. The fox outwitted the pack quite often, most spectacularly as in Edith's description of the Manch run at Christmas 1886. Whether we read their humorous stories or their serious novels we continually encounter lyrical descriptions of communion between horse and rider, or the excitements of the chase; and even those who have never ridden a horse are carried along by the author's enthusiasm. Learning to ride and hunt was, for women like Edith and Martin, an important step in learning confidence and competence in a pursuit where they could freely compare themselves with men. Lord Dunsany, in his *My Ireland*, gave a story that startlingly illustrates how women were learning to believe in their own competence and right to be to the 'fore in the hunting field. In the second half of the nineteenth century the Meath Hounds were splendidly managed by John Watson, the Master. He was a powerful, huge-voiced, imposing man who completely dominated the hunts of the Meath Hounds. Towards one woman rider he was unfailingly polite, no matter what she did, after the following initial contretemps. One day Mrs Dewhurst's horse, in the excitement of the chase, had careered on unrestrained, far beyond the range of many of the exhausted field. Furious with Mrs Dewhurst for putting unnecessary strain on the field, who had followed her lead, John Watson galloped up to her and bellowed, in his huge voice: 'Woman! Go home.' Mrs Dewhurst did not go home, but turned to him and said: 'Go home yourself, you damned son of a bald-headed Carlow onion.'

That great escaper from traditional femininity, Florence Nightingale, wrote:

> As for riding, no 'hockey', no games, will equal it for improving the circulation all over and exercising the muscles and animal courage. A live horse and the sympathy of 'the horse and its rider' is worth all the bats and balls put together. So 'drat' hockey and long live the horse! Them's my sentiments.

After publishing *The Silver Fox* in 1897 Edith and Martin, in the eyes of their agent, J.B. Pinker, went into a decline and enjoyed inertia. Pinker was one of the best-known agents of the time, acting for Henry James, Arnold Bennett and many of the best writers. He worried over the writer's block that seemed to be afflicting Somerville and Ross. He worried and harried them into creating *The Irish R.M.* Edith recalled Pinker in her memoir *Happy Days*, describing a day when the two writers were on holiday in Étaples with a group of painting friends:

> We had a taskmaster, a little man of iron determination, A Literary Agent . . . and he did not forget us . . . In my diary at the date July 16, 1898, appears the fateful entry: 'Heard from Pinker again. He says Watson of the Bad Mag is shrieking for hunting stories . . .' And then heaven intervened . . . there befell a day so cold and wet that the extreme measure of staying in the house and doing some work became our only resource . . . Gradually we talked and argued into existence one after another of the little group of men and women who were destined to become for us intimate friends . . . The weather, that had severely discouraged painting and picnicking, now decided to support literature . . . there prone on the yellow sand, we lay, and talked and wrote, bit by bit . . . and Great Uncle McCarthy's ghost, with its 'fumbling hand and inebriate shuffle' materialised, and Flurry Knox and Slipper began to assert themselves.

Although Edith and Martin wanted to avoid portraying characters too clearly based on living originals, we can identify characteristics of the R.M.'s cast in many of Edith Somerville's relatives. The R.M. himself, with his public school uprightness and happy flights of pedantry, was, like Herbert Greene, Edith's faithful suitor, a Magdalen man and a Classicist. His wife, Philippa, an Englishwoman suddenly pitched into Ireland on her marriage, may have been modelled on Aylmer Somerville's first wife, Emmeline Sykes. Bobby Bennett shares many characteristics with Edith herself.

Here and on the following pages: Illustrations from the Badminton Magazine *of R.M. characters.*

Philippa on her bicycle

'Miss Sally and the cockatoo moved away'

Denis O'Loughlin

'Mrs Knox extended a skinny hand'

Peter Cadogan

My friend Slipper

Quite clearly Aylmer Somerville served as the model for Flurry
Knox; M.F.H. of the West Carbery Hounds, alone of the family he
spoke in a strong brogue. The anti-hero Willy of their first novel *An
Irish Cousin* was a trial run at the character of Flurry and was recognized by relatives, Mrs Somerville, as we have seen, hotly objecting to
this portrayal of her favourite child. When Edith was discussing casting
for a stage version of *The Irish R.M.* with her nephew, the younger
Nevill Coghill, she wrote to him: 'If only your Uncle Aylmer were
available to play Flurry Knox ... the Half-Sir is not an easy part to
play.'

In her preface to the 1928 edition of *The Irish R.M. and His Experiences* Edith stated firmly: 'I should like, once more, to declare that of
them all, Slipper and Maria alone had prototypes in the world as
Martin Ross and I knew it.' And in 1946 she reiterated, when remin-
iscing about the birth of the R.M.:

Lady Knox

> One after the other of Major Sinclair Yeates' friends and
> neighbours came effortlessly to our call. It seemed as if we had
> always known them. I can truly say that in order to identify an
> actual representative of any of them, it would be necessary to tear
> each to pieces, and collecting the fragments, resume them into a
> sort of human ragbag.

Searching for an image to illustrate their creative technique she
quoted from Gilbert's *Patience*:

> Take of these elements all that is fusible,
> Melt 'em all down in a pipkin or crucible,
> Set 'em to simmer and take off the scum,
> And a Heavy Dragoon is the resid-u-um!

and commented: 'So we simmered Flurry Knox, and old Mrs Knox,
and the rest of the company.'

Egerton Coghill's outrageous water spaniel Pastel was the model for
Maria, Major Yeates's dog. Pastel was a celebrity in her own time;
Lord Dunsany was introduced to her when shooting near Skibbereen:
'I remember how thrilled I was to meet even a dog out of that famous
book *The Experiences of an Irish R.M.* It is perhaps hard on my pub-
lisher to say it but the bare fact remains that readers will get more of
Ireland from that book than from anything I can tell them.'

The local hero nicknamed 'Pack', who was the model for Slipper,
was an even more gifted speaker than Rickeen at Ross. He spoke with
a full-blown theatricality, always playing to his audience. Even his
death was public. He made his last appearance in the main street of
Skibbereen, leading a badly broken stallion that turned on him and
trampled him to death. In his introduction to a series of readings from
the R.M. stories for the B.B.C., Nevill Coghill said: 'I knew Slipper
well myself in real life and all that is said of him in these books is

The redoubtable Mr Tomsy Flood

*'Drinking strong tea and eating buns with
serious simplicity'*

speakingly true to his nature. He was a sort of horse-coping poacher and generally sporting rascal, with astounding gifts as a liar and a lord of language.'

'*Bernard hanging on to his tail, belaboured him with a cane*'

'*At this juncture Maria overtook us with the cockatoo in her mouth*'

'*I felt as if I were being skilfully kicked downstairs*'

CHAPTER 8

Horse-Drawn and
Water-Borne: Getting About

Few South Pacific Islands are now as isolated as was, in those days, –
I speak of ninety or one hundred years ago – Castle Townshend ...
Each estate was a kingdom, and in the impossibility of locomotion,
each neighbouring potentate acquired a relative importance quite out
of proportion to his merits, for to love your neighbour – or, at all
events, to marry her – was almost inevitable when matches were a
matter of mileage, and marriages might be said to have been made by
the map.

From *Irish Memories*, 1917

All readers of Somerville and Ross are familiar with the appearance
of a Bianconi car, a sidecar or a trap; we are less sure of what a two-
horse jingle, a spring-back gig or a coal boat looked like. In rocky,
hilly seaboard country, most transport of heavy goods was by water.
Into Castletownshend came the coal boats from Bristol to the coal
quay; passing up the river to Rineen flour mill went the flour boats.
Smaller cargo boats constantly came and went from the landing stage
at Sheehys, whose store for salted provisions was in the long building
opposite the Castletownshend pier, on the other shore. The smaller
craft, many made by the O'Mahony boat-building family, were the
fishing boats, the sailing dinghies and pleasure craft of the gentry.

Wheeled vehicles capable of travelling the rough roads had to be
well made and strong. The narrow escapes and outright disasters of
travel in horse-drawn society figured large in the writings of Somerville and Ross, as in their lives. Martin, as we have seen, was to die as
a result of a fall from a horse, and there are many distressing descriptions of her slight body being pitched from cabs and traps.

Although there was a large visiting circuit at Castletownshend
which could be walked, horse-drawn vehicles extended the range of
family visiting greatly, so that cousins ten to fifteen miles away could
be called on. In the early 1800s wheeled traffic between Skibbereen and
Castletownshend was infrequent; the easiest method of travel was on
horseback. The countryside was crossed by a bewildering mesh of
bridle paths and bohreens, both obscured by the great ditched banks
that were such a catastrophic feature of West Carbery hunting. When

*Martin and Edith sailing up the river. Edith
is at the helm.*

The Kathleen and May, *the last Bristol coal boat to deliver to Castletownshend.*

Castletownshend itself was a centre for trade and provision, of such importance that it had its own majestic customs house, travelling to Skibbereen was not of much importance to its inhabitants. But as the road system improved, and stage coach services reached Skibbereen and beyond, to Bantry, the trading centre moved inland from Castletownshend to Skibbereen. Consequently the road was improved.

The Poole family was based at Mayfield, a house, with estate, near Bandon. A diary written by Judith, Horace Poole's wife and Hewitt's mother, for the first months of 1857 gives a detailed visiting round. The extent and frequency of visits, and distances travelled, even for a day trip, are astonishing. The first week of January lists:

> Tuesday. Drove to Newcourt and surprised them all – very cold day.
> Wednesday. Drove to Whitehall in the morning. Caulfields and Townsends spent evening night and morning with us.
> Thursday. Drove to Drishane, saw H and Mrs Bushe, wet day. Annie and Theo stay with us.

Drishane was thirty miles from Mayfield, and Newcourt and Whitehall were even further. The system of transporting Somervilles to Pooles, or vice versa, for long visits, is explained by this entry:

> 23rd February – Met the Drishane carriage at Clon. arrived at Drishane, found poor Mrs Somerville very low.

So that carriages set out from each house and exchanged passengers at Clonakilty.

Sailing boats in the harbour,
Castletownshend, c.1890.

These distances, travelled by heavy family carriages, are impressive when we compare them with Edith's own best rate for cross-country driving in a trap. During the 1920s, much of Ireland's railway system was disrupted by the frequent explosions and malicious damage caused by the Troubles. Edith, on a visit to Kerry, discovered that she could not return to Drishane, as planned, by train. She sent a telegram to Mike Hurley, her groom, asking him to send her horse, trap and mackintosh to her, and drove back alone, covering fifty miles a day. She was at this stage in her sixties.

Many travel books were written by journalists, or authors in need of money, who came over to Ireland, rushed about it at speed, and turned out amusing, shallow books. Thackeray did this, but Trollope, in his Irish novels, achieves a deeper, more intimate portrait. They were both equally observant of Irish modes of transport, and from them we have detailed information on what it was like getting about Ireland during the early and mid nineteenth century. When Thackeray travelled through Ireland in 1842, writing up his *Irish Sketch Book*, he passed through Skibbereen on the stage coach:

> Near Dunmanway that great coach, 'the Skibbereen Industry', dashed by us at seven miles an hour; a wondrous vehicle. There were gaps between every one of the panels; you could see daylight through and through it. Like our machine it was full, with three complementary sailors on the roof, as little harness as possible to the horses, and as long stages as horses can well endure - ours were each eighteen-mile stages. About eight miles from

Skibbereen a one-horse car met us, and carried away an offshoot of passengers to Bantry ...

Before you enter the city of Skibbereen, the tall new Poor-house presents itself to the eye of the traveller; of the common model, being a bastard-Gothic edifice, with a profusion of cottage-ornée (is cottage masculine or feminine in French?) – of cottage-ornée roofs, and pinnacles, and insolent-looking stacks of chimneys. It is built for 900 people, but as yet not more than 400 have been induced to live in it, the beggars preferring the freedom of their precarious trade to the dismal certainty within its walls. Next we come to the chapel, a very large respectable-looking building of dark-grey stone; and presently, behold, by the crowd of blackguards in waiting, the 'Skibbereen Perseverance' has found its goal, and you are inducted to the 'Hotel' opposite.

Before railways reached Ireland, long journeys to the West and South-West could be made by canal boats. Trollope, in his *The Kellys and the O'Kellys*, gives a detailed picture of the mechanics of getting across to the West of Ireland:

We will now return to Martin Kelly. I have before said that as soon as he had completed his legal business, – namely, his instructions for the settlement of Anty Lynch's property, respecting which he and Lord Ballindine had been together to the lawyer's in Clare Street, – he started for home, by the Ballinasloe canal-boat, and reached that famous depot of the fleecy tribe without adventure ... [He] at last reached Ballinasloe, at ten

Rose Marie Salter Townshend in a wicker safety seat on a donkey.

o'clock the morning after he had left Dublin, in a flourishing condition. From thence he travelled, by Bianconi's car, as far as Tuam, and when there he went at once to the hotel, to get a hack car to take him home to Dunmore.

In the hotel yard he found a car already prepared for a journey; and on giving his order for a similar vehicle for his own use, was informed, by the disinterested ostler, that the horse then being harnessed, was to take Mr Daly, the attorney, to Tuam, and that probably that gentleman would not object to join him, Martin, in the conveyance. Martin, thinking it preferable to pay fourpence rather than sixpence a mile for his jaunt, acquiesced in this arrangement, and, as he had a sort of speaking acquaintance with Mr Daly, whom he rightly imagined would not despise the economy which actuated himself, he had his carpet-bag put into the well of the car, and, placing himself on it, he proceeded to the attorney's door.

Railways began to appear during the Famine; many of them were constructed as relief work, the Great Southern and Western line through Charleville and Mallow to Cork and Bandon being one of these. In the 1850s extensions were made from Cork to Midleton, and from Queenstown to Carrigtwohill. A branch of the Cork and Bandon line was complete to Kinsale by 1863. The Cork and Macroom Railway and the West Cork Railway from Bandon to Dunmanway were both opened in 1866. Skibbereen and Bantry were not connected by railway with Cork until the 1880s. The arrival of the railway at Skibbereen created a sensation. Edith noted in her diary (21 July 1877): 'All went up to Skib in honour of the opening of the railway. Great fun and speechifying - ate enormously. Hordes of people - an old man told Papa it was a beautiful vessel he had brought to Skibbereen.'

In order to alleviate poverty in the Baltimore area the Baroness Burdett-Coutts and others had revived the fishing industry there, and a railway extension was taken to Baltimore, the fish catches reaching Cork and further afield as a result.

The proliferation of branch lines, although useful when shipping hunters to meets by rail, was to prove infuriating to Edith when she first attempted to visit Martin at Ross:

The journey from Drishane to Ross was first made by me in February, 1889. As the conventional crow flies, or as, on the map, the direct line is drawn, the distance is no more than a hundred miles, but by the time you have steered east to Cork, and North-West to Limerick, and North to Ennis, and to Athenry, and to Galway, with prolonged changes (and always for the worse), at each of these places, you begin to realise the greatness of Ireland, and to regard with awe the independent attitude of mind of her railway companies. It would indeed seem that the 'Sinn Fein

movement "Ourselves Alone" ', might have been conceived and
brought forth by any one of the lines involved in the *trajet* from
Cork to Galway.

The coincidence of a fine stretch of sailing water with a clutch of
gentry houses resulted in the Castletownshend Regatta; all inhabitants
were accustomed to rowing, sailing and the delights of racing. Edith
seems to have enjoyed sailing in her youth, but rough sea yachting
made her uncharacteristically weak. A diary entry, describing a trip to
Glengarriff, gives a revealing picture of what could happen to women
on a 'pleasure cruise': 'On board Gyneth at eleven, peaceful run as far
as the Mizen. Fainted in a rough swell after the Mizen. Mrs Warren
sick overboard.' Later, in the dark: 'We go on the rock, pulled off, set
out for hotel in punt'. The hotel was full and Edith had to change into
evening dress in the boot cupboard. The entry concludes: 'To Glengarriff Castle to see the Whites. Very wild people.'

Pleasure boats ranged from Sir Joscelyn Coghill's splendid schooner

Ierne, *Sir Joscelyn's schooner, under sail
going out of the harbour.*

Ierne, to the yachts like *Thea*, *Gyneth*, the *Haidee*, down to the delicately built racing gigs like the *Miri Chi*. Diary entries for the summer of 1879 show Edith on a yachting holiday with a party of friends who sailed off and wandered about the West Coast of Ireland. The party included a very eccentric yachtswoman, who raced the *Haidee* single-handed, called Sydney Robson, who was a niece of Lord Avonmore. She and Edith sailed the *Haidee*, in company with Miss Robson's white cockatoo, and survived numerous scrapes. Twenty years before the writing of 'The House of Fahy', its elements were laid away in Edith's mind.

When Somerville and Ross describe wealthy Anglo-Irish society, able to afford the new forms of transport, they base their knowledge on a section of Castletownshend society that was wealthy by marriage with, or inheritance from, English women. Several of the brothers of Edith Somerville married wealthy women, and the wealth of such men as Percy and Eddy Aylmer explains how there was still a monied and leisured society at Castletownshend when landlord families like the

Ierne *in Castletownshend harbour.*

Ierne *converted to a houseboat. Like the Somervilles, the Coghills sometimes leased their house in the summer, to keep afloat financially, and moved on to the houseboat. She broke up on rocks in a bad storm in 1917. Sir Joscelyn had given her the first name ever recorded for Ireland: 'Ierne' was the name given to the island by Greek geographers. Like his nephew, Boyle Somerville, Sir Joscelyn was a keen amateur Irish historian.*

The Miri Chi. *Something of a wooden horse, this boat was given to Edith by Herbert. He named it* Miri Chi, *which is Romany for 'My Girl'. The gift enabled Herbert to commandeer more of Edith's time and also to instruct her. The cox is Herbert Greene, the stroke Martin. Edith is in the bow, and Hildegarde and Emmie are seated in the stern. Boyle Somerville is lying in the bows. At the launch of the* Miri Chi, *Edith made a quick cartoon, which shows a remarkable talent for likenesses and not unpleasing caricature.*

The Nadine *moored at Eton, on a misty morning in the 1870s.*

Coghills were in difficulties because of non-payment of rents. One of Edith's many Coghill aunts was married to John Aylmer of Walworth Castle, Northumberland. Percy and Eddy were their sons; Percy was a close and lifelong friend of Edith after he came to live in Castletownshend when his parents and elder brother were killed in an appalling railway accident in North Wales on 20 August 1868. All the passengers on the Irish Mail were burnt to death when an oil wagon up-line got loose and ran back into the oncoming Mail down a steep incline. The sons Percy and Eddy became wards of their uncle, Sir Joscelyn Coghill; they continued to live at Castletownshend, two elderly bachelors, until after the First World War. They were sailing fanatics, and it was their steam launch that provided the model for the *Serpolette* of *The Real Charlotte.*

Ramshackle Ross, with its one usable trap and the ungainly Daisy for transport, had nothing to compare with the racing gigs, steam launch and splendid yachts of Castletownshend. The big house and all its trappings, used beyond their natural life, and without careful maintenance, were worn out. There was no money to run the house with, let alone purchase the newer toys of transport. Martin, trying to harness Daisy with mouldy old tack, complains to Edith of its 'lengthy interludes of string'.

Transport for Edith and Martin meant, ideally, riding, and they were both outstanding riders. Harnessing horses for the trap or car, and driving them, was as familiar to them as walking. The importance of a good seat, firm hands, balance, and a grasp of the mechanics of driving might mean the difference between life and death. Diaries of the pre-motor era in West Cork abound with asides such as 'killed by a cob', 'killed by a toss', 'killed by a bicycle', 'trampled'.

The strength of forearm, wrist and back required for hauling about the wildish ponies that drew their traps remained with Edith and

Hildegarde into their old age. In October 1938 Hildegarde leapt from
the trap in which she was driving Edith, in order to lead by the head
the pony that had gone wild with alarm at a disturbance in the hedge.
She was seventy-one at this date. Edith still drove alone in her trap
when she was in her eighties. On the last Sunday of October 1939, she
drove alone to the church to play the organ. Geraldine Cummins,
staying at Drishane at this time, noted with horror that one of Edith's
days consisted of rising at five, driving eighty miles through filthy
weather to Midleton, where she bought a mare at a horse fair, and
being back at Drishane at five in the afternoon. She was eighty-one
years old, and to the end of her life delighted in being driven fast in
a motor car.

Edith and Martin had to cope with many a horse-drawn disaster.
They always made light of these, but it is difficult to forget that death
was then a shade too close. One such incident is described in *Wheel-
Tracks* (1923):

*The Glen Barrahane motor. Hildegarde with
Katharine, her daughter, and a friend.*

> The first horse that was absolutely mine, bought with money
> earned by myself, was a pretty, little well-bred mare, called Dodo,
> she and Mr Benson's novel coming into action at the same time. I
> bought her, half-trained, from a farmer, and she had the name –

before she received that of Dodo – of being 'a very airy mare, and as loose as a hare'. In view of these qualities it seemed well to give her a spell of discipline with long reins before saddling her. It happened, on the day following on that of her arrival, that Martin Ross and I were driving homeward in a high dog-cart, and with a decidedly 'airy' horse in the shafts, a hunter, whose foible it was to jump the nearest fence, dog-cart or no, if anything agitated him. We were at the foot of a long hill when we saw from afar some creature coming down the hill to us at that rate of speed that is picturesquely, if obscurely, described as 'hell for leather'. Soon we realized that it was a riderless, runaway horse; I pulled Sorcerer as close under the fence as he would go, and we awaited events with some not unpleasant excitement. Like a flash the horse went by us, in a whirl of lashing ropes and reins, and Martin and I, looking at each other, aghast, said but the one word:

'Dodo!'

She was out of sight in a few seconds, flying back to her birth-place, four miles away, by the hard high road.

'She shot into the yard to me like a thrain!' said her late owner, 'she'd a great gallop in her always!'

I got her home at once, and she stood all night in bran poultices, and was none the worse. Airy though she undoubtedly was, she became reasonably steady with hounds, and was chiefly given to misbehaviour on the road, where, on small provocation, such as a humming in telegraph wires, or a donkey grazing on what is called 'the long meadow' (i.e. the grass of the roadside), she would, as someone said, 'go into the sky and stop there for five minutes'.

It once happened that on a market day, in a street in Skibbereen, a large pig ran across the road so directly in front of her that she came on her knees on its back. Before I had time to think, Dodo had hopped like a kangaroo, on her hindlegs, clean over the pig, and no one was any the worse. The owner of the pig said it was by the Mercy of God that the pig was there, the way the mare's knees didn't meet the road. But he agreed that the mercy might have been still greater had the pig been elsewhere.

Unprotected bodies, great weights and high speeds made transport at all times a dangerous enterprise. The chief difference from our modern motorized monotony was one of sound: the varying rattles of the light gigs and cars, the thundering rumble of heavy drays. Somerville and Ross readers may feel and hear what this was like at traction rallies, where historians of transport drive their restored horse-drawn vehicles. The trembling ground and the rush of air as a vehicle passes close enable one to realize at once the dangers and pleasures that were everyday experiences to Somerville and Ross.

A Castletownshend racing gig in store.

Martin's competence at harnessing operated in the most strained of circumstances. Here, in a letter to Edith from Ross, in 1901, is a description of one of the more strained:

> We did not achieve church this morning without some difficulty. I went round to the yard after breakfast to see if things were *en train*, and was informed by Rickeen that he had not fed the grey pony, as he had found a weasel in the oats, 'and sure there's some kind of pizen in thim'.
>
> Being unable to combat this statement, I desired that the pony should be given hay. This was done but at the last moment, just before she was being put into the shafts, she 'sthripped a shoe'. Mama's old pony, Killola, was again a little lame – nothing for it but the monster Daisy, browsing in the lawn with her foal. It was then 10.45. I had on a voile skirt of stupendous length, with a floating train, my best gloves and other Sunday trappings, none the less must I help Rick to harness Daisy. Then the trouble was to shut her foal into the barn. In the barn was already immured the donkey, filled with one fierce determination to flee over to the White Field, where was Darcy's donkey. I had to hold Daisy, and combat her maternal instincts, and endure her ceaseless shriekings, I had also to head off the donkey, which burst from the barn, with gallopings and capers, while Rickeen stuffed in the foal, who, like its mother, was shrieking at the top of its voice. I also was weak with laughing, as Rick's language, both in English and Irish, was terrific, and the donkey very ridiculous. Rick finally

Above. Guillemot.

Right: *Miss Somerville makes for a stair head on a rough crossing in the Bristol boat.*

flailed it into what he called 'the pig-shtyle' . . . then the harness had to be torn off the grey, in the loose box . . . then we pitched Mama on to the car and got off. Daisy, almost invisible under her Buffalo mane, as usual went the pace, and we got in at the First Lesson, and all was well.

Martin's mother had an almost divine calm that sustained her through many a terrible catastrophe when travelling, a characteristic that she passed to her daughter. Edith, in *Irish Memories*, recollected that:

Mrs Martin's contempt for danger was one of the many points wherein she differed from the average woman of her time. Indeed, it cannot be said that she despised it, as, quite obviously, she enjoyed it. Martin has told of how she and her mother were caught in a storm, in a small boat, on Lough Corrib. Things became serious; one boatman dropped his oar and prayed, the other wept, but continued to row; Martin, who had not been bred to boats on Ross Lake for nothing, tugged at the abandoned oar of the supplicant. Meanwhile her mother sat erect in the stern, looking on the tempest in as unshaken a mood as Shakespeare could have desired, and enjoying every moment of it. Neither where horses were concerned did she know fear. I have been with her in a landau, with one horse trying to bolt, while the other had kicked till it got a leg over the trace. Help was at hand, and during the readjustment Mrs Martin firmly retained her seat. Her only anxiety was lest the drive might have to be given up, her

only regret that both horses had not bolted. She said she liked
driving at a good round pace. An outside car might do anything
short of lying down and rolling, without being able to shake her
off; her son Robert used to say that on an outside car his mother's
grasp of the situation was analogous to that of a poached egg on
toast - both being practically undetachable.

Travelling abroad became something of an industry for Edith and
Martin during the nineties, when they were commissioned to write
travel books and articles. They toured France and Denmark, and were
both accustomed to using Bradshaw and surviving long periods in
boats, trains and cabs. Edith always cut things fine, travelling as cheaply
as possible and giving away *en route* all food and monies not strictly
necessary. Her fatal impulse to generosity must have frequently infuriated Martin. Edith worked out how much money she needed immediately and gave away the rest. More than once, coming back from
art-study in Paris, she would arrive at some relative's house in London
and have to rush in and borrow the money to pay the cab fare. The
Irish Sea crossing was done usually Passage West to Bristol, but if
hard-pressed for money, Edith would take a train through Wales to
Milford Haven and take a Cork bound boat from there, as it was far

*Glen Barrahane, the 'Moorish' end. As a
house Glen Barrahane was a happy medley of
styles. It is now demolished.*

The Point House, Castletownshend, as it was when owned by Major John Somerville and his wife, Aunt Fanny (Herbert). This house came into the hands of Aunt Fanny's dreaded niece, Emily Herbert, on whom Edith was to model the character of Charlotte Mullen. Martin never met Emily – she had died before The Real Charlotte *was finished. This plain and pleasant house, even in this photograph, is beginning to suffer at the hands of amateur improvers. The bold move of throwing out a bay window has not been without its effects above. The house was later completely transformed, by Kendal Coghill, into a rambling Swiss cottage. Dreadful things were done to houses by their imperious owners. Madam Townshend, she of the unique rockery, accidentally demolished the family house of the Townshends that preceded the present Castle. She objected to the low ceilings, and decided to remedy this by lowering the floors. When several sets of beams that tied the fabric together had been removed, the entire building gently collapsed.*

cheaper. Cattle boats, and cattle trucks, in which she hitched lifts happily, were not unfamiliar to Miss Somerville.

During the twenties all Anglo-Irish families had to decide whether they were to the left or the right of the hyphen. Most chose the former and resettled in England. Landing at Bristol, many Anglo-Irish menfolk gravitated naturally to Oxford and surrounding counties; some, seeking a coastal landscape like that they had left, settled in Cornwall or Devon. A large proportion of West Cork Anglo-Irish society established itself in the West Country/Oxford area during the Troubles, and the visiting circles revolved again; the 'picnic in a foreign land' was over.

CHAPTER 9

'How Will They Ever Understand Us?'

Who could hope in half a dozen lines, or in as many volumes, to state their views about Ireland? No one, I fear, save one of those intrepid beings, wondrous in their self-confidence, who lightly come to Ireland for three weeks ... Some such have come our way, English people whose honesty and innocence would be endearing, if they were a little less overlaid by condescension.

From *Irish Memories*, 1917

In belonging to a class no longer of any substance, either in Ireland or in England, save now in anecdote, Somerville and Ross have passed into the same limbo as that other Irish non-sequitur, the Irishmen who served in the First World War. The Rising in Dublin at Easter 1916 involved 1,600 Irishmen, of whom 450 were killed; of the British army 116 were killed. At the same time 150,000 Irishmen were at the Front, two thirds having joined up since the outbreak of war. Approximately 50,000 Irishmen died during the 1914-18 war. These men also had a vision of an Irish nation. Initially they joined up in support of 'little Belgium', a small nation, predominantly Catholic, overrun by the giant Germany. They hoped to demonstrate, by their valour, their own fitness for nationhood, and the Irish regiments' demonstration of their 'Irishness' during the war was intense.

The first completely Irish Division into the field was the 10th, commanded by Sir Bryan Mahon, the Galway cavalry officer whose flying column had relieved Mafeking in the South African war. Each battalion in this Division had its piper, and when the Division was inspected by the King on 25 May 1915, it marched to the once forbidden song 'A Nation Once Again'. In August it was in action in the

Arthur Townshend studies the cup and ring marks on the slab at the entrance to Knockdrum fort on a hill overlooking Castletownshend. The panoramic view on page 10 was taken from its rampart. Many resident Anglo-Irish made a determined effort to understand the history and culture of Ireland. In Castletownshend the district's archaeological remains were recorded by Boyle Somerville and others; the Irish language was taught by Violet Townshend at the Castle – to Edith and Martin among others.

disastrous Dardanelles campaign, where it was decimated. A soldier of the 10th Division wrote home after 'The Dardanelles': 'I am proud to be Irish ... Ireland may mourn, but the Irish may hold up their heads and be proud of their losses.'

The execution of the leaders of the Easter Rising replaced this pride with another, and it was a pride that Somerville and Ross found difficult to share at that time.

At the outbreak of the war *Some Experiences of an Irish R.M.* was well established as a classic of humorous writing – stories from it were included in the broadsheets sent to the Front by *The Times*. Edith and Martin had many appreciative letters from Irishmen at the Front, and through their two suffrage societies they supported the war effort in every way possible.

Edith was adaptable, in a way that Martin was not; had she lived, Martin as a Unionist would have been unable to accept the road to separation that Ireland took, or the force that took it there. In comparison with Martin, Edith was a Nationalist, of an individual kind. In December 1915, Martin died, and at first Edith had no impulse to work, or conviction that she could carry on alone. She spent the first months of 1916 in a stunned loneliness, and was in London at the time of the Rising. As communications were cut, accounts in *The Times* were sparse. The leader on Wednesday 26 April describes the 'insane rising' as German-backed: 'It is evidently the result of a carefully arranged plot, concocted between the Irish traitors and their German confederates.' An Irishman called Thomas Polson wrote a letter to *The Times* on 2 May headed 'An Irishman's Remedy', and his reaction must have been typical of many at the time. He suggests that the 'invertebrate government' hang all the leaders and conscript the rank and file: 'The majority are simple, misguided fellows, who, once removed from the baleful influence of their leaders, would make as fine soldiers as any we have got, and they are already partly trained.'

By 7 May the reports of the execution of the leaders were being published, beginning with Pearse, Clarke and MacDonagh on 4 May, and Edith must have seen that the reprisal was severe, and must have feared over-reaction from the berated Asquith government. She sat up on the night of the 7th, writing a letter to *The Times* which was published on the 9th.

It is an astounding letter – the first and only *Times* letter at this critical period to plead for clemency. She signed herself 'An Irishwoman', presumably wishing to remain unknown as all of her brothers were serving in the war. She blames the inaction of England for the growth and power of Sinn Fein. This letter tells us little about Edith's Nationalism, as it is slanted to an English audience, but it does show her considerable powers as a writer, and is unusual in having been published between Martin's death in December and the date in June

Boyle Somerville photographed many standing stones and made accurate surveys of many West Cork Stone Age alignments. Edith came with him on his surveys. She appears, rather worn out, sitting on a recumbent stone.

1916 when Edith became convinced that Martin was writing with her again in spirit:

The Rebel Rank and File

Sir, It has been pointed out in your columns, and elsewhere, that the Sinn Fein organisation, which had started its career as a somewhat academic league of conventional patriots, began, by a singular coincidence, to give practical life to its ideals at the moment when the Liberal Government entered upon its reign of peace and love. A new spirit was breathed into Sinn Fein.

Love, we all know, is blind: in the case of the large souled administrators of Irish affairs it was also deaf. Sinn Fein, unpropitiated by the indulgence of its rulers, proceeded to sharpen its claws.

Its officials were at no special pains to conceal either their opinions or their methods, and, as they found 'freedom slowly broadening down', they took every advantage of their favoured position. Financed by Germany, tutored by America, sheltered by England, the Sinn Fein propaganda ran through Ireland like an epidemic in a South Pacific island. The Gaelic League was turned from its ingenuous programme of jig dancing and warbling passé treason in modern Irish, and was set to more effective issues. . .

. . . I have heard of more than one state-supported school in a remote part of Munster – fuller particulars of the locality, might, perhaps, be obtained from Ireland's most recent invader – in which the greatness and generosity of Germany, and the reptile villainy of England, were given as themes for the essays of the 'little Scholars'. The boys of nine or ten years age, quick as ever to learn the romance of revolt, ready as ever to absorb sedition, as white blotting paper soaks up ink, have grown into these senseless, reckless, slaughtering idealists of to-day, out not for plunder or outrage (unworthy, there, of their German instructors), but out of the mad dream of Ireland a Nation. It seems improbable that any English government, past or present – the methods of Cromwell, who was also an idealist, being impracticable – would propose that a couple of thousand or so of young men should either be hanged or imprisoned for life because they risked everything for a vision – 'Their Country, right or wrong!'

But what is the alternative? To send them back to Ireland to be jeered at, admired, abused, to brood over their failure, and to plan, perhaps, a more excellent way; or to slam them into 'English dungeons' for as long as may serve to sour their wild blood and slacken their eager limbs, but not long enough to provide a time for repentance; and is Eternity long enough for an Irishman to lay down his vision and take up with expediency and submission? Can prison discipline turn a thwarted rebel into a loyal subject, or

sightless staring at the walls of a cell make a dreamer forget his dreams? England sat quiet while these lads were being taught disloyalty to her as assiduously as a Japanese child learns patriotism; the fault is not wholly on their side. Let her send these captives to join their brothers in the trenches, there to find out what manner of man the German is. The mother of Shamus O'Brien, rebel of '98, had but one plea, but today it seems sufficient – 'The craythure is young. Ah! Spare him, my Lord!'
Yours, etc.
An Irishwoman
May 7

In the first months of the war in 1914, the British forces had experienced the staggering death tolls of the battles of Mons, the Marne, Alsace and Ypres. In just over a year of battle, up to 9 January 1916, over half a million men had been killed. At Easter in 1916 the battle of Verdun was raging. Verdun was a great German offensive planned late in 1915; it was not over until July 1916. As Mr Polson had remarked in his letter to *The Times*, the coalition government, under Asquith's leadership, was 'invertebrate', and owing to its failure to act over the Dublin crisis, control was taken by the military. Edith was very aware of the temper of mind of an officer core seasoned by the war in which it was engaged with Germany. She was quick to realize that, in trying the leaders of the Rising, the British military court would be judging it as an act of treason such as desertion under fire. It is not surprising that officers who, at the Front, would unhesitatingly have shot one of their own men, if he deserted, should have administered the rough justice that they did in Dublin.

Although pleading for clemency, Edith was infuriated by the Nationalist delusion that the Irish and the Germans had a natural affinity and brotherhood, and this must have caused her to be uncharacteristically savage – 'warbling passé treason in modern Irish' and a few other phrases give substance to Edith's reputation for a ferociously cutting tongue when roused.

During the week that Edith's letter was published, the captive leaders were executed, and the revulsion experienced by the Irish people, and the exalting to martyr status of the leaders, effectively ended any hope of a peaceful transition to self-government. After this turning away from England, volunteer Irishmen, who continued to fight, and enlist, throughout the war, were in a strange position. Now 'out of line' with a new, neutral Nationalist Ireland, they were also in an anomalous, difficult position in the British army. They continued to win V.C.s – having won seventeen up to the time of the Rising.

As the Irish regiments passed through Boulogne, they sang and whistled 'Tipperary', the song that was to become one of the great marching tunes of the war; the people of Boulogne cheered and pelted them with flowers.

The Irish regiments were renowned for their 'dash', exhilaration and speed in the face of extreme physical danger; many accounts exist of their valour, written by soldiers of other regiments. Their war-pipes, their gold and green banners with the harp emblem, their priests and prayers before action, made them extraordinary. English officers remarked 'at the order "advance", they shouted "Erin go Bragh", and at the order "fix bayonets", they sang "God Save Ireland".'

Edith hoped that England would come to see, particularly by Ireland's efforts in the First World War, that Ireland was deserving of a separate nationhood. In the 1920s, her friendship with Dame Ethel Smyth produced a series of letters that show the nature of Edith's Nationalism very well. Dame Ethel irritated Edith intensely by her lack of understanding of the Irish and her support for the force known as the 'Black and Tans'; in her irritation Edith retorts with sharp clarity:

> I half think of writing an article about the absurdity, if it were nothing else, of grinding and crushing Ireland to death. Oh yes, I admit the assassinations, but I still can't see why the Irish should not wish for freedom as they have wished and struggled for it since Henry II's time. If the English smash us to pulp, you will have nothing left to laugh at (yes, *you* and all the good and well-intentioned people who think they know what is best for Ireland) . . .
>
> In all these centuries of disaffection and disappointment one simple thing has never been tried – giving Ireland what she asks for. If I said I wanted to go hunting, I shouldn't be consoled for a refusal by being given a ticket for a Sunday concert at the Albert Hall.

Roughly half of the British army in the nineteenth century was made up of recruits from Scotland and Ireland. These men were tough and of fine physique, inured to hardships; as the century wore on, two factors reduced the intake of Scots and Irish, who were replaced by poor specimens from the English industrial areas. In Scotland the Highland clearances, which replaced peasants with more remunerative sheep and deer, caused the class that provided soldiers to emigrate. In Ireland the Famine and the consequent agitations and emigration reduced the entry into the British army drastically. On the other hand, the flow of Anglo-Irish into the services increased, as there was no prospect of continuing income from landlordism.

The Anglo-Irish in the British army were eccentrics; their high spirits, dash and impulsive overriding of the regular 'right thing' made them sometimes anathema, although always curiosities, to the stolid British officer. There is no better example of an outstanding Anglo-Irishman in the Victorian army than General Sir William Butler. A

*Mrs Warren and Boyle Somerville both
recorded scenes and practices that they saw to
be passing. These four studies – which might
be by either, as they exchanged prints – show
Rineen Mill (above), salting fish on the
League (top right), gutting fish on the Quay
(middle), winnowing (bottom right).*

Catholic, and younger son of a small farmer in Tipperary, Butler had a magnificent physique, stamina and an acute, quick mind. In 1856 he entered the army on the recommendation of a relative, General Sir Richard Doherty. Butler's family was a branch of one of the most powerful Anglo-Norman families, unusual in that unlike most Butler branches it had not changed over to Protestantism.

Butler communicated his drive and enthusiasm to the men in his command, and was popular in the ranks, if not with his colleagues. He was gazetted a Brigadier General in 1886 and given a K.C.B. In his impulsive efforts to put right what was obviously wrong, although annoying his British fellow officers whose impulse generally was to let things be, he had much in common with many Anglo-Irishmen serving in the British army (like Colonel John Townshend, of the Castle family, who initiated many reforms of the conditions of life in the ranks). His un-English nature springs out from a phrase in one of his obituary notices: 'He had an inexhaustible fund of pity, and indignation quick as a flame.'

Impulsive acts, close to madness, were part of the nature of Anglo-Irish soldierly valour. Even Sean O'Casey celebrated the bravery of Nevill Coghill, Egerton's eldest brother, saving the colours at the Zulu battle of Isandhlwana, for which he received a posthumous V.C. And Edith records with admiration her father's action at the battle of Inkerman, in the Crimea, when the Colonel of the 68th Durham Light Infantry urgently needed to identify some troops approaching through a thick fog. As they could have been friend or foe, the Colonel said: 'What would I give to be able to decide!' Edith's father, on hearing this, said: 'I'll soon let you know!' and threw open his grey great coat to reveal his scarlet uniform. There was a hail of bullets, and the 68th was able to retrieve itself. Edith's father was one of the very few infantry officers to serve throughout the Crimea, winning all clasps with his Crimea medal. His return to Castletownshend was celebrated throughout Carbery, the village raising a triumphal arch for the hero.

However 'English' the Irish themselves may have thought their landlord class to be, that same class in England was considered 'Irish'; certainly the Somervilles and Martins of Edith's generation and of her father's were at home only in Ireland and felt natives of that country. They did not feel English to any degree. Edith berates a brother who dares to suggest that he has come to consider himself English:

> Nonsense about being 'English'! I don't mind if you say 'British' if you like, but the only pallid trickle of *English* blood comes from *one* marriage, when Hester Coghill married Colonel Tobias Cramer, *a pure blooded hun* – if not Jew! You might just as well say you were German! . . . My family has eaten Irish food

Step-dancing at the Castle, 1920, a Kodak by Sir Patrick Coghill. His inscription on the back: 'Mrs Norris (left) and Betty McCarthy from Reen step-dancing at the Castle 1920.' There were several notable male step-dancers amongst the young at Castletownshend. The boys learned the madly exciting intricacies of footwork when small and never forgot them.

and shared Irish life for nearly three hundred years, and if that doesn't make me Irish I might as well say I was Scotch, or Norman, or Pre-Diluvian!

For 17 March of every year Edith and Hildegarde picked, packed and posted to each of their brothers a clump of shamrock for St Patrick's Day. Edith was an adept performer of popular music, and often she was requested to sing or play at parties and concerts one of her set pieces. Not surprisingly she specialized in Nationalist tunes and songs, and most frequently played 'Let Erin Remember', and sang her greatest favourite 'The Wearing of the Green'. She was deeply moved by these songs – their sentimentality was simplest logic to her soft heart. But she was no simple-minded romantic Nationalist. Here is a verse of 'The Wearing of the Green' that she so often sang:

Oh Paddy dear and did you hear the news that's going round,
The shamrock is by law forbid to grow on Irish ground,

No man Saint Patrick's Day shall keep his colour can't be seen
For there's a cruel law against the wearing of the green.
I met with Napper Tandy and he took me by the hand.
Said he 'How is old Ireland and how does she stand?'
'She's the most distressful country that ever could be seen,
For they're hanging men and women for the wearing of the
    green.'

Singing this, the name of Napper Tandy always stuck in Edith's throat before she forced it out; for this is what she thought of him:

> Mr Napper Tandy makes his *début* in Irish History in the year 1780, when he appears to have begun to qualify as a Professional Patriot . . . He is described as being 'an ugly little man with no talent but for speech' . . . In Mr Tandy's later years he was seldom sober; he has been described as very vain, very quarrelsome, and very drunken, and to these pleasing qualifications Wolfe Tone has added, grimly, of his fellow conspirator, that he was 'boastful and mendacious' . . . Napper Tandy fled to France and safety. There he found it advisable to remain, but in 1798, after long years of plotting, he succeeded in persuading the Republican Government to make him a General, and to entrust him with the command of a corvette, the *Anacreon*, in which, with a small force, he was to invade Ireland, and, incidentally, to reinforce General Humbert's expeditionary army. To accomplish this, General Tandy landed at a remote harbour in the County Donegal, and took possession of

The avenue to Inishbeg, home of the McCarthy Morroughs, an army family, Catholics and good friends of the Somervilles. There was not a particularly rigid division between Catholicism and Protestantism at all levels of society until the Troubles. The best-loved servants were Catholics. Hildegarde's Bridget Driscoll and Gungie Minehan, and Edith's Mike Hurley, were members of the household in a way inexplicable to English visitors. Edith once turned her rage on a Drishane house guest because she had 'treated Mike like a servant'. This easygoing integration was sorely tried in the twenties, but Edith, by an incredible effort of will, weathered even Boyle's murder and kept faith with her favourite Catholics, chief among them being Mike Hurley.

Edith was in charge of the graphics of Somerville and Ross books and made these as distinctively Irish as she could. Their monogram uses Irish letter forms and interlace. As a memorial for Martin she designed a mosaic floor using a design from the Book of Kells, *a splendid graphic image to commemorate their writing together. Called upon to design her brother Aylmer's gravestone, she chose a monolith of local rough stone with a small bronze plate.*

the village, improbably named Rutland, from which all its inhabitants had unhesitatingly fled to the mountains on the arrival of their saviours . . . he then learned that Humbert and his army had been taken prisoners. It was obvious that an immediate evacuation of Ireland – or, certainly, Rutland – was indicated, but the cloud of disappointment was not without its silver lining. The conqueror, having seized the village and its public houses, seized also the fortunate opportunity of getting blind drunk on good Irish whiskey . . . and after eight hours on shore abandoned the conquest of Ireland, and was carried back to the corvette on the backs of his warriors, dead to the world. After various adventures, he arrived in Hamburg, 'still drunk and incapable of acting' (as was deposed by one of his friends), and having been surrendered to England by the Senate of Hamburg, he was the cause of a preposterous declaration of war by the French Directory against his late hosts. Finally he was tried for treason, sentenced to death, contemptuously released by Lord Cornwallis as being 'a fellow of so very contemptible a character' that he was incapable of further mischief, and he was permitted to return to France, where, soon afterwards, he died.

Napper Tandy's name has survived, preserved in the sad old rebel song 'The Wearing of the Green'.

It is one of the bitter jests of the ironic Muse of History that she should have chosen to embalm his unworthy name in that poignant broken cry.

Robert Emmet is another of Ireland's Nationalist heroes whom Edith sang about in her rebel songs; she classified him with the 'sincere and honourable visionaries', but her historical knowledge of him, though intimate, was not inspiring. Edith had access to two sets of letters which she used when she wrote her account of Emmet's Rising in her *Incorruptible Irishman*, letters showing Emmet in different lights. On the one hand Edith read Emmet's letters to his lover, Sarah Curran, and Sarah's letters to Anne Penrose, her great friend, to whose home, Woodhill, she fled after Emmet's execution. These letters had passed to James Penrose, the husband of Ethel, Edith's 'Twin'. On the other hand, and giving the Anglo-Irish Establishment's view of Emmet, she owned the letters of Charles Kendal Bushe and his wife Nancy Crampton, who were present at Dublin Castle on the night that Lord Kilwarden was murdered by Emmet's insurgents. Such deep personal knowledge of the minute by minute workings and complexities of these huge historic events enabled Edith to realize the past in her writing in a vivid and convincing way.

Robert Emmet spent a great deal of money – inherited from his father – in providing pikes and firearms for an Irish uprising and travelling to France to plead for French aid. But in France exiled United Irishmen considered him impractical and advised against supporting him. None the less Emmet planned a rising for the night of 23 July 1803. He had a uniform made for himself of green cloth with gold epaulets worn with a white feathered cocked hat and tight white breeches. The conspiracy was doomed by spies and incompetence. Insurgents coming into Dublin from afar were turned back by false reports that the rising was abandoned. Late in the evening Emmet himself was given a false report that soldiers from the Castle were alerted to the rising and in action. He put on his glorious uniform, and at the head of about three hundred men, set out for Dublin Castle. Many of the men he led were by now crazed with drink.

Meanwhile, at the Castle, the Lord Lieutenant, Lord Hardwick, had no intelligence whatever of a rising planned for that day, and a dinner party was going ahead. Charles Kendal Bushe and his wife Nancy Crampton were among the guests waiting for the late arrivals of Arthur Wolfe, Lord Kilwarden, his daughter and nephew. Kilwarden's coach had the misfortune to run into Emmet's mob. They dragged out Kilwarden, who was Chief Justice of the King's Bench, and his nephew and daughter; they piked the men with the pikes bought with Emmet's money. Emmet entreated them wildly not to kill, but could not control them. A passing gentleman drew his sword to assist the Kilwarden party, and he also was piked to death. Miss Wolfe, in the confusion, ran for her life to the Castle; she burst into the reception room, hysterical, with her white gown stained with blood 'from breast to hem'.

Lord Kilwarden had been 'completely mangled' by the pikes, but breathed for half an hour more. He had been a liberal and humane judge, whose last concern, in horrible pain, was that the men who killed him should have a fair trial and by the laws of his own country. Doubtless Lord Kilwarden had recognized Emmet, as Emmet's father was well known and highly thought of by the legal fraternity in Dublin. Emmet's trial caused great complications when John Philpot Curran, a great friend of Kilwarden's, undertook to defend Emmet out of his friendship for Emmet's father. But Curran had to drop the defence when he discovered that his daughter Sarah and Emmet were lovers, and that in hiding the ever thoughtless Emmet had been sending letters to Sarah at the Curran home, which incriminated the whole family. Emmet was captured by that same Major Sirr who took Lord Edward Fitzgerald. Ignoring Emmet's vanity, incompetence and disregard for others, Edith wrote of him:

> The disastrous story of young Robert Emmet has often been told. His character, with its strange mixture of childishness, and faithful love and courage, of determination, and of entire lack of the power of organisation, is one that inspires affection as well as profound compassion.

Edith believed that the power of organization could be developed in Ireland; what she could do, in fostering improvement, employment and self-help, in her immediate neighbourhood of Carbery, she did. Who can forget Edith's delight, in *The States Through Irish Eyes*, when during her American lecture tour in 1929 she discovered that enthusiasts were prepared to pay £5 for her autograph. So she signed and signed and signed until she had made enough to complete a long-established fund to support a District Nurse for West Carbery, and a long-time ambition was fulfilled.

Edith was proud of her connection with Maria Edgeworth. They had, as literary ladies, a number of characteristics in common, but they were most alike in their social concern. Although Maria wrote the following passage, it shows exactly Edith's temper of mind, absorbed by improving and putting things right:

> What do you think is my employment out of doors at this moment – making a gutter, a sewer and a pathway in the streets of Edgeworths Town and I do declare I am as much interested about it as I ever was about writing anything in my life ... I find that making said gutter and pathway will employ 20 men for a fortnight or 3 weeks and feed them well with a meal – with Mrs E's assistance my gutter goes on famously.

Unlike Edith, Martin felt deeply that Ireland was incapable of looking after herself, and her letters give glimpses of the depressions into which she was thrown by Irish incompetences and lack of forethought. She was exasperated by the fluxes of temperament, the unexpected eruptions of activity, the infinities of dreaming sloth – perhaps because she herself fluctuated in this way. When Ross had fallen into one of its frequent frozen stills, motionless and soundless, she wrote to Edith:

> I told you that the Oughterard races were yesterday, Old Holloran who has been cleaning the avenue, went there and has never turned up today. Nurse D says its drowsy he is after the races. I think it is far more likely that he has crawled into Oughterard to sell Robert's trousers and buy lemons and sodas therewith – everyone about has been drunk, even that wretched deformed boy at the gate.

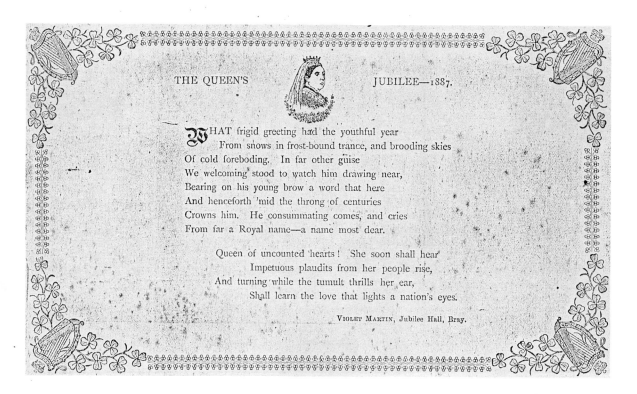

THE QUEEN'S   JUBILEE—1887.

WHAT frigid greeting had the youthful year
    From snows in frost-bound trance, and brooding skies
Of cold foreboding. In far other guise
We welcoming stood to watch him drawing near,
Bearing on his young brow a word that here
And henceforth 'mid the throng of centuries
Crowns him. He consummating comes, and cries
From far a Royal name—a name most dear.

    Queen of uncounted hearts! She soon shall hear
    Impetuous plaudits from her people rise,
And turning while the tumult thrills her ear,
    Shall learn the love that lights a nation's eyes.

VIOLET MARTIN, Jubilee Hall, Bray.

Martin's attitude was typical of those Unionists who wished to 'kill Home Rule with kindness' – an attitude that she probably absorbed through her brother Robert, a close associate of Gerald Balfour and his brother Arthur. Martin's inability to comprehend that a class of Irishmen existed who were capable of governing as fairly as they were governed from London is brought out vividly in a heated exchange of letters with the Nationalist M.P. Stephen Gwynn which started on 1 February 1912. Martin cannot believe that an Independent Ireland could organize such a benefit to society as the Old Age Pension, just instituted by Lloyd George:

Martin's Unionism inspired her to write this tribute to Queen Victoria, published by the Irish Times in a book of Jubilee sonnets. If we compare its sentiments with those of Edith's letter to The Times in 1916 on the Easter Rising, we see at once the deep difference between them.

> . . . I wondered deeply and sincerely whether Home Rule could increase the peacefulness, or whether it will be like upsetting a

basket of snakes over the country. These people have bought their
land. They manage their own local affairs. Must there be yet
another upheaval for them – and a damming up of Old Age
Pensions, which now flow smoothly and balmily among them, to
the enormous comfort and credit of the old people? My cousin
and I, in our small way, live in the manner that seems advisable
for Ireland. We make money in England and spend it over here.
We are sorry for those who have to live in England, but Ireland
cannot support us all without help.

This letter inspired an instant, spirited response from Stephen
Gwynn:

> Your letter filled me with a desire to talk to you for about 24
> hours concerning Ireland. Why snakes? . . . We have too much
> abstract politics in Ireland, we want them real and concrete. I
> don't for an instant believe that the pension will ever be cut
> down, but I do think that an Irish Assembly ought to decide
> whether farmers should qualify for it by giving their farms to
> their sons . . . I think we ought to be able to tackle the whole
> transit question. Poor Law, the whole Education system – all these
> things want an assembly of competent men, with leisure and local
> knowledge. You think we can't get them? That is the trouble
> with people like you. You know the peasantry very well; you
> don't know the middle class . . . There are plenty of men in
> Ireland – men of the Nationalist party – brilliant young men, like
> Kettle [Professor Kettle was killed, fighting in France with the
> Royal Dublin Fusiliers, at Ginchy, September 1916], who has also
> courage and enterprise . . . Of course in many here you feel the
> want of an educated tradition behind. No one can count the harm
> that was done by keeping Catholics out of Trinity College Dublin
> . . . To my mind the present system *breeds* what you have called
> 'snakes'. In Clare, among the finest people I have ever met in
> Ireland, you have the beastly and abominable shooting, and no
> man will bring another to justice. They are out of their bearings
> to the law, and will be, until they are made to feel that it is their
> own law. For Gentlefolk who want to live in the country Ireland
> is going to be a better place to live in than it has been these past
> thirty years – yes, or than before, for it is bad for people to be a
> caste . . . You and yours stand for so much that is the very choice
> essence of Ireland, that it fills me with distress to see you all
> standing off there in your own paddock, distrustful and not even
> curious about the life you don't necessarily touch.

Martin responds with a clear definition of what she feels 'snakes' to
be:

> There are dangerous elements in Ireland, and strong ones, Irish-

American, Gaelic League, Sinn Fein, and what I feel uncertain
about is whether straight and genuine and tolerant people like
you, will have the power to control them. With the Home Rule
banner gone, what is to keep them in hand?

This prophetic strain in Martin had no counterpart in Edith, who
was not, as Gwynn described Martin, 'in a paddock, distrustful', but
who did try to do as Gwynn suggested and, like all Anglo-Irish resi-
dents who made this effort, was to suffer agonies during the Civil War
and Troubles of the twenties that Martin so clearly foresaw. Stephen
Gwynn, at the time of these letters to Martin, obviously had no knowledge at all of the deep difference between Somerville and Ross. As to
Home Rule and Nationalism Martin and Edith were not, and never
had been, in the same paddock. He seems to have had the popular
notion of the pair as thinker and artist, and possibly did not suspect
Edith of deep thoughts, or any at all, on the subject of Nationalism.

Edith kept herself in ignorance of Celtic duplicity. She could not
bring herself to believe that she had untruthful relationships with those
Irish people that she knew well and loved, until the Troubles, betrayals
and brutality, forced her to agree, in some measure only, with Martin's
gloomier view of Irish character. In *Irish Memories* she concedes:

> how gravely and anxiously she thought about her country, and
> events have written a grim endorsement on certain of her
> apprehensions. She was never one of those who can be content to
> regard Ireland as a pleasant place for sport, full of easy laughable
> people: or she would never have understood Ireland with that
> intensity which can be felt even in her humour. If her letters show
> that she was often angry with her countrymen, they show too
> that it was because she could not be indifferent to the honour of
> Ireland.

That Martin, left to her own devices, unmoved by an inspiring
Edith, would have developed into a political commentator of deadly
seriousness is suggested by another tired letter from Martin to Edith
on 17 April 1888:

> I have had a notion of a feeble kind for a story in my mind for
> a little time and will try conscientiously to work it. But indeed I
> don't feel it my line – I feel more like writing pompous papers on
> emigration and such things and even occasionally vex my soul
> with wonderings as to what germ of truth might be in Fenianism.

Edith was a perfect representative of that section of the Ascendancy
who worked hard and long to merge with a new Ireland, and to make
that new Ireland good. The driving force of this party was Sir Horace
Plunkett. Plunkett, like Edith, had grasped that the battle over landownership had obscured the problems of land maintenance and

A page from Edith Somerville's Irish exercise book

Above: *The simplest way to demonstrate
Irishness was to speak Irish. Schools teaching
Irish such as that advertised here in the* Irish
Review *flourished during the Celtic revival.
Edith and Martin worked their way through
Professor O'Growney's Irish Primer,
volumes I–III. They reached 'advanced
conversation' level in theory.*

Right: *Advertisement for the* Irish
Homestead. *Founded in 1895 as the journal
of the Irish Agricultural Organisation Society,
Edith and Martin were both contributors.*

improvement, and how best to produce and distribute agricultural produce. He set up the Irish Agricultural Organisation Society in 1894, and the journal of this Society, the *Irish Homestead*, was founded in the next year. He, with George Russell (the poet and mystic Æ) as Secretary of the I.A.O.S., organized an effective dairy co-operative system. In its first ten years of existence 876 societies were established, with an annual turnover of three million pounds.

In 1904 Plunkett published *Ireland in the New Century*, which only too clearly pointed out what he saw as Irish Catholic defects – 'they especially require the exercise of strengthening influences on their moral fibre'. Plunkett took his natural position as a strengthening influence too much for granted, and the new Ireland rejected him. No

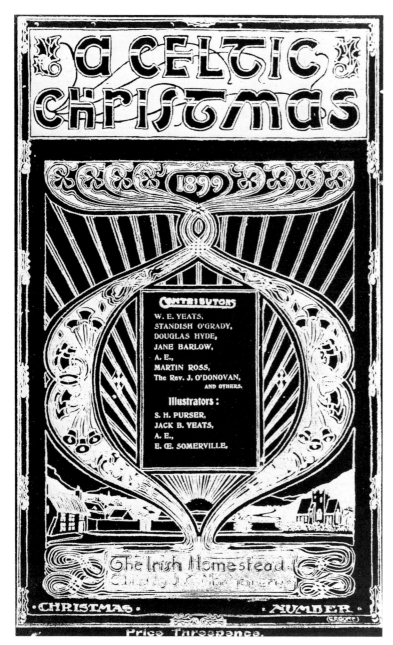

Cover for the Christmas number of the Irish Homestead, *1899. This and the cover opposite are a graphic illustration of the Somerville and Ross Anglo-Irish balancing act.*

Cover of the Badminton Magazine *for January/June 1899. This contained the second batch of Irish R.M. stories, which came out in the 'Bad Mag' in serial form from late 1898. Redolent of the great days of Empire, it contains stirring articles to while away the time of sportsmen and women when off-duty, such as: 'An Amateur's Honeymoon on a Forty-Tonner' by Miss Barbara Hughes, 'Loafing on the Limpopo' by O.E. von Ernthausen, 'Forty Miles on the Neckar in a Racing Four' by D.D. Braham, and 'Shooting in the Sunderbunds' by Lady Westmacott.*

man could have spent more time, money or strength in such a cause than Plunkett did; his rejection shows how absolutely all Ascendancy members were to be damned by their class, regardless.

Determination to smash every sign of Ascendancy presence resulted in the burning of Sir Horace's house, Kilteragh, where Martin and Edith had been guests, the destruction of many more beautiful houses, and the alienation of Irish Protestants from their homeland. Divisions were accentuated, civilization became the absentee. Irish Protestants

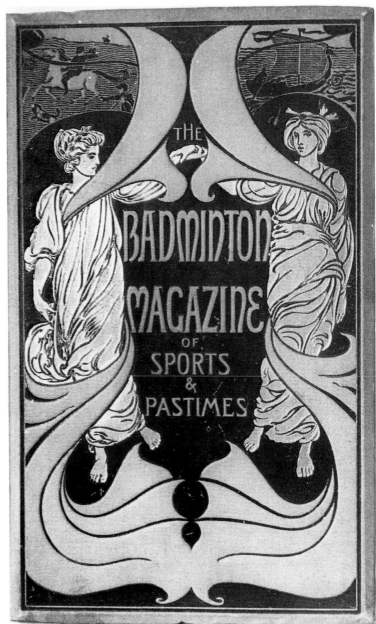

became defensive, as did Yeats in his splendid 'we are no petty people' speech as a concessionary Irish Senator. Edith, numbed, saddened, but still refusing to move, wrote: 'With the casting out of the unique product of centuries of breeding from the best of two races, there comes tumbling down more than half a civilisation.'

Far-seeing members of Edith's circle foresaw the time when they would, as Irish people, have to reject England, so sure were they of their Irishness, and of the voluntary nature of their link with England.

Far-seeing as they were, none saw that they themselves would be rejected as being non-Irish by an independent Ireland. A letter from Constance Bushe to Edith makes this startlingly clear. She was writing to congratulate Edith and Martin on one of their novels:

> I am glad you insist on the idealism of the Irish, and their need of some object of adoration. That has never been fostered by England, and it would have been a powerful asset. But the creatures! How will they ever understand us? They who have no answering quality, and whose utmost effort of comprehension is usually summed up in – 'You are mad!'

Constance asks 'How will they [the English] ever understand us?' (including the Anglo-Irish with the Irish) without the slightest suspicion that there were coming generations of Irish men and women who would be as incapable of understanding Constance Bushe and her class as Constance Bushe felt the English to be incapable of understanding the Irish.

Edith's belief in the essential goodness of Irish people was often strained in the years of the Troubles, but having survived into the 1930s the greatest blow to her faith was delivered on the night of 24 March 1936, when her best-beloved brother, Boyle, her staunch fellow Nationalist in all the fraught family debates on Unionism versus Nationalism, was assassinated in Castletownshend by Irish extremists; the assassins were outsiders who had gathered the information that all servants would be that night at a concert in the village hall. Edith's diary entries are concerned, remarkably, with the anguish and depression into which the murder had flung her groom, Mike Hurley. When the family gathered at Castletownshend for the funeral, there was nothing to distract from, or relieve, the shock. The assassins gave as the reason for Boyle's execution the fact that he had written many letters of recommendation for local boys wishing to enter the British navy.

Two of Boyle's nephews, Hildegarde's sons Nevill and Ambrose Coghill, in order to occupy themselves at such an awkward and speechless gathering of the family, went through Boyle's papers and talked to local people in order to discover how many boys Boyle had 'helped to the navy'. Boyle was popular and sociable, he never refused to see callers and he always wrote recommendations at the request of boys whom he knew personally, or whose parents he knew. Fishermen in such a poor district encouraged their sons to become sailors – the navy was an excellent prospect as a career, compared to fishing the Carbery coast. Edith enters in her diary on 28 March 1936: 'Nevill and Ambrose making a list of the boys he [Boyle] has helped to the navy, 292.'

She did not blame the villagers for the tragedy. As a memorial to Boyle, Edith had Seamus Murphy carve a seat at the gates of Drishane 'for the use of the people of the village'. Inscribed on it, in fine uncial

The Somerville brothers and sisters, August 1924. Edith has written on the mount that this was the first time they were all together at Drishane since Boyle went away to sea, at the age of seventeen. In 1880 he served in H.M.S. Shannon during the Chilean–Peruvian War. Aylmer died in 1928, and Boyle was murdered in 1936. The family, like many other Anglo-Irish families, was violently divided on the subject of Nationalism. Of these seven they divided into Nationalists: Edith and Boyle with Cameron falling in behind them; Unionists: Jack and Hugh. Hildegarde was the peacemaker, and Aylmer non-committal. The violence of the arguments between the brothers and sisters left Edith exhausted and flushed with rage and angry tears, Hildegarde distraught and weeping. From left to right: Aylmer, Boyle, Edith, Cameron, Hildegarde, Jack, Hugh.

Seamus Murphy's design for the memorial to Boyle at the gates of Drishane. 'Cómharsa maith' means 'good neighbour'.

IRELAND'S CHOICEST.

DOES Miss E. Œ. Somerville ever fail to win lovers for her Ireland? Not, certainly, among those to whom the high heart and the laughing eyes are treasures to be cherished wherever they may be found. In her new book, "An Enthusiast" (Longmans, Green, and Co., 8s. 6d.), she adds some notable portraits to her gallery, drawn, as always, with kindly humour and subtle perception; it is not, however, her happy hunting people that supply the models, but all the warring classes in the troubled land.

Miss E. Somerville.

The enthusiast is a man of the old landlord stock who, eschewing politics, devotes himself to constructive work among his farmer neightbours. But, grateful though they will be of the new understanding they gain of conditions in Ireland, most readers will follow with a more absorbed interest the story of the hero's heart; for, with him,

> A spirit in my feet
> Hath led me—who knows how?
> To thy chamber window sweet.

A moving story, told with dignity and restraint.

Among modern Irish novels and stories none have a higher literary value thos. written by Miss E. Œ. Some and "Martin Ross." Death has unfortun broken that happy and fruitful nership; but the surviving member has not laid aside her pen. Her story, "The Enthusiast" (Longmans, G & Co, 37, Paternoster Row, London, is not in the least degree inferior to the of those written in collaboration. "Tales of the R.I.C." it depicts Ireland the Sinn Fein "rebellion," but is wr from a somewhat different point of view. two books are complementary, not mut contradictory, and no one who reads o them should fail to make himself mast the other.

Some reviews of An Enthusiast (1921) *– a page from Edith's scrapbook.*

Irish, are the words: '*cómharsa maith*': 'good neighbour'. Mike Hurley, a reserved man, astonished friends and mourners at Edith's funeral by weeping throughout the entire service at the graveside.

In reading the books published in the years after Martin's death Stephen Gwynn came to realize Edith's sincerity and involvement in Ireland's predicaments. The novels after 1915 bravely tackle serious Irish themes, and where before reviewers had been delighted to remark upon 'the complete absence of politics' the late novels take their themes from contemporary Irish issues. *An Enthusiast* of 1921 refers to the political events of the previous year. Stephen Gwynn wrote of this novel and *Mount Music*: 'These books are documents, not only because they show how far the minds of Miss Somerville and her comrade were modified by the social revolution which was in progress through their whole lives.'

As tor comes there are several
friends about you to day
I see that one lady puts to
the front calling herself C.
and of course the White Lady
and Boyle and Ethel also
your father who ever came
before He asks me to remind
you of that favourite saying
of his which you wrote as
a memorial to him "God
the Lord the strength of him
salvation thou hast covered
my head in the day of battle"
He wants you to of — that
these words apply to his family
in the coming perilous months
they an tall will be well if you

CHAPTER 10

Extra-Mundane Communications: 'You and I Have Not Finished Our Work'

It would seem that there are but two alternatives: either the creature who has left us is so changed in that supreme moment of transit that all he once loved has become nothing to him (in which case it is idle to talk of the Resurrection of the Dead, since the individuality, which is the precious thing, has perished); or, if we believe that the human soul we knew is still existing, can we for an instant imagine that he is not – as we are – longing to call through the darkness, to say to those who are left behind: 'Peace, it is I!'

Edith, in 'Extra-Mundane Communications',
an essay in *Stray-Aways*, 1920

Belief in spirits, which has been described as the minimum definition of religion, is called 'animism'. When Margaret Mead, the anthropologist, was making a study of animistic religions, she went to live with a tribe called the Manus. She found that their religion was 'a special combination of spiritualism and ancestor worship. The dead males of the family become its guardians, protectors, censors, dictators after death' ... 'the Will of the spirits is conveyed to mortals through seances ...'. Margaret Mead would have found much of interest in the synthesis of religion and spiritualism practised at Castletownshend by Edith Somerville and her sister Hildegarde. In the twenties, during the Troubles, Castletownshend was watched over by the 'Guardians' - spirits of relatives who had died. They were organized in a group by Kendal Coghill, who died in 1919. His spirit voiced the opinion of the 'Guardians'. Hildegarde and Edith both had psychic powers, and because of the unusual attitudes taken by the Somerville and Coghill families towards spiritualism, they felt no moral restraint in using these powers. This was unusual at a time when the calling-up of the dead was forbidden by the Catholic Church and many branches of the Anglican Church. Even Madame Blavatsky advised against communicating with the dead, on the grounds that the medium had no control over the force that might enter her, and evil might manifest itself.

But there were less sensational aspects of spiritualism and the psychic

'Astor comes ...' Automatic writing by Geraldine Cummins. Astor was her control, or spirit guide. In automatic writing the pen is not held by the fingers but rests between the thumb and forefinger. The medium, in a light trance, makes no pen-lifts, so that the writing is in a continuous line, the word breaks being added later. An attendant to the medium moves the sheets of paper when they are covered with writing and the hand moves to the top of the next clean page and continues.

that were of general interest, and many distinguished members of the Establishment, like the Balfours and the Sidgwicks, declared in favour of investigating paranormal powers. Gladstone said that psychical research was 'the most important work being done today'.

Spiritualism was established in Castletownshend by those three siblings, Sir Joscelyn Coghill of Glen Barrahane, Colonel Kendal Coghill of Cosheen and their sister Adelaide, the mother of Edith. Seances were attended in London, and an enthusiasm for amateur psychic investigations and seances quickly became an accepted part of Castletownshend life. In the 1850s spiritualist journals were full of instructions on how to form a 'Family Circle'. A non-professional medium, John Jones, advises in the *Spiritual Magazine* of February 1862:

> Let the members of the family sit around a good size table, in a calm but cheerful spirit and in a child-like manner ask the privilege of witnessing the phenomena – to sit at a certain hour three times a week for a month or two and I am sure that in 95 cases out of a 100 the result would be the occurrence of spirit action in their own families.

The *Spiritualist* magazine in 1869 and 1870 was frequently advising on 'How to Form Spirit Circles', articles that show clearly that their writers thought that all human beings could develop psychic abilities: 'An experimental trial at home among family friends and relatives often gives the most satisfactory evidence of the reality of spiritual phenomena.'

In her late teens, Edith Somerville's psychic powers were recognized and used by her uncle, Kendal Coghill. He supervised Edith at sittings where she wrote, unconsciously, in the character of an ancestress, Elizabeth Cockhill. Edith's reaction to being used as an 'interpreter' by a spirit was one of interested appreciation – yet she often wrote scornfully of Uncle Kendal's 'gubs' and 'gubbing parties'. She was friendly towards ghosts and spirit manifestations, unlike Martin, who disliked them. Edith was never disturbed by the sometimes unnerving effects of her power. A small table once followed her across a room, and she sometimes received scripts from Elizabeth Cockhill even when conversing with her brother Boyle. It is unusual for an automatist to be fully conscious during the writing of a script, but the Society for Psychical Research does record a similar case. In her diary for 25 August 1878 she wrote: 'Aunt Flo's basket trunk has suddenly (11.30 p.m.) become possessed by an evil spirit and has waved its lid about of its own accord. I am going to sleep with her in my character as materialiser and strengthener.' It was probably Kendal Coghill who was responsible for describing Edith as a 'materialiser and strengthener'. The phrase gives us a valuable image of Edith at twenty.

Amateur circles like the Coghills' increased in numbers and soon a

From a distinguished Cork medical family, Geraldine Cummins spent her life as a professional medium in London, with frequent visits to Ireland. She was thin, with a thrillingly sepulchral voice and a sense of humour that was appreciated by Edith. Surprisingly, she was a fine hockey player and played for Ireland as an international. Her biography of Edith, Dr E.Œ. Somerville: A Biography, was published in 1952, three years after Edith's death.

London-based Society was formed. An open-minded and down-to-earth attitude pervaded the Society for Psychical Research, compared to the wilder reaches of spiritualism. Sir Joscelyn was a founder member; a skilled photographer, he attempted 'spirit photography'. His fellow countryman, Sir William Barrett, Professor of Experimental Physics at the Royal College of Science for Ireland, was the most formidable of the scientists involved in psychical research. The Society, particularly in its exposure of Madame Blavatsky as a trickster, caused a split in the ranks of the spiritualists. They divided into 'materialists' and the more airy-fairy theosophists like Æ and Yeats, who disdainfully objected to 'proofs'. The Coghills, and Edith Somerville by inheritance, were 'materialists' – serious, sensible and convinced. Sir Joscelyn, at a seance with the celebrated medium Daniel Dunglas Home, was levitated in an armchair. He had the presence of mind to whip out a pencil and sign his name on the ceiling before re-entry into normality.

The Society for Psychical Research was founded in 1882 by four learned and curious men: Professor Henry Sidgwick, Sir William Barrett, Edmund Gurney and F.W.H. Myers, lecturer in Classics at Trinity College, Cambridge. The Society hoped to establish, by the most rigorous scientific investigations, that personality and mind could operate independently of the body and continue to communicate after death. Just as Darwin's evolutionary revelations forced a new 'scientific' approach to the Bible, the founders of the S.P.R. believed that they could demonstrate that psychic 'supernatural' communications, popularly dismissed as evil fraud or self-deceiving hysteria, were a natural extension of man's sensibilities. They used the word 'super-normal' rather than 'supernatural'.

F.W.H. Myers died in 1901. Apart from Classical studies he had published a book called *Human Personality and Its Survival after Bodily Death*, and he had confided to his friend, Sir Oliver Lodge, his intention of writing another such work. In 1924, Geraldine Cummins, who practised in London as a medium and was a remarkable trance-writer, received by automatic writing the text of a book purporting to be written by F.W.H. Myers. Miss Cummins knew little of Myers himself and had not read *Human Personality*, but she knew that he had been a great friend of Sir Oliver Lodge.

She accordingly sent the manuscript to Lodge, asking him if it could be Myers' work. Lodge, like many at this time, was in daily communication with the dead. His 'contact' was his son Raymond, killed in the First World War. He communicated with Myers through Raymond and was satisfied that Myers was sending his book through Cummins, whom Myers called his 'interpreter'. Lodge also checked on Cummins through the medium Mrs Osborne Leonard, who also confirmed Myers' intentions. Mrs Osborne Leonard was surely the most investigated medium in history, for the S.P.R. conducted experiments and tests on her over a number of years. She was undoubtedly a genuine medium, the conductor of thoughts from people beyond her knowledge, and beyond bodily life.

Having agreed that the script received by Cummins came from the mind of Myers, Lodge wrote the foreword to the book. The title page reads:

> *The Road to Immortality:* Being a description of the After-Life purporting to be communicated by the late F. W. H. Myers through Geraldine Cummins. Foreword by Sir Oliver Lodge, F.R.S., D.Sc.

When receiving automatic scripts, Miss Cummins would fall into a light trance. Her hand would be placed, by a companion, at the top of each sheet and would travel at great speed in a continuous line, in clear writing that was not her normal hand. The word breaks were inserted later. The speed of writing was unusual: rates of 1,140 words in sixty-five minutes or 2,600 words in two hours without a break were not uncommon. Once, in the presence of five witnesses, Miss Cummins wrote 2,000 words in one hour and a quarter.

These speeds are significant, for Miss Cummins was normally a painfully slow and laborious writer, and it was not unusual for her to take seven or eight hours to write a short article of 800 words. Reading *The Road to Immortality*, we are immediately impressed by the style and use of unusual words. Miss Cummins was to become the friend of Edith Somerville and author of her first biography, which, despite her affection for Edith and her collection of excellent material, is awkwardly written, with clumsy constructions and a tired use of words. Here is the opening of *The Road to Immortality*:

> Many wonderful speculations have been made about the whence and whither of Man's destiny. Few have directly attempted to discuss why man was created, why the material universe spins apparently for ever and ever through space, its elements ever continuing, nothing lost, seemingly immortal, changing but in its imagery. 'A vast purposeless machine.' Such was the epitaph the scientist of the last century wrote of it, and in so doing he declared the faith of the thinking man of his age, namely, that there is no why. There is, therefore, no fulfilment. Matter is the only reality. And this terror, a purposeless mechanical drama of motion and life, must, with ghastly monotony, play on for ever and ever.
>
> Now, truth is far from us all; but it was immeasurably remote from those who came to this melancholy conclusion.

After Martin's death, early in 1916, Edith was consoled by reading the sermons of Basil Wilberforce. He eloquently preached that the continued existence of the individual after death was but simple

A drawing of Martin made by Edith when Martin was dying. Edith concentrated coolly on this drawing. She always preferred to conceal personal grief, and the making of this drawing must have been a necessary distraction. She wrote to Jack: 'There isn't much to say. Just that a life, that has always been a happy one, has fallen in ruins. It is ungrateful to say I have no future left ... but the innermost part, "my share of the world", has gone with Martin, and nothing can ever make that better. No one but ourselves can ever know what we were to each other ...'

Christianity: 'Believe that God's life in you is your immortality, that life in the body is but a brief stage in an endless career, that there is a consciousness within you wholly independent of the body.' He insists that those living keep faith with and maintain their love for those dead:

> The heart strains and yearns in the track of the loved spirit that has passed into another dimension ...

> > They do not die
> > Nor lose their mortal sympathy
> > Nor change to us.

And I confess that I cannot see in what our Christian religion is better than Materialism if we allow ourselves to change to them.

From the same volume by Wilberforce, Edith took down a prayer that shows both the chaste depth of her Christian belief and her openness to spiritualism:

> Suffer her to know, O gracious lord, if it may be, how much I love her and miss her, and long to see her again; and if there are ways in which her influence may be felt by me, vouchsafe her to me as a guide and guard, and grant me a sense of her nearness in such degree as thy laws permit.

The same insistence that faith must be kept with the dead is made by the living Myers in a passage quoted by Edith at the close of her essay 'Extra-Mundane Communications'. It shows that Edith was familiar with the work of Myers many years before her meeting with Geraldine Cummins:

> Not then, with tears and lamentations, should we think of the Blessed Dead. Rather should we rejoice with them in their enfranchisement, and know that they are still minded to keep us as sharers of their joy. Nay, it may be that our response, our devotion, is a needful element in their ascending joy.

Edith and Martin shared with the Irish a belief and intense interest in premonitions, apparitions and the workings of Fate. Their interest in spiritualism was an extension of this aspect of Irish life. As they were both devout Christians they did not dwell on their belief in a more primitive ancient animism, but it often features in their work, as in *The Silver Fox*; in their daily lives we often find evidence of their patient reliance on the benign intervention of a kind Fate, and in opposition to this an impatience and boredom with the organization of the Church of Ireland.

After Martin's death, spiritualism came to be a subject that Edith took very seriously, which we cannot say of her attitude to the Church of Ireland and its rectors; her religious views were tolerant and opposed to pomp and circumstance. Her behaviour with the rectors of Castlehaven parish was decidedly non-reverential. When one of her terriers howled at the start of the sermon one Sunday, the rector sent up a note to the organ-loft asking Miss Somerville to put her dog outside. Both Miss Somerville and terrier swept out, and the service staggered on with no music. On 12 August 1883, she wrote in her diary: 'Church. Had the new man Mr Horace Townshend – the manner and matter of his sermon was eminently adapted to infant negroes.'

Many things survive as evidence that Edith's mind wandered in church: a sharp little drawing of Martin's head from the side during one of her first choir practices at Castletownshend; numerous drawings of children and congregation members taken from the back, as Edith leaned over and observed from her place at the organ; Edith telling Martin that when Charlotte Payne Townsend told a long 'funny' story: 'My mind wandered as if it were the Litany.'

Kirk and its institutions, the choral society, choir, bazaars, absorbed everyone of the Protestant persuasion. Edith played the organ at St Barrahane's for sixty-five years. When not playing the organ, her mind wandered; she often took her pocket sketchbook out and pencilled – hence, the studies of members of the congregation from behind, and to the side, her subjects being limited to the front rows of the gallery where she sat at the organ.

Edith's comments on the quality of Castletownshend preachers and their sermons are more scathing than Martin's, who was often simply amazed and interested by human behaviour, whereas Edith would be irritated into a rage. Here is Edith's reaction to a sermon that Harry Becher had been ordered, by the law of the Diocese, to deliver 'against drunkenness' on the first Sunday in Lent, 1902. An account of the sermon was sent to Hildegarde:

> ... He preached entirely in extenuation of drunkenness! I nearly walked out I was so furious ... Colonel Morris said to me as we met on the steps 'has Mr Becher shares in a brewery?' While Mattie [a servant at Glen Barrahane] said to Nurse 'ye'd say he had a public house round the corner.' ... He said that 'there were many worse sins than drunkenness' (which tho' true was not to the point) ... he had taken for his text the story of the ten lepers who were cleansed, of whom only one gave thanks – 'But, Brāthren, whaat happened to the Nine? Doubtless they went away

and contracted other diseases!' I presume this means that if you
kept yourself blind drunk you would not be able to do a
successful forgery – He would be wholly intolerable if he were
not so amusing.

Edith and Martin were both conscious of the world of mind independent of those living. Martin, after being chloroformed by a Dublin
dentist, wrote a description of the experience to Edith. Her conception
of an 'innermost being' independent of, but in control of, the body
and personality is expressed in terms familiar to spiritualists:

> This morning I had a tooth out under gas. I am quite sure that
> all gassings and chloroformings are deeply uncanny. One dies, one
> goes off into dreadful vastness with one's astral body. That was
> the feeling. A poor little clinging M E, that first clung to the
> human body that had decoyed it into B . . . 's chair, was cast loose
> from that, and then hung desperately on to an astral creature that
> was wandering in nightmare fastnesses – quite separate – then that
> was lost, and that despairing ME said to itself quite plainly 'I am
> forsaken – I have lost grip – I don't know how I am behaving – I
> must just endure.' Long afterwards came an effect as of the gold
> shower of a firework breaking silently over my head. Then a
> radiant head appeared in a fog . . . I am sure these visions happen
> when one dies, and I am convinced of the existence of an
> innermost self, who just sits and holds on to the other two.

Martin swung from engagement to disengagement with the physical
world quite consciously; in her periods of disengagement she would
think, inert and alone, and sometimes write; when engaged she would
work energetically about Ross, as hard as a man, restoring the house
and immediate grounds that had been badly damaged by tenants
during the seventies and eighties. In a description of a typical household disaster at Ross, written to Edith in 1895, she uses a phrase that
shows how well she knew herself – she either 'pervaded space' or did
not:

> . . . Andy set to work on the kitchen chimney. No one knew
> that the old oven had a special flue of its own, and it was down
> this flue that the soot elected to come. I was fortunately pervading
> space that day, and came in time to see a dense black cloud issuing
> from the oven's mouth into the kitchen. I yelled to a vague
> assembly of Bridgets in the servant's hall, all of whom were
> sufficiently dirty to bear a little more without injury.

She was also deeply superstitious, and wore a silver Maltese charm
against the evil eye. She had strong ideas about when it was propitious
to act and when it wasn't. It was not unusual for her to instruct Edith
in this way: 'Come on Thursday week next and you will do well –

[in small writing:] – don't come on Friday, I write it small because I am ashamed of being superstitious, but consider it said.'

Edith's counterpart to Martin's Maltese charm was a curious collection of silver oddments all looped together on a chain. She called it her 'Luck', and had assembled it by her seventeenth year. It is what she seems to be wearing in the portrait by Chancellor of Sackville Street, Dublin. Trust in their luck carried them through their tours and the extraordinary situations they often found themselves in. Martin had absolute faith in Edith's competence and ability to move mountains. One of her chaffing exclamations at Edith was: 'Faith, ye have a great power of attack.' In 1904, when Edith was at Drishane, involved, as their Master, in the running of the West Carbery Hounds, Martin fell ill, with bronchitis and a high temperature, in London. Her doctor ordered her to travel as far south as possible, to a rest home or spa hotel, and not to return until mended. Edith received this information at Drishane, handed over the Mastership to Aylmer, packed a very small bag and set off. For what became a six-week stay Edith, including what she was currently wearing, took one light frieze skirt and coat, a black skirt for evenings, a pair of holland skirts and coats, two flannel shirts, underclothes, one travelling hat, one straw hat, one pair of canvas shoes, one pair of brown walking shoes, and a pair of boots for rainy days.

She took it into her head to go to a place called Amélie, in the French Pyrenees. Collecting the fevered and inert Martin in London, trusting to luck and Bradshaw, Edith got them safely to Amélie. Until they got to Toulouse she could not convince anyone that Amélie existed, but she stuck to her recollection of a lyrical description in a guide book that had stressed how inexpensive the resort was out of season. Amélie proved a perfect place, and because of its cheapness they were able to stay for six weeks. Martin recovered well, and it was during this rest period that *Dan Russel the Fox* was born. Edith always kept the happiest memories of Amélie, and in *Irish Memories*, writing of the strong impulse that had guided her there, triumphed: 'Irrational impulse was justified of her children.'

Martin respected the strong spiritualist beliefs that she encountered in Castletownshend. Staying in St Andrews in 1895, she discussed Stainton Moses' book *Spirit Teachings* with Andrew Lang, the celebrated Scots author. She wrote to Edith:

> I spoke of *Spirit Teachings* with caution and respect and he gave one of his dreary crows of laughter ... he seemed unfeignedly amused when I said that I had several cousins who put *Spirit Teachings* above the Bible (your mother being one) even as literature.

Although respecting spiritualist beliefs, she did not become involved in spiritualism, and seems to have reserved judgement on the subject;

but she certainly thought more deeply than Edith about life after death.

Until Edith's mother died, when Edith was thirty-seven, she had never seen anyone dead. Martin was very familiar with the sight of death and the ceremonies associated with it in Ireland. From her youth, she had been to wakes, and visited and attended dead and dying tenants at Ross. In January 1895, she wrote to Edith:

> I often wish you had seen someone dead – I should like to
> know how you felt about it, and I think it does one good, though
> it is excessively painful. But yet I should try to shield you from it
> when it came to the point.

Martin was not at Drishane, in December of that same year, when Edith's mother suddenly became ill, and died. Edith and Hildegarde nursed her through great pain. Edith's relationship with her mother had been intense and unhappy, with terrible depths of feeling. She wrote to Martin on 6 December:

> I could not feel that it was she. It was a beautiful mask that her
> soul had worn, and now that it had been cast aside it had taken on
> a cold sort of serenity, a character of its own, quite apart from
> hers – in a curious way, seeing what had been her, reconciled me
> to her in the cold half dark silent room. I felt that she was not
> there – I thought of her meeting Aunt Florrie and telling Minnie
> what a success *The Real Charlotte* had been and how, for her part,
> she had much preferred the mad dog Paris story.

After her parents' death, Edith constructed a kind of icon out of a portrait of Henry and a portrait of Adelaide and a crucifix. This hung above the head of her bed.

As Edith and Martin were apart for much of the working year, it was important for them to be able to sense each other's thoughts. Martin did not reside permanently at Drishane until after her mother's death in 1906. By this date they had been collaborators for twenty years. When they were together, each instinctively knew what the other was thinking and this spurred the racing pace of their humour; when they were apart, a continuous awareness of the other's mind affected all their reactions, notes and projects. They communicated at this intense mental level for almost thirty years, for Martin died just twenty-six days before the thirtieth anniversary of their meeting.

That Edith believed she continued to sense Martin's thoughts when they were finally physically separated is not difficult to understand or accept. The quality of the writing did change. Edith unassisted could not now reach the heights of humorous writing; a blacker humour pervades the work. We must remember that Martin thought they had reached their peak of achievement with *The Real Charlotte*. In 1895, she had written to Edith: 'I will take my stand on Charlotte I think and learn to make my own clothes and so subside noiselessly into middle age.' Nevertheless the overall quality of a book such as *Dan Russel the Fox*, which they wrote together in 1911, is not measurably greater than, for example, *The Big House of Inver* or *Mount Music*, which were among the fifteen books written by Edith, with Martin in mind, after 1915.

Automatic writing done by Edith alone in the Studio in 1933. Edith eventually learned to receive automatic writing without the aid of Jem Barlow. She sat alone in the Studio every evening. In the January entries, in smaller writing, she is alone; in the December entry Jem Barlow is with her.

The Big House of Inver is as great an achievement as *The Real Charlotte* – if we see more of Edith's rambling, untidy sense of structure and finish, it is not the less impressive. Martin could not physically control the finish, as she had so thoroughly when living. No one but Hildegarde was close enough to Edith to be accepted as an editor or adviser, but she did not start to read her manuscripts aloud to Hildegarde immediately. As soon as she did, Edith avoided unspeakable disasters like the love scenes between Larry and Christian in *Mount Music*. The confusion of Edith's and Martin's intelligences, after thirty years of collaboration, was so great that it seems quite reasonable to suppose that Edith, whose capabilities were enormous, could maintain two minds in one head.

In the first few months after Martin's death Edith could not believe that she would ever write again. But by April, as we have seen from her letter to *The Times* on the Easter Rising, she was in good form, in a literary sense. She felt no desire to communicate with Martin in a seance, which was cool and controlled of her when we remember that she lived in a circle where seances were a very common occurrence.

Edith and Hildegarde, seated centre foreground, at Tim Chavasse's christening in 1931. Jem Barlow is in the row above Hildegarde, slightly to Hildegarde's left.

" Sad is the death of a Comrade.
But we may say 'Death comes
not untimely to him who is
fit to die. The briefer life,
the earlier immortality.' "

Florence Nightingale –

(G.P.V.A – Feb. 21. 1916.)

*A loose sheet tipped in to the end paper of
Edith's 1916 diary during her stay at Lismore
with Ethel and Jim Penrose after Martin's
death. It shows the quotation, misused by
Maurice Collis, from the Ven. Basil
Wilberforce's sermons, published as 'New (?)
Theology' [sic]. Two of Edith's first cousins
were close enough to her to sense what would
comfort her. Percy Aylmer gave her this poem
by Florence Nightingale, and Ethel gave
Wilberforce's sermons.*

" Only goodnight, Beloved, not farewell."

Dec. 21. 1915.

Jan. 1. 1916.

June 16. 1916

Ven. Basil Wilberforce's Sermons.

"New Theology."

LISMORE CASTLE,
LISMORE,
IRELAND.

Suffer her to know, O gracious God,
if it may be, how much I love her and
miss her, & long to see her again; & if
there are ways in which her influence
may be felt by me, vouchsafe
her to me as a guide & guard,
& grant me a sense of her near-
-ness in such degree as Thy laws
permit.

If in anything I can minister to her
peace, be pleased of Thy love to let this
be; & mercifully keep me from every
act which may hinder me from union
with her as soon as this earth – life is
over, or mar the fullness of our joy
when the end of the days has come.

At such an everyday sitting in Castletownshend on 16 June 1916, Edith
was calmly present and asked to assist in contacting a Colonel Isher-
wood. A message came in automatic writing via the local medium Jem
Barlow. It was from Martin: 'You and I have not finished our work.'

CHAPTER 11

'The Traditions of the Harem': The Society of Victorian Women

Not the Woman's Place. Time was when there were but few forms of healthy, normal enjoyment to which these words, pregnant of prunes, prisms, and prisons, did not apply. Regarding the matter dispassionately, by the light of literature, as well as that of social history, it would seem that the sole places on God's pleasant earth to which this warning placard was not affixed were those wherein The Woman was occupied with her dealings with the other sex; directly, as in the ballroom, or indirectly, as in the nursery. The indoor traditions of the harem governed the diversions and relaxations of the early Victorian ladies.

Edith, in '*Not* the Woman's Place', an essay in *Stray-Aways*, 1920

Edith published some unequivocal statements about her relationship with Martin, such as the following passages from *Irish Memories*:

> For most boys and girls the varying, yet invariable, flirtations and emotional episodes of youth are resolved and composed by marriage. To Martin and me was opened another way, and the flowering of both our lives was when we met each other.

> The doctrine that sincere friendship is only possible between men dies hard. It is, at last, in the fulness of time, expiring by force of fact ... The outstanding fact, as it seems to me, among women who live by their brains, is friendship. A profound friendship that extends through every phase and aspect of life, intellectual, social, pecuniary. Anyone who has experience of the life of independent and artistic women knows this; and it is noteworthy that these friendships of women will stand even the strain of matrimony for one or both of the friends. I gravely doubt that David saw very much of Jonathan after the death of Uriah.

Her successful professional life with Martin shielded Edith from accepting a marriage of convenience to Herbert, which she came perilously close to accepting.

A woman in her proper place. Hildegarde Somerville with her father and great-uncle, Dr Jim Somerville, in 1896. Her first son, Patrick, is on her lap. Edith Somerville was ten years older than Hildegarde and there was a great gulf between them until Hildegarde came to her late teens. Edith grew up holding her own in the society of her brothers, and spent much time with her adored grandfather and father. Many characteristics of hers are masculine as a consequence. Her toughness, her slang, the habit of concealing her deepest feelings she learned from the company she kept as a girl.

Although Edith showed fondness for Herbert in the early 1880s, by
the time she had settled into a pattern of writing with Martin, his
attentions, and the man himself, began to irritate her; for poor Herbert,
despite his love for Edith, was handicapped by the millstones of male
pomposity and excessive self-assurance. A letter from Edith to Hildegarde dated 6 August 1893 illustrates vividly Edith's frustration and
unspoken anger. Herbert obviously lacked any sympathy with Edith's
depths:

> Herbert is really too provoking with his stirk against the grass
> court – his sisters are all mad with him for his rudeness, but of
> course he does not consider that he can be rude to any of the
> family, his theory is that such civilities are mere conventional
> usages of other places. They do not obtain in C–T. This in itself is
> exasperating. I must say he is a most wearing person in his
> madness for expeditions or exercise, and in his resolve to boss
> everything, and his conviction that he knows this place better than
> we do becomes very maddening. Fancy his trying to assure me
> that Papa and I were both mistaken in supposing that there was
> any strand near the Dutchman's Cove on which cowries could be
> found 'of course he meant Poul Ghurrum' he said patronisingly.
> 'He did nothing of the sort' I said 'he meant Russet Cove, where
> I found cowries long before you ever came to the place – I think
> Papa ought to know his own strands', I concluded indignantly.
> Herbert then turned to *Jack* to ask him if I was right! Could you
> imagine anything more maddening. Then I must say he riles me
> awfully in his persistently ignoring that I have any work to do – I
> have told him a dozen times that to give up the afternoon is the
> most I can do, and yet every morning I have to undergo the same
> botheration about playing tennis (on the gravel) or going out in
> the boat – I hate seeming ungrateful and he is a very good fellow,
> but a more tactless creature I have seldom met – Martin and I are
> worrying on with the Welsh Aunt [an early title for *The Real
> Charlotte*] through great disadvantages.

This passage provides an excellent picture of the conditions under
which *The Real Charlotte* was written, as well as of traditional male
attitudes to women, their competence and capacities.

In December 1897, Edith received her last onslaught from Herbert.
Herbert pressed his proposal of marriage before Christmas. The poem
already quoted (on page 40) comes from a Christmas letter of 1887.
Towards the end of 1897 Edith became very ill with an infected jaw
and fell into a deep depression. However she responded to Herbert's
proposal, it was not with the usual negative. The Greenes' home was
on St Stephen's Green in Dublin. It was a general clearing house and
stopover place for all Castletownshend people. Herbert's mother was
Edith's aunt, an aunt of whom she was very fond, as surviving letters

Hildegarde and Egerton on their wedding day, 11 July 1893.

to her show. Herbert spent Christmas here with his mother, and communications between Herbert and Edith led him to believe that Edith had, at last, accepted his proposal.

We cannot know what actually passed between Edith and Herbert at this time, as Edith left her diary blank for these crucial months, an indicator of mental turmoil and depression. She filled them in later, sketchily, from Martin's diary. Herbert's confidence that he was to marry Edith was absolute, and he told his mother that they were to marry, and Edith would move from Castletownshend to become an Oxford don's wife. Another aunt of Edith's, Georgina Chavasse, visited her sister Sylvia, Herbert's mother, at home in Dublin. Sylvia told Georgina the good news. Georgina returned to her lodgings and wrote to Edith to congratulate her:

21 Lower Baggot Street
Dublin 14.3.98

Dearest Edith

Altho' you have not written to announce the fact yet having been told it 'on the very best authority' I must send you a line of hearty congratulations on your engagement to be married. You were very clever to keep your secret so well, but now as it is out of the bag I suppose there is no use in trying to capture the feline again. I hope you will have a very happy future in store for you. I hope that the changed state will not bring art and literature to an end. Hildegarde will find it hard which to rejoice or bemoan, as she will wish to share in your happiness and yet C–T will be a very different place to her without you. Hal's letter is ready for the post and as he will have given Aylmer all the news so I will only add best love and best wishes, ever yr loving Aunt Gig.

The two trees decorated by the villagers for Hildegarde and Egerton's wedding day. A banner on the trees proclaims 'Cor unum, via una'. Though Edith knew Egerton to be an enchanting man and saw that he and Hildegarde had a vital love, she still disapproved of the physical ill-effects that childbearing had on Hildegarde and saw her strength consumed by marriage. Martin confessed to Edith that observing her elder sisters' marriages had much dismayed her when she saw them overlook behaviour in their own children that they strongly objected to in others'.

Whatever the nature of the crisis in Edith's life at the beginning of 1898, this reaction to Edith's supposed engagement, which survives in the Drishane House papers, is extremely illuminating. Firstly, it shows that Edith's close relations considered that she had the option to marry. We know that many of them often dwelt upon Herbert's predicament – would he or wouldn't he get Edith after such long faithfulness and adoration? But most striking of all in Aunt Gig's letter is the fact that there is no mention of Martin, except obliquely as 'art and literature' – it is Hildegarde to whom Edith's marriage will mean most.

Edith somehow extricated herself from this situation, helped by the upheaval caused by her father's death and her accession as mistress of Drishane. This spring of 1898 was a crucial one for Edith. She took the responsibility as head of a house and family, refused for the last time a proposal of marriage, and chose a true independence. It was also in this spring that Edith's appearance began to change. In January of 1898 she had all of her lower-jaw teeth removed after almost two months of debilitating pain and sickness. Almost imperceptibly the photographs begin to show her jaw thrust forward. In the splendid studies by Elliott and Fry of 1905, it is not noticeable, but by the 1920s she had a pugnacious set to her mouth, giving a faint Habsburg effect. The accidental pugnacity of her jaw, allied to the bright fierceness of her eyes, must have contributed much to the frightening impression that she made on small children who could not appreciate her charm.

The three people who loved Edith most intensely through their lives were perpetually aware of her, and conscious of her every movement; we have two instances of Edith's life being saved by this consciousness. Hildegarde, on board *Miriam* in Youghal harbour, woke in the night, aware that Edith was in danger. Edith, who walked in her sleep, was up on deck and about to saunter overboard when Hildegarde stopped her. On another occasion, Herbert Greene, walking with Edith and a group along the cliff-edge walk from Drishane to the west, caught Edith bodily as she slipped. Martin's awareness of Edith, wherever she was, is acutely shown in the letters. When Edith was away in Paris, studying, Martin would read world weather reports to know how cold it was in Paris and write to Edith reminding her to wear heavy clothing: 'You are very precious and haven't anyone to bully you or take care of you.' Edith was notoriously careless of herself. When they were apart, Martin also used train and ship timetables in order to know exactly where Edith was and what she was doing.

Considering their own restrained physical manners and suppressed sexuality, Edith and Martin surprise the reader of *The Real Charlotte* with their knowledge of passion in men and women. When Charlotte Mullen loses her self-control over the letter from Roddy Lambert, whom she loves, a letter that tells her he has married Charlotte's niece,

Francie, the authors preface the astounding description of Charlotte's physical rage with this:

> A human soul, when it has broken away from its diviner part
> and is left to the anarchy of the lower passions, is a poor and
> humiliating spectacle, and it is unfortunate that in its animal want
> of self-control it is seldom without a ludicrous aspect. The weak
> side of Charlotte's nature was her ready abandonment of herself to
> a fury that was, as often as not, wholly incompatible with its
> cause, and now that she had been dealt the hardest blow that life
> could give her, there were a few minutes in which rage, and
> hatred, and thwarted passion took her in their fierce hands.

Just as Edith and Martin were different physical types, they could not have been more different in their emotions.

Edith was passionate in the extreme; the letters and diaries map out a Richter scale for Edith's tempers; her moods were publicly readable in her face. The drama critic who wrote of Edith's performance in *Pinafore* – 'Little Buttercup in her gaudy red-striped dress and scuttle bonnet was represented in a very lively and droll manner by Miss Somerville who possesses considerable powers of facial expression' – saw the extent to which Edith could control and express her emotions to amuse others; but, off stage, there were times when Edith knew not what her face was doing, for she could not control her blood. Edith was very aware of what she called her 'temper-line' and kept herself tightly reined as a result; in a letter to Martin from Paris on 22 March 1887 she writes of the irritation of stupid criticism by a fellow art student: 'I felt my arm stiffening with fury, my tongue clave to the roof of my mouth (as well for her that it did).'

She flushed easily, and in deeper anger all of the blood would leave her face, so that even her lips were white. She cried easily, and cried, sleepless, through three nights after the death of her beloved dog Patsey at Ross; she could also cry instantly – though that did not prevent her from action – at the sight of a human or animal in pain. Whether the colours given to Edith's tempers by those who experienced them were symbolic or actual reflections of appearance, we do not know, but she is described as flushing deep crimson, and as fading to white-faced shock. Edith describes herself as 'getting blue with rage'; and what she looked like in the ultimate storm of a 'black passion' one dreads to think.

Martin, on the other hand was cool and detached. In writing *An Irish Cousin* she showed a positive dislike of passionate romantic passages that dwelt on physical love. It was Edith who, backed up by her mother's protestations, overrode Martin and put in 'most fiery love' (first edition, Chapter IX), and it was Edith who wrote the intense proposal scene where Willy and Theo so distress each other, for it was she who had had experience of, and had the capacity for, passion. But when we come to define their love for each other, one fact stands out clear: there was no passion in it.

The letters show intimacy of a chaffing, familiar, sisterly kind. Their modes of address over the first ten years of their correspondence change from the formality of 'My Dear Edith ... Yours Affectionately V. Martin' to 'My Dear Edith ... Yours' or 'Yours Ever – Martin'. Edith, more interestingly, writes 'My Dear Girl', 'My Dearest Child' or, most frequently, 'My Dear Martin'; and, astonishingly, she sticks to the formality of signing herself E.Œ.S. until 30 September 1888 – there are more than two years of correspondence before she signs herself 'Edith'. By March 1889 she has settled for 'Yours Ever, Edith'. Their P.S.s are informative. For instance, from Martin to Edith: 'Goodnight again, you were a nice woman to write with' or 'Goodnight dear Edith and I am sure you are having a pleasant evening with your soldiers' (refer- ring to a dance at Drishane). Typical of Edith's P.S.s is 'Be a good child and take care of yourself.' There is a remarkable amount of chaffing rudeness, particularly from Edith to Martin. Martin is berated variously as 'ye great gommaun' (for forgetting something important) or 'lazy slut' (for not doing something important) and, gloriously, on 14 June 1896, 'You are the Queen of Pigs feet' (for no apparent reason). This is not the language of a Sapphic sexual love.

They did not sleep together habitually; at Drishane, when Martin was sick and Edith wanted to be at hand to fetch things for her during the night, she slept in Edith's room; and after Martin's hunting fall on 1 November 1898: 'The wretched E couched on a sofa in my room.' Both diaries calmly record where and with whom they slept, as the inhabitants of Castletownshend wandered about, often sleeping in whichever house they happened to dine at. Edith writes 'Slept with Hildegarde', 'Slept with Ethel', 'Slept with Martin', presumably to indicate where she was. Martin loved bed – she wrote there, thought there, and when at Ross, up in her attic bedroom, liked nothing better than to have the visiting Edith all to herself, in bed. But to Edith, who bounded out of bed and into action, and to whom bed was a place where she crashed out and rapturously slept, it seemed a matter of no importance who was with her. She writes to Martin about the problem of beds at her hotel at Paris, just before Martin's visit; the rooms were small, so it would be better for Martin to be in one on her own 'as I am afraid it would be rather a squash in mine'.

It is significant that at family crises, such as at the death of their mother, Edith and Hildegarde slept together for company and comfort. The bedrooms at Ross and Drishane were icy cold for a large part of the year, and we know that Hildegarde enjoyed Edith's warmth in bed because of an 'Edith' retort. When Hildegarde strayed too close to Edith, so that she was shoving her out of bed on Edith's side, Edith would slap Hildegarde hard on the backside with a 'kindly remove your fishmonger's slab!' Both Hildegarde and Martin were cold in bed,

Above: *Hildegarde's four children. The boys, from the left: Ambrose, Paddy, Nevill. Her only daughter Katharine is held in Paddy's arms.*

Left: *Hildegarde in 1895 in the garden at Glen Barrahane.*

and Edith was in some demand as a hot-water bottle. Although Hildegarde was bulkier than Edith, she was not the heating plant that Edith was. We know that Martin enjoyed Edith's physical warmth because of this remark in a letter from Ross, just after Edith's departure: 'I found it hard to sleep on Monday night and felt as if I could not get enough bedclothes about me to make up for the absent animal caloric.'

The undemonstrative nature of their affection for each other is shown by a letter from Martin to Edith dated 23 January 1895. After nine years of knowing Edith, Martin is embarrassed to write of physical affection:

> I am all right about money for the present, having just had
> £50 from Ross – I have paid some debts, and will pay more –
> You are – what you always have been in offering to stand by –
> My Dear – if it were not so awfully foolish I could put xxx's in
> that place like the children – you will understand that I have not
> done so because I don't want you to laugh at me.

This is the first mention by Martin of any expression of physical affection. She does mention that she would like to express her fondness for Edith, but, no doubt feeling that it went against Edith's down-to-earth nature, does not. She refers to such impulses as 'foolishness' and writes:

> Old Flanagan inquired for my sister and hoped she had
> materials in her head for another novel. I said 'I hope so' and hid
> among the tribe for fear of having to explain – the fat young one
> that the puppet adored said when she heard you were gone
> 'Won't you miss her very much?' I smiled with sickly idiocy and
> murmured foolishness. I could even write foolishness now, but
> will cease – it being bedtime – and just the time I miss you most –
> Yours Ever Martin.

But this is a strain of affection that does not exist in the breezy, chaffing letters of Edith, who never loses the matronizing, elder-sister tone. Edith appears to have converted all of her affections into mothering; her skill in restoring invalid humans and animals to wholeness and health never left her, which is why she is so often referred to as 'the mother of the animals' or the 'dog's mother'. She referred to her books as 'my illegitimate children', ruefully. Though it is chiefly Martin who springs to mind as the invalid maintained by her strength, Edith also bore up many desperately ill people, like her brother Cameron through his last illness, or Geraldine Cummins, very ill after a major operation. Though unmarried and technically childless, Edith was a matriarch on the same grand scale as her sister, Hildegarde. That Edith was a lesbian has gained general acceptance through an unlovely combination of affected liberalism, ignorant salaciousness and the sad assumption that huge vitality and strength in a woman implies masculinity.

Edith hardly ever wrote anything intimate about herself in her letters to Martin, and never anything intimate about their own relationship. But Martin, in 1895, after almost ten years of close association with Edith, wrote a letter to her from Drishane when Edith was away studying in Paris. It shows how reserved Edith was, how much Martin

respected her reserve, her authority, and how much both Mrs Somerville and Martin had fixed their affections upon her. Martin was astonished at how much she enjoyed society at Castletownshend when Edith
was not there:

> I suppose people used to think that I only cared for your
> society, and I have always told you that I am at my worst when
> you are by. It is quite true – you make me shy and cross in some
> mysterious way – and I think your mother is like that too. She
> prefers your company to anyone's, but it seems over-stimulating.
> So don't tell me again I don't get on well with your mother – I
> can get on with her for ever when you aren't there. It is *you* who
> fight, and then my heart takes part with you and I turn horrible.
> It is a very intricate position, and it has often made you justly
> angry with me, but believe me there is a basis of good feeling and
> always was, and it has often lately touched me to see how your
> mother has suppressed, in talking to me, the home truth that in
> the early days would have flown from her lips and would have
> roused the spirit of combat in me. This is a strange dissertation,
> and confused – but I thought of it all a good deal and I think I
> had better stay at Drishane only when you are away in Paris –
> and I am sure Hildegarde would agree with me. She used daily to
> cross herself regarding the Millenium harmony. But for all that
> your mother and I would rather fight and have you there –
> strange as it may appear . . . Did I tell you that Mrs Warren and I
> developed into great amity in your absence, and she looks at me
> now with most sane and kindly eyes and is agreeable. (There it is
> again – you make me nasty to everyone when you are there
> because I am so anxious to please you.)

Nothing in all their correspondence shows so well as this letter that
the bond between Edith and Martin was mental and not physical.
Martin would not be able to write 'I had better stay at Drishane only
when you are away in Paris' if it were otherwise. Women writers and
professional women were aware that they were channelling their sexual
energies into creativity; often we find them referring to their concerns
as their children. Winifred Holtby presented her first book to her
parents with: 'Here is your first grandchild.' Florence Nightingale,
returning from the Crimea and upset by the jubilation at her return
when so many had died, wrote: 'Oh my poor men; I am a bad mother
to come home and leave you in your Crimean graves – 73 per cent in
eight regiments in six months from disease alone – who thinks of that
now?' Edith wrote of her books as having conception, periods of
gestation and births. None the less she called her books her '*illegitimate
children*', as though the sublimation of biological creativity into artistic
was held improper for a woman.

Hildegarde target-shooting. She was a dead shot, a skill she kept into old age. Jimmy Penrose taught Ethel, Hildegarde and Edith to shoot.

What Edith thought of lesbianism in the flesh we know, because in September 1919 Ethel Smyth fell in love with her. Ethel Smyth was, in many ways, a great woman as a composer and writer, but she was an unrestrained sensualist, who barged through life, flesh first; she tried to seduce Edith physically and experienced a most humiliating rejection. Edith admitted that she loved Ethel, and quite calmly defined her love as exclusive of physical feeling. Hildegarde's son, Nevill Coghill, who became Professor of English Literature at Oxford, wrote a clear account of their relationship:

> My Aunt adored Ethel's tornado character. In fact they got on famously, both being fiercely courageous, pro-feminist, generous, instant in repartee, passionate, geniuses, and gentle folk ... I mean they had real *style*. At first sight each knew she had met her

match. My Aunt was a little shocked by Ethel, especially in the
matter of her terrific romantic passions in the past (Ethel has told
the world about them in some of her books). My Aunt who so
far as I can learn, never had any such relationships and, in
conversation anyhow, regarded the symptoms of them as
ridiculous, and verging on the disgusting, was prepared to make
an exception of Ethel's passionate attachments, incomprehensible as
they were to her. But she certainly was shocked.

Ethel was also shocked by her rejection. She wrote two very intense
letters to Edith on the subject of Edith's apparent sexual inhibition, one
on 25 June 1920, the other on 11 July. Edith had insisted that her and
Martin's love was not physical and had suggested that Ethel should
have physical relationships elsewhere. Ethel replied:

> ... your instincts and education made you fastidious and ...
> rather virginal. Well and good. Your charm is to be thus – that
> your law is not my law – that I can do and risk things you could
> not – because in your case the inner sanction is lacking ... Well, I
> don't mind. I don't mind you feeling as you do. You and V M. It
> goes with your type. It is yourselves ... The idea that I, who I
> think, have more experience of life stored in my little finger than
> you have in your whole body (I mean of a certain type of
> experience), should not be capable of judging whom to do what
> to seems so odd to me ... You innocent – you know I *can* put
> my shoulder to other wheels. Why, why should you imagine that
> I had not done so? (and far more cleverly and energetically than
> any man would be capable of doing) for myself?

In this same letter Ethel makes an analysis of Edith that shows how
different the two women were in manners; Ethel is objecting to Edith's
reserve on meeting new people:

> How often are you paying attention – you villain – you cloudy
> aloofer? You don't understand people in a flash unless they happen
> to enchant you ... people don't deeply interest you. You are one
> of those who don't wish to dig too deeply into hearts – on
> principle and because hearts are not your field of exploration,
> unless in the field of your own creations. I am deeply interested in
> humanity – have handled it all my life.

Edith, who destroyed her side of this correspondence, probably
because she had never discussed homosexuality or physical love before
and thought it embarrassing, seems to have responded with a severe,
censorious letter (11 July 1920) that infuriated Ethel into insults: 'Certainly the being incapable of a certain kind of entrainment in matters
physical is not a human being,' and later – 'I go with my father in
preferring a "rip" to a spiritual pedant – a righteous pedant.'

Hildegarde (centre), Violet Coghill (left) and Sylvia Townshend (right). Three members of the Old Clyde Crew, the local ladies' boat that took on all comers at the Regatta in August. (16 August 1890.)

Their friendship survived, because of Edith's good humour and level-headedness. Edith, perhaps with feelings of relief, calmly took a position in the chorus when Ethel fell madly in love with Virginia Woolf. The private nature of Edith's personality reduces us to laughter when we find her entering in her diary, as a note of the receipt of Ethel's harrowing letters: 'Hear from E S, her ears bad;' and 'letters from E S, ears intermittently better and worse.'

Edith was obtuse in the extreme when she had to analyse any affection that might be directed at her. She must have felt herself officially disengaged from sexuality. When Ethel Smyth fell in love with the little-knowing Edith, she arranged a romantic trip to Sicily. Edith invited Hildegarde and Egerton to come along, too. Ethel was astounded, but not as much as Edith was to be at Ethel's declaration of physical love.

As feminists neither Martin or Edith were separatists. They could not envisage a satisfying life without the bounds of the family, without

men. Both had the same reaction to the story of the Ladies of Llangollen, who in the late eighteenth century had fled from their unhappy
families in Ireland. They described a visit to the Ladies' home during
their tour in North Wales in *Beggars on Horseback* in 1895; they referred
to the 'grotesque romance' of their lives. Completely unsympathetic
to the impulse that caused the Ladies to leave their families, Martin, in
a later letter to Edith, wrote: 'I never could tell the wearisome grind
of those blessed hags of Llangollen.' Edith had no wish to cut herself
off from the society of men, as we can see from her speeches as
President of the Munster Women's Franchise League:

> The woman who has had to sit at home while her husband, her
> sons, her servants, play their part in making the laws and fixing
> the taxes which she, as well as they, must obey and pay, now sees
> windows opening into life. She can leaven politics, she can debate
> topics of national interest and moment, with men and women, on
> equal terms. She can think of them as she goes about her
> household tasks, and feel that she is part of the thinking world,
> not merely a minister to its bodily needs. She will become the
> companion, in a new and higher way, of her husband and her
> sons, and her brothers. She will provide for them an infinitely
> more interesting and entertaining home, an interest and
> entertainment that will raise home-life to its highest possibility,
> and will endure, unimpaired, into old age.

Both Edith and Martin were freaks within their families in being
independent women. They were both stubborn in growing firmly
from girlhood into the unconventional types that they were. They
were not young and unformed when they met.

> When we first met each other we were, as we then thought,
> well stricken in years . . . not absolutely the earliest morning of
> life; say, about half-past ten o'clock, with breakfast (and all traces
> of bread and butter) cleared away.

They had made the best use of the education that they got, be-
grudged them as it was.

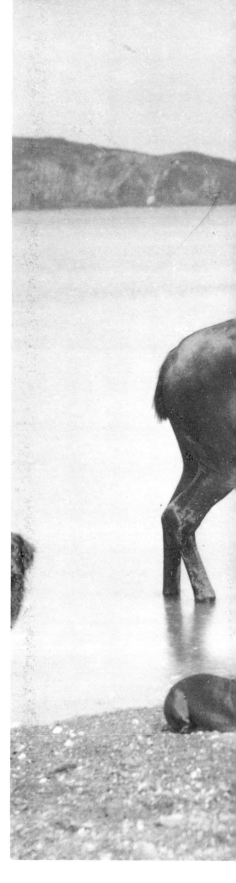

*Edith and Hildegarde on the Strand. Edith is
walking a horse through sea water. Wherever
the sisters went, a crowd of dogs followed.*

CHAPTER 12

'To Us Was Shown Another Way': New Women

> The last piece of writing that Martin and I undertook was a pamphlet entitled 'With Thanks for the Kind Enquiries'. It set forth to the best of our power the splendid activities of the various Suffrage Societies after the Great War broke out, and it pleases me to think that our work together was closed and sealed with this expression of faith that was and is in us.
>
> From *Irish Memories*, 1917

Edith photographed for Vogue *in 1948, the year before she died. She is in her room at Tally Ho, the house on the Main Street to which she was moved for convenience in 1946. She is looking at Hildegarde. Their relationship became even closer after Egerton's death in 1921. Edith's writing brought in very little money after Martin's death, but she made a windfall or two with successful exhibitions of paintings such as the one at the Goupil Gallery in London in 1920. She went to America in 1929 and made a great deal of money with an exhibition at the Ackermann Galleries in New York. She was also selling hunters to American enthusiasts at this stage. Her mind remained very alert, ever game for a new venture, and she reviewed books on spiritualism for* Time and Tide.

For Edith and Martin women's education and rights were closely connected. The founding of Alexandra College, Dublin, in 1866 clarified attitudes to the status of women as well as beginning the improvement in their education and opportunities so long overdue. The *Alexandra College Jubilee Book* in 1919 opened:

> The middle of the last century saw the dawn of Women's Education. It is not now our task to recall the darkness before the dawn, nor to tell the story of the wide movement for the 'higher education' of women, but to trace the history of Alexandra College, which in its dates coincides almost exactly with the general movement in England.

Somerville and Ross, both Alexandra girls, grew up at a time when only a few benign men had the notion that women also had minds that could be educated.

That disadvantaged darkness is beyond the recall of most modern women. It is salutary to remember the position before 1857, when women were first allowed some legal rights against their husbands. For women, marriage was the only fulfilment – the nursery and household was their world. Single women could hope for little more than upper servant status as companions and general helpmeets in those households that kept them. As head of the household the husband voted and dealt in law and property for the women of his household. Before 1857 a husband could divorce his wife for adultery, but there was no redress for her in the case of his infidelity. Husbands had exclusive rights to children no matter what the case, and property was in the control of the husband. The convenience of this system meant that most men could see nothing but futility in any attempt to educate women.

It was not until 1846 that an educational qualification for women was established. This was the Diploma for Governesses instituted by the Governesses' Benevolent Institution, but from then on, women gradually worked their way towards equal footing with men in educational terms. Archbishop Trench, co-founder of Queen's College, London, and of Alexandra College, insisted: 'There is no need to break the bread of knowledge smaller for young women.' From the beginning it had a flourishing Irish Society. Its magazines had sections in Irish. Patrick Pearse taught Irish there.

Edith Somerville attended Alexandra College for two terms in 1875, her education before this having been sketchy. She 'disposed of a series of governesses' and her mother had a low opinion of her potential. Both Edith and Martin, left to their own devices, read widely and were particularly well versed in the Bible; their range of words, metaphor and allusiveness is impressive when one thinks of them in their unschooled childhoods, patching together an 'educated' writing style.

Edith's ambition to be a self-supporting professional artist led her to train abroad in some hardship, exactly like Sarah Purser, who was aiming at independence from the male world in the same way. The boredom and futility of life at home irritated Edith. In a remote place like Castletownshend, housekeeping for women included upholstery, framing, painting and decorating, and Edith was able to turn her hand to anything. Before she met Martin her diary teems with descriptions of the Pooter-like embellishment and restoration of household goods, much given to collapse: 'Spent the entire morning doctoring old chairs with Boyle and glue.' There is a period of months in 1880 when Edith and Ethel Coghill did nothing but 'black presses', that is paint cupboards black, and stencil Japanese effects on top. Apart from the distractions of her art and hunting Edith railed at the futility of her life. In March 1883 she wrote: 'Began a very original book "my trivial life and misfortune, by a plain woman".'

After meeting Martin in 1886, Edith found absolute fulfilment in their work, as this delightful excerpt from the diary in mid-March 1888 shows: 'Nothing to record, a peaceful life of uninterrupted shocker [they were writing *An Irish Cousin*]. The General ceases from troubling, the Canon is at rest. Violet copies the first part, all is pure and good and holy.'

During the nineties – the most productive years of Edith's and Martin's collaboration – numbers of educated and eloquent women began to appear, as agitators, on the political scene. In 1897 the National Union of Women's Suffrage Societies was founded. In 1910 Edith became President of the Munster Women's Franchise League, and Martin one of the Vice-Presidents.

There were two kinds of organized agitation for women's rights.

"Taxation without Representation
is Tyranny."

MUNSTER WOMEN'S FRANCHISE LEAGUE.

MEMBERSHIP CARD.

President:—MISS EDITH Œ. SOMERVILLE.

Subscriptions to be sent to the Hon. Secretary—
MISS DAY,
Myrtle Hill House,
Cork.

OBJECT.

To obtain for women the Parliamentary Franchise on the same terms as it is or may be given to men.

METHODS.

1. Action entirely independent of all political parties.

2. Energetic agitation upon lines justified by the fact that women have at present no voice in the making of the laws under which they live.

3. Education of public opinion by Public Meetings, Debates, Demonstrations, Deputations to Public Representatives, and such other non-militant methods as may be necessary.

4. To promote the Election of Candidates selected by the League for Boards of Guardians, Town Councils, etc.

MEMBERS.

Women of all shades of political opinion who approve of the principle, object, and methods of the League are eligible for membership.

ASSOCIATES.

Men who approve of the principle, object, and methods of the League are eligible as Associates.

Please tear off here.

I approve of the principle, object, and methods of the Munster Women's Franchise League, and hereby enrol myself a member.

Name

Address

Amount of Annual Subscription

The membership card, front and back, of the Munster Women's Franchise League.

Left: In February and May of 1929 Edith made a successful lecture tour in America. She first published a series of articles about this tour in Vogue *then extended them into a book:* The States Through Irish Eyes *(Boston and New York, 1930). She was over seventy years old and her little marginal drawings made in America are still sprightly and crisp. She followed hounds in Virginia, was enthralled by Negro spirituals, and tore after Drag Hounds at Aiken, S.C., in a horse buggy. The tiny drawing of the buggy keeling over shows the Hunt Master and Edith driving hell for leather after hounds. Close behind them was Hildegarde, driving the following buggy.*

The Suffrage Leagues and Societies like Edith's were non-violent, but the number of women prepared for violent agitation grew, and the Women's Social and Political Union, the members of which did not baulk at large and violent demonstrations, was founded in Manchester in 1903.

Very few women at this time had learnt to recognize their strength, let alone use it. Women like Ethel Smyth were extraordinary in their physical vigour and demonstrated strength. Neither Edith nor Martin were of the type of feminist who wanted to break away entirely from men and traditional female roles. They wanted to revolutionize women and attitudes towards them, within the framework of the family, and without offending tradition. Edith often insisted in her speeches to the Munster Women's Franchise League on the importance of each woman realizing that she herself was the example of womanhood to her immediate family, and that their opinion of women would be based on the knowledge that they had of her as a sister, mother, wife or aunt:

> Every man, consciously or unconsciously, judges women by the women he knows best, and it rests with each of us to form that opinion. We are asking men to give us the share of power that should, in abstract justice, be ours. Let us show them that we are competent to use it, not only for our own advantage, but for that of the Commonwealth. It is time for us, in Ireland, to bestir ourselves, and to relinquish the more agreeable pose of Looking On.

Edith and Martin were very aware of the attitude of women who did not take issue with men, who accepted their appointed roles, mutely. This retreat, the refusal to engage except at a sexual level, was later called, by Margaret Mead, 'the retreat into fecundity', and Edith and Martin had intimate knowledge of two examples in their own mothers. Edith wrote:

> My mother was of that race of professional mothers that seem
> to have been a special product of the Victorian Age: mothers who
> took seriously their trade as such, and devoted themselves
> unflinchingly to their offspring. (I have heard of one who, being
> asked of which she thought most, her husband or her son, replied
> indignantly, 'Me son, of course! Why wouldn't I think more of
> me own son than a strange man!')

Neither Mrs Martin nor Mrs Somerville could understand their daughters' urge to work, and to be unmarried and independent. Numerous diary and letter comments by the daughters make clear the gulf between mothers and daughters. The mothers were liable to interrupt or erupt into work at any time, and retreat into childishness if offended. Martin writes to Edith:

> Nothing on God's earth has the same power to rouse me to
> fury as being talked to while I'm writing. One of the worst battles
> I have ever had with Mama was last year when I wasted a whole
> goodly evening . . . I would not answer her conversation – and
> there was no work out of that.

The battles between Edith and her mother were terrible and painful to both, and only a great deal of careful handling by Martin and Hildegarde made life possible together for them. Edith wrote, quite rightly, of her mother: 'She is as headstrong as a child and often much more foolish.'

Edith and Martin might often have pondered on what their mothers might have become, given proper education and opportunities, for they were both sharply intelligent and critical women. In a speech to the M.W.F.L. called 'The Educational Aspect of Women's Suffrage', in December 1911, Edith, with the simplest of words, instils revolutionary ideas:

> I have said that the Women's Suffrage Movement is a
> momentous one, and I believe that no one, as yet, can even dimly
> apprehend its ultimate effects upon the character of the women of
> this country. It is in its educative power, in its unique capacity for
> touching and stimulating the very springs of character, that lies
> one of its most important characteristics. Education is what
> women want. Practical education, that shall arouse their
> constructive sense, shall make them want to improve things, shall
> make them critical.
> But there is remarkably little use in being constructive or even

critical, if you have no power to give effect to your ideas. Want of power causes want of interest, and want of interest causes stagnation, a sodden acquiescence in things as they are, or a peevish and uncomprehending acceptance of reforms that are imposed by main strength, as by Masters upon Slaves.

You cannot reform a slave. Reform must have its feet set upon freedom. It is the sense of Power that creates the sense of responsibility, the desire to better things, that wakens the character to say 'These things are wrong, let us make them right.'

Edith was the first President of the Munster Women's Franchise League, and in the first year of its existence, 1910-11, they held sixteen public meetings and established branches in Waterford and Skibbereen. Edith travelled a Suffrage circuit: Cork, Waterford, Bandon and Skibbereen. She evolved a precise, compacted speech for Suffrage meetings, of which this conclusion to a 'Votes for Women' speech is a good example:

Ladies – I support the Extension of the Franchise to qualified women for four reasons.
1st. For the Good of the State – because the state has to make laws for women as well as men, and wants all the help it can get from both sexes.
2nd. For the Good of Women. To educate them. To give them equal pay for equal work and to raise their general status.
3rd. For the Good of Men. To enlarge their Mental Horizon and Sympathies.
And lastly, because Taxation without Representation is Injustice.

Edith's League had over two hundred members in 1911, a surprising number when we remember that the extreme sensationalism of the press reportage of militant English suffragist violence meant that to declare oneself a suffragist was to take an eccentric stance. But Edith was quite clear in her speeches that although she did not approve of the methods of the Women's Social and Political Union, she by no means disowned them:

Their methods are not universally approved of, and they have been consistently, and persistently, abused and misrepresented by the Anti-Suffragist newspapers. But whether we, Non-Militant Suffragists, approve of their methods or not, I have not the smallest doubt but that it is their courage and their reckless self-devotion that has made a live question of Votes for Women.

That Edith had admiration for these brave women is shown by her careful copy of a very long letter from a Cork suffragette, Miss F. Allen, to Miss Day, Secretary of the M.W.F.L., describing an enormous rally at the Houses of Parliament in November 1910. Edith

cherished the letter, which vividly illustrates the bright hope and intelligence of suffragists at that time, and their difficulties:

On arriving at Caxton Hall I was shown into the room where
the Irish contingent were awaiting their deputation badges. Mrs
Cousins immediately asked me if I would represent Cork, as I was
the only Cork woman among them. Of course I gladly consented,
and I laughed to think of my small self representing you and your
committee ... 'General' Drummond arranged us in sections of 11
or 12; the Irish party were in the 4th section. Mrs Pankhurst, Mrs
Garrett Anderson, Mrs Ayrton, and other well-known women
formed the 1st section. There is an old law which forbids
deputations to the House to consist of more than 13 persons, and
so our 400 had to be all arranged in sections of 10 or 12, and left
Caxton Hall with intervals of a few minutes between each section.
We all had, previously, full directions as to tactics, mode of action
in case of arrest, etc. etc. The Irish 10 were hugely cheered as they
left Caxton Hall; we walked smartly into Parliament Square,
where we met a crowd that helped us by making way as far as
they could for us. This was not the case, I hear, in all parts of the
crowd, but we were fortunate in coming into a section of
sympathisers ... So we, the Irish, got through, and then I learned
that Sections 2 and 3, which had set out before us, had not yet got
through, and Section 1, with Mrs Pankhurst, had only arrived
after a struggle ... from the steps of the House I saw some
horrible sights. I saw some police who quite lost their heads, and
handled the women brutally. Especially if they happened to be
working women, or women not fashionably dressed. I am certain
our Irish police would not have behaved so. One would think a
man would naturally be nicer to a woman of his own class, but in
England it is not only Cabinet Ministers who are 'respectors of
persons'. A fashionable hat and a certain carriage mean a good
deal in dealing with the London Police, and I realised on Friday,
as I never did before, that it is we, well-fed, well-housed women,
who must face street scrimmages, prison, etc. It is not suitable
work for our poorer sisters, they are too roughly handled.
Remember the greater number of the police were all extremely
good tempered, I think they are too fat to be anything else. It was
quite funny to see an agile girl dodging three fat policemen, it
reminded me of Tennyson's 'Little Revenge'; but there were other
scenes that were horrible, these heavy creatures throwing the
whole weight of their bodies against some fragile girl, or elderly
woman ... Of course you know our quarrel is not with the police
... but in spite of all they had to arrest 119, and, as any arrested
girl passed, we cheered. At Cannon Row (the police station) they
were met by Suffragettes with refreshments, and were bailed out

for the night by Mr Lawrence [husband of Mrs Pethick-Lawrence].

Mrs Garrett Anderson went into the House with Mrs
Pankhurst, indeed Mrs Garrett Anderson was the first to pass the
cordon of police, then came Mrs Pankhurst, but even they had
some little struggle to get through, while dear old Miss Neligan,
aged 75, was, I believe, quite roughly handled. You know she
nursed through the Franco-Prussian war, and was Head Mistress
(First Head Mistress) of that beautiful High School in Croydon. I
felt proud to think we Irish could claim her as a Cork woman.

. . . Friday has left a strong impression on my mind. 1st –
Cabinet Ministers don't speak the truth unless they are obliged to.
2nd – we shall get nothing but what we fight for, 3rd – the
women are bricks, and stand grandly together. . . .

In abandoning their traditional sexual roles, suffragists and suffragettes entered a no-man's land in which their sexuality was difficult to
define. All too easily, with the aid of sensationalism and intellectual
laziness, their feminism has been equated with inversion. The injustice
of men ordering the whole of a woman's life around her breeding
season, or possibility of breeding, which generally absorbs only a
quarter of her life, appalled and infuriated Edith and Martin as much
as they were appalled and infuriated by women who were simply
stockbreeders. Edith wrote:

Men's professions, whether great or small, invariably remind
them of their position as part of a community, while the persistent
effort of hundreds of generations of husbands has been to isolate
and insulate their women.

Husbands were remote beings to their wives. They were so often
away, at wars, law-courts, hunting, sailing; those marriages that were
able to sustain a romance after the second or third child in the first
few years of marriage were rare indeed, and neither Edith nor Martin
saw any romance in their mothers' marriages, whatever the stories of
long-past courtships. Here is Adelaide Somerville writing of her husband in her diary on 11 August 1868: 'Played a game of croquet with
my Husband and won it. He said I played in a mean manner as I
changed from one to two handed strokes *but he lied.*' They had been
married for more than ten years.

Minutely intimate relationships were reserved for a special woman
friend, often a sister or cousin, who would be at hand during childbeds,
illnesses and death. It is not straining language to classify these strong
loves as 'romantic'. Both women might be married; it is surprising
how often accounts of deathbeds include the information that the close
woman friend of the woman dying, usually in childbed or its aftermath, is temporarily mistress of the house. The last experience for
many women then was the delirium, agony and cold sweat of a death

from general septicaemia. Mary Wollstonecraft died in this way, by
the filthy hands of her own doctor. An instance from Anglo-Ireland
is the death of Hewitt Poole's mother, Judith, who died of peritonitis
on 16 September 1861:

> Lily Poole and Marianne Walker put her to bed. As she was
> again expecting a baby they thought perhaps that this accounted
> for her illness but it was soon plain it was something more serious
> ... All the evening she grew worse. They sent for Dr Garde, who
> arrived about ten, and was mystified ... Every hour she grew
> worse ... Dr Wood came from Bandon and he also was entirely
> puzzled... About eight o'clock on the morning of the sixteenth
> Jane Leslie came in and told Lily: 'It is hopeless. No one in such
> agony could live.' ... Sometime after eleven o'clock that morning
> – in the presence of those whom she had most loved, her husband,
> her son, her sister Lily Fleming and her friend Jane Leslie, Judith
> Poole died.

Immediately Horace Poole, Jane Leslie and Lily Fleming became in-
competent with grief; the servants left, and on the following day the
household fled: 'Horace fled from Courtmacsherry the next day. He
was crazy with misery, stunned by shock, unable to eat.' The house
was left in chaos, with jewellery and clothes scattered about, and in
sole attendance upon the dead Judith was her sister-in-law, Lily Poole.

It was Edith who held Drishane together during the many grief-
stricken times when close members of the family died. A critical time
for Edith, and a time when the whole weight of being mistress of
Drishane fell suddenly upon her, was at her mother's death. None of
the male members of the family seem to have been competent in grief.
Her mother died just before midnight on 3 December 1895; having
been in great pain, she had been drugged with morphia by Dr Hadden.
Edith remained calm through nursing her mother, helped by Egerton
and Hildegarde. When she died Hildegarde, who was pregnant, broke
down and had to retire. Edith immediately had to see to getting her
brothers, who were away on service, informed, arrange the funeral,
and deal with the floods of sympathetic visitors and telegrams and
letters. But the first thing that Edith did sheds such light on her delicacy
of feeling, on the practicality of her love for people, that we cannot
wonder at the number of people that found her lovable. She instantly
prepared the old blue nursery as a new room for her father, and moved
him from the set of rooms that he had shared with Adelaide, as the
blue room had been his nursery and he would be in a room 'of which
he only has happy memories'.

At Mrs Somerville's death, Martin sent a letter to Edith suggesting
that she should leave Drishane and stay down at the Cottage, Egerton
and Hildegarde's home in Main Street, to get away and recover. Edith
retorts very sharply – 'Martin – how could you?' – with a letter that

harrowingly describes the utter collapse of the household, and what an act of desertion, and unfeeling desertion, it would be to leave. Edith was instantly mistress of Drishane, and incomparable. Martin's impulse to leave the scene and return later illustrates a deep difference between them. There was a weakness in Martin, a fragility that had led her to attach herself to Edith's huge strength, not so much as to a protector but as to an anchor. Martin had a very close relationship with Hildegarde. At times of crisis it was to Hildegarde Martin went, at Glen Barrahane, and not Edith at Drishane, as at the death of Edith and Hildegarde's father, Henry. Martin enters in her diary at Ross: 'Heard from E.Œ.S. and Hildegarde. The latter wants me to go to her – accepted – sent notice of Uncle Henry to *Irish Times*.'

By the end of the nineteenth century there were enough educated women for there to be a market for feminist books. One of the best was Olive Schreiner's *The Story of an African Farm*, published in 1883, and both Edith and Martin had read it by 1889. These books suggested that women might expect more of life than to be at most the mistress of a house and a mother, and to expect more of marriage than an initial animal passion followed by boredom and stunned years of co-parenthood. Olive Schreiner was fascinated by the possibilities of relationships between men and women that combined mental and physical communication. She has her characters, the male Waldo, and the female Lyndall, converse deeply on sexuality, the synthetic aspects of 'femininity'; here the woman speaks:

> The less a woman has in her head the lighter she is for
> climbing. I once heard an old man say that he never saw intellect
> help a woman so much as a pretty ankle; and it was the truth.
> They begin to shape us to their cursed end, she said with her lips
> drawn in to look as though they smiled ... the curse begins to act
> on us. It finishes its work when we are grown women, who no
> more look out wistfully at a more healthy life; we are contented.
> We fit our sphere as a Chinese woman's foot fits her shoe, exactly,
> as though God had made both – and yet He knows nothing of
> either. In some of us the shaping to our end has been quite
> completed. The parts we are not to use have been quite atrophied,
> and have even dropped off; but in others, and we are not to be
> less pitied, they have been weakened and left. We wear the
> bandages, but our limbs have not grown to them; we know that
> we are compressed, and chafe against them.

Olive Schreiner came to the sad conclusion that friendship was impossible between men and women, if sexual compatibility was to come before personal. She had hoped for a relationship with a man that would combine a physical and mental compatibility. A friendship with one's husband must have been difficult to attain when women were confined to the department of home and nursery affairs.

When Maria Edgeworth met Mrs Bushe (great-grandmother of Edith and Martin), Edith wrote: 'She lost no time in falling in love with her "very dear Mrs B".' An example of the tone of affection of Maria's letters to Mrs Bushe is: 'In everything that has affected you since we parted I have keenly sympathised – Oh that we could meet again. I am sure our minds would open and join immediately.' Five years later, in August 1832, she writes:

> I wish dear Mrs Bushe we could ever meet again, but this world goes so badly that I fear our throats will be cut by order of O'Connell and Co very soon, or we shall be beggars walking the world, and walking the world *different* ways. It is good to laugh as long as we can, however, and whenever we can.

Maria's sentiment here on laughter was to be echoed by Edith and Martin, who believed utterly in the cleansing and healing powers of laughter. They wrote the R.M. stories during a period in Ireland even more turbulent and distressing than the 1830s.

Despite his interest in the potential of women, Maria Edgeworth's father seems to have reserved his deeper thoughts and feelings for his close men friends Thomas Day and Erasmus Darwin (grandfather of Charles). Here we have examples of exactly that kind of deep friend-

Hildegarde, Edith and Sylvia Warren, an American friend, at Clonakilty Horse Show, 1936.

ship between persons of the same sex that appears to be unremarkable between men, but remarkable between women. Constant lengthy letters flowed between the friends. The intensity of feeling was so great, and so respected by his wife, that when Erasmus Darwin collapsed and died at his writing desk, in the middle of a long letter to Richard Lovell Edgeworth, Mrs Darwin saw to it that a note was appended explaining why the letter was unfinished, and it was duly posted to Edgeworthstown.

When women were regarded as heir-containers only, men did not require their continuous company, so that companionship or compatibility – what Montaigne calls 'the consonance of wills' – was hardly necessary. Victorian women who chose companionship with their own sex rather than marriage could hardly have done otherwise in their overriding urge to be other than annexes of men. This was not an attempt to do without men, a retreat, or a deliberate sexual inversion, but rather an attempt at self-discovery and independent growth. Many pairs of women who had powerful and productive lives, living in friendship together in the first years of 'New Womanhood', wished to base their lives, not on sexuality, in the service of men and children, but on growing out of their enforced minor status into adults, educated, competent, capable of achievement.

It is a frivolous masculine judgement of such relationships that one of all such pairs must be 'masculine', that a sexual fixation and the physical possession of the weaker of the pair by the stronger must be involved. Very few of these women thought so much of masculinity as to wish to ape it sexually. Mutual adoration in these cases infrequently involved sexuality, though often sensual affection. Homosexuality may involve a dissatisfaction with sexual identity that causes one of a pair to adopt the sexual behaviour of the opposite sex, so that in expressing their love the pair engage in synthetic acts of generation.

Those feminists who did love other women enthusiastically, and physically, like Ethel Smyth, clearly thought that they had developed sensuality to a high art, infinitely superior to the fleeting, brute sexuality practised on women by men. As we have already seen in her letters to Edith, Ethel was proud of her skills in this field, and flaunted them. For Ethel, her sensuality was directed only towards the physical fulfilment of the individual, and had no connection with reproductive instincts or delusions of sexual possession. For some women this type of sensual fulfilment and appreciation was part of feminism, an alternative to a sexual fulfilment that involved childbearing. But Edith, a traditionalist and fine genealogist, who wrote magnificently on the pride of generation and of family, in women and in men, was not sympathetic to such affections.

Martin had considered the moral reprehensibility of homosexuality, probably more closely than Edith. Though their strong moral sensi-

bilities put the subject of homosexuality out of court for discussion,
Martin did make this comment on reading *The Picture of Dorian Gray*
(23 December 1890):

> Finished 'Dorian' – which I think a vulgar variation on Dr
> Jekyll – the only reason I can imagine for the Chimp [Edith's
> brother Cameron] lending it to you is that he thought you
> wouldn't understand it – if it is what I darkly surmise it to be, it
> is the most daring beastliness ever I struck – but keep this to
> yourself – certainly I would be afraid to own to having read it, to
> a man.

To the end of her life, Edith violently condemned immorality and
refused to meet or entertain those whom she considered 'fallen'.

The upper classes had always had the time and leisure to investigate
the by-roads of sexuality, and were blasé on the subject, as the letters of
early bluestockings, or those in social circles such as the Polignacs',
show. After Oscar Wilde's trial in 1895, the subject of homosexuality
was one that could not be avoided, in any class. It is wrong to assume
that Martin and Edith were in complete ignorance of the Wilde trial
and its details. Oscar Wilde was known to both of them personally.
The judge, giving his ruling at the Wilde trial, regretted that Sir
William, Oscar's father, had prevented his son from converting to
Catholicism, as the strict codes of Catholicism, the judge felt, would
have prevented Oscar from his later indulgence in 'moral obliquity'.
Edith admired the Catholic Church for the same reason.

Martin, writing in about 1910, said of her own mother: 'In her
outdoor life, she was what, in those decorous days, was called a "Tom-
boy", and the physical courage of her youth remained her distinguish-
ing characteristic through life.' However many different interpretations
may be put upon undertones or overtones of homosexuality by those
scholars who have studied the papers of Somerville and Ross, the
already quoted aside by Martin, in a letter to Edith in 1898, 'I never
could tell the wearisome grind of those blessed hags of Llangollen',
seems unequivocal.

It is deeply saddening that Edith's appalled realization (after Ethel
had enlightened her on the subject of physical love between women)
that Martin's letters to her, containing frequent expressions of affection,
might be mis-read caused her to edit some sentences with heavy over-
scoring. One of these deletions is, however, still legible. Martin wrote:
'I have the wish for travel in my blood now – I looked up into the
blue Connemara hills and could have cried that I wasn't in among
them. . . .'

Here Edith has made a great scored blot – she has tried to delete
'with you'. It is astonishing that Edith should have decided that this
sort of remark would be misleading, while calmly leaving in all of
Martin's remarks about missing her company in bed, or Martin's re-

ference to Edith laying her hand on her head, as Edith and Egerton
(who was involved with healing through mesmerism and physical
contact) both treated neuralgic headaches with massage. Martin
suffered badly from neuralgic headaches. Truly, when Edith
grappled with the subject of sexuality in relation to herself, she was
obtuse.

Though they held differing views on the perfectibility of relationships between men and women in years to come, Edith being far more
optimistic, they were united in their continual awareness of the low
status of women, and in their detestation of those women who played
up to men in confirmation of their expected feminine roles. Their
diaries, letters and even published works are shot through with acid
and scathing comments on women in society. Here Martin writes to
Edith from Atlantic Lodge, a boarding house in Galway, on the running of the household:

> The principal servant is called Miss O'Brien, she being the sister
> of the owner's wife. Her brother-in-law invariably calls her 'Miss
> O'Brien' and does it as often as possible to show the respect that is
> due to her – there is then her niece, aged fifteen, called Mary
> Kate. They are distinguished from servants by the fact that neither
> wears a cap or apron.

More gentle, but just as acute, is Edith's comment on her great-
grandmother, Nancy Crampton, wife of Charles Kendal Bushe, beloved by Maria Edgeworth:

> I grieve that I have been unable to find any of Mrs Bushe's
> early letters. She was a brilliant creature in all ways, and had a
> rare and enchanting gift as an artist, which, even in those days,
> when young ladies of quality were immured inexorably within
> the padded cell of the amateur, could scarce have failed to make
> its mark, had she not, as the Chief [Charles Kendal Bushe], with
> marital complacency, observed – devoted herself to 'making
> originals instead of copies'.

To look into the face of men directly, intelligently, with no feigned
meekness, was unusual and disapproved of; General Butler called
women who did so 'man-eyed', and his refusal to allow his daughter,
Eileen, to eat any meat was probably not unconnected. Edith and
Martin were both direct in looking at, and talking to, men. Unex-
pectedly, it is Martin who provides evidence on this point. Martin was
a very able debater, who quoted Blue Books by the column; her subtle
mind and political instincts, her determination never to lose an argument, must have frightened, disconcerted or just displeased many men
and women. Edith admired Martin's relentless logic, but she herself
avoided long verbal engagements in argument because of her explosive
temper. When Martin was annoyed with someone, she frightened

them with cleverness; when Edith was annoyed she was sarcastic and could demolish the opposition with one blistering remark.

Martin wrote to Edith on male notions of women quite often. In December 1887 she writes: 'Rossetti had but one idea of life – to be in love – with perhaps religion thrown in – of a glamoury, inamoury sort and I think in all his sonnets he had not the right idea of a woman.' Martin was aware of the feminine expression in the eyes, the signal of mental truce, or surrender, that men expected: 'Why did not Tom Becher come – with him I could have faced the meek-eyed sentimental Mrs Harry and her Madonna superiority?' she wrote to Edith of a party in 1888. Edith pours scorn on male novelists' representation of women in *Irish Memories*:

> Let us think of Mrs Proudie, of 'The Campaigner'; of Eleanor,
> 'The Warden's' daughter, who bursts into tears as a solution to all
> situations; of the insufferable Amelia Osborne. Consider John
> Leech's females, the young ones, turbanned and crinolined, wholly
> idiotic, flying with an equal terror from bulls and mice, ogling
> Lord Dundreary and his whiskers, being scored off by rude little
> boys. And the elderly women whose age, if nothing else, marked
> them in mid-Victorian times, as fit subjects for ridicule, invariably
> hideous, jealous, spiteful, nagging, and even more grossly imbecile
> than their juniors. Thackeray and Trollope between them
> poisoned the wells in the 'fifties and the water has hardly cleared
> yet.

In her affection for her father, grandfather and brothers, particularly her deep love for her brother Boyle, Edith was quite different from Martin. Martin was the youngest of a large family, treated as a pet by her elders; she was a remote child, headstrong and wilful, who had no deep voluntary attachment to a person until she met Edith, and that was final. All her life through, her sisters were to send for her whenever they wanted assistance of a sisterly sort, and commandeer her time, with this sort of reaction from Edith, because Martin had just recovered from a heavy cold (she is writing to Hildegarde from London on 14 July 1895):

> Her filthy sisters want to hunt poor Martin back to Ross and
> all they want her to do is *arrange a bedroom for Jim's two boys*! As if
> Nanny, or even Selina couldn't do that – I am in a fury – She
> would only stay there a few days, but I had hoped she would
> have travelled home with me, and you must write and expostulate
> at being thrown over, for such nonsense! She is so absurdly good
> and obedient to them that I can hardly rouse her to revolt.

Although Martin enjoyed being accorded gentlemanly attentions, deep down she reserved a cold, almost prejudiced attitude towards close male relatives that shows particularly in her comments on her brother Robert. She writes, on 2 October 1890, to Edith from Ross, on why she thought that people should be allowed to retire to bed after dinner:

> I think the social evening is a tiring thing especially when your elder brother entertains the company for most of it with stories you know and respect of old and scarcely recognise through their exaggerations. Most especially of all when the stories have been told by yourself to that brother . . . I had to sit and listen and smile the permissive smile of the jester's relative . . . I could wish that Robert's voice was a little less penetratingly loud – he shouts down a whole dinner table and I feel sick.

We have a curious sidelight on received form at Castletownshend for male-female reciprocal behaviour in a letter from Edith to Hildegarde (19 August 1893):

> You would have smiled to see Aylmer at the supper here . . . he had placed himself, as usual, between Mildred and Fanny Morgan, and from their piercing shrieks I judged he was making himself even more agreeable than usual, and so he was, he was putting his chewed grapeskins down their backs. 'Oh, it was delicious', they said.

Edith knew what a good relationship between a man and a woman might be because of her relationship with Boyle. She wanted Martin to love him as much as she did, not realizing that Martin's possessive love of her made this difficult; here she tries to explain to Martin why Boyle was lovable (he has just returned after four years serving in Japan):

> My Dear Martin, Boyle is full of anxiety to meet you and is prepared to love you very much – he is curiously unchanged except in size – He is about 5′ 11″, and his shoulders are like those of a bull – In fact I think he has a nice figure and tho' not good-looking, he has an awfully nice face – He is full of art fads and theories which we assure him are Youngrot. . . . His own boxes have not come yet, he says he has lots of nice things – which I can well believe as he has excellent taste . . . he is unaffectedly keen about Rossetti's sonnets and poems, and has a book of them. . . . He does not seem to think it is any merit on his part to like nice books, but just does it because he was built that way. He is excellently appreciative of any sort of story and will soon have quite as good (and more intellectual) a grasp of the Squaw jests and converse as Aylmer . . . I think you would like him very much. He is anything but an 'overflow meeting' being singularly independent in his ideas and calmly determined in expressing and holding to them. You *must* come down here before he goes; as goodness knows when there will be another chance of your seeing

him, and I want you to do so more than I can say. I think he is a
dear boy and a fine fellow – Quite seriously.

Martin was quite contrary, and a month later Edith is still trying to
make her see Boyle:

> Only for Boyle I would much prefer going first to you, i.e.
> after the wedding. But I should feel the most selfish brute in the
> world to go away while he is at home – He plays about with me
> all the time – I couldn't leave him. I never knew a boy so
> thoroughly nice all round as he is. He has not one dirty turn in
> him – I *insist* on your coming here and seeing him yourself.

An extraordinarily intelligent polymath, Boyle Somerville published dictionaries of the languages of New Hebrides, New Georgia
and the Solomon Islands. He published several books. He was the first
archaeologist mathematically to measure and survey stone circles, his
work in this field being so thorough that his published papers on this
subject are still referred to. He was also a psychical researcher, and was
present and transcribing at many of the Castletownshend seances. He
and Edith had a most harmonious relationship. In the Drishane House
papers there are meticulous technical drawings of stone circles discarded
by Boyle, which have been used by Edith on the backs for pencil
drawings. Together Edith and Boyle compiled the *Somerville Family
Records* and after his assassination in Castletownshend on the night of
24 March 1936 Edith saw through the press his last book, *Will Mariner*.
When Edith was talking to Geraldine Cummins, shortly before her
death, when she was far from any self-consciousness, she spoke of the
relief of crossing over to the spiritual world, and of how, when she
awoke, she wished to see 'Boyle and Martin' (in that order) 'and then
Ethel' (Penrose).

However many delightful and civilized men Martin and Edith
knew, their portrayal of marriage is jaundiced. In *The Real Charlotte*
alone, there are these awful representations of the delusions, illusions
and façades of marriage: Mrs Lambert to Lambert, Francie to Lambert,
Lady Dysart to Sir Benjamin, the marriage-to-come of Hawkins and
his heiress. It is as though they could not bring themselves to believe
in, and depict, a union between a man and woman that could be deep,
truthful and fruitful of more than children.

It was allowed that women writers could achieve a close appreciation of the physical world, of appearance and the senses; it is easy to
appreciate, for example, Colette, in such a way without perceiving
what else is there, so strong is the surface impression. What was not
expected was a sense of logic, justice and history. Schopenhauer diag-
noses female limitations with clarity:

> She is . . . a mental myopic in that her intuitive understanding
> sees very clearly what is very close to her but has a very narrow

field of vision from which what is distant is excluded; so that
what is absent, past, or to come makes a very much weaker
impression . . . the fundamental defect of the female character is
the lack of the sense of justice.

Somerville and Ross took a huge stride into a male preserve with
their R.M. stories. Their wit and knowledge of masculinity – rough
justice and all – caused many readers to deny, adamantly, that Major
Yeates and his fellows could have been the creation of feminine minds.
In their novels they counterbalance their knowledge of the domestic
world of women with an absolute understanding of masculine occupa-
tions, sports and frames of mind, and achieve an unusual grasp of the
engagements of animus and anima, in love and in war.

Martin died in the second year of the First World War, so that she
did not see the immense change in attitude towards women that came
as a result of women proving themselves during this war. Women did
the physical work of the absent men, and served at the Front in nursing, ambulance and despatch service. It is ironic that some of the very
first awards made to women for gallantry were to those nurses who
left the Front and came to serve in Dublin during the Easter Rising of

*Munster Women's Franchise League
ambulance. As soon as the First World War
broke out the M.W.F.L. started a fund-
raising drive for ambulances.*

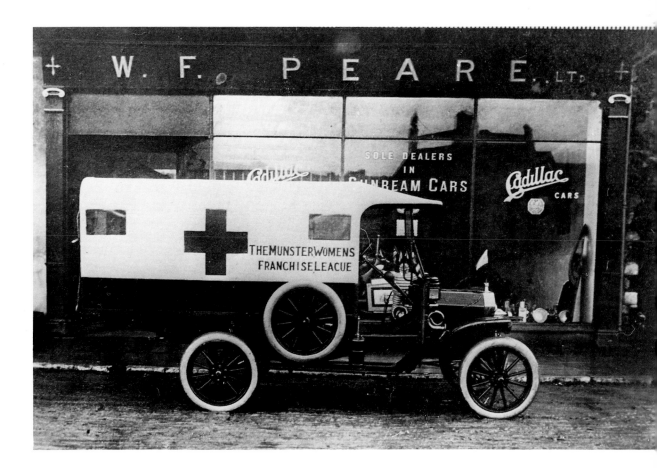

No. A 4988

BRITISH RED CROSS SOCIETY

— AND —

ORDER OF ST. JOHN.

Received from _Miss Somerville_

for Sale for the benefit of the Sick and Wounded :—

The "Irish R.M." MS.

with grateful thanks.

This Gift is received upon the condition that same may be sold by public auction or by private treaty
at such time and at such price as the Committee decide.

Accepted for Sale when and where it is deemed most advisable

Date _27/2/18_

Charles Russell

Chairman Red Cross Sale Committee.

p.p.

1916. It became easier for women to become professionals. It is impressive that a number of women in Edith's and Martin's immediate circle achieved professions when this was still very difficult. The Royal College of Physicians in Ireland had opened its examinations to women in 1877, and three women M.D.s were well known to Edith. Egerton Coghill's sister, Violet, was one and Geraldine Cummins, who came from an outstandingly gifted medical family, had two M.D. sisters, Dr Mary and Dr Jane; another sister of Geraldine's was the first woman to qualify as an engineer in Ireland. A curious memorial to the general intelligence of women in Edith's circle is _The Intelligent Woman's Guide to Socialism_, written by George Bernard Shaw for his sister-in-law, Cissie Cholmondely, Edith's close friend from childhood.

A Red Cross receipt. Towards the end of the war Edith donated the manuscript of the first R.M. stories to a fund for the sick and wounded. Edith found ways to overcome shortage of cash. Hildegarde instituted a collection for chloroform for the French army, providing a supply that lasted through the war. She was awarded a Diploma of Honour by the French Red Cross.

Edith and Martin succeeded in their chosen profession; as humorists their place in literature is assured, and a growing reappraisal of *The Real Charlotte* bodes well for their future reputation as serious novelists. They have had such popular success as humorists, so fine is their writing, dateless and genderless, that their achievement has been too easily accepted by those who forget their sex and its difficulties at the time they were setting out as writers. The firm clarity, pace and substance of their writing might shame modern feminists who have retreated into dissonant jargon.

In *Women Writing about Women Writing*, a collection of essays published in 1979, Anne Stevenson, in her essay 'Writing as a Woman', moderately wrote:

> I am not convinced that women need a specifically female
> language to describe female experience . . . language is difficult to
> divide into sexes. A good writer's imagination should be bi-sexual
> or trans-sexual. . . . A flight of fancy prompts me to imagine a
> woman's language which appoints itself guardian of the traditional
> beauties of English as opposed to the speed-road efficiencies of
> American. Imagine a woman's language which preserves the
> dignity of the *King James Bible* and the *Prayer Book* which forbids
> the use of technical jargon.

We may rest our imaginations; it is written.

In 1895, the year after the publication of *The Real Charlotte*, when Edith was thirty-seven and Martin thirty-three, Edith went up to Ross on a visit. When she had gone, Mat Kenealy, a servant at Ross, talked to Martin about the strong impression that Edith had made. Mat was unfamiliar with the creations of Somerville and Ross, though his words were transcribed into many of them. Martin, describing his talk to Edith, who was back at Drishane, wrote:

> He never seen the likes of a lady like you that would have that
> – 'undherstandin' of a man's work; and didn't I see her put her
> hand to thim palings and lep over them! Faith I thought there was
> no ladies could be as souple as our own till I seen her. But indeed
> the both o'yee proved very bad that yee didn't get marri'd, and
> all the places yee were in!

How thoroughly we must disagree with his conclusion.

Somerville and Ross possessed qualities that men found disturbing, even singly, in women. They were feminists, spiritualists and hunting women who spent their lives in a professional literary partnership unlike any other attempted by women at the time. Male critics had a lot to swallow before evaluating their work, but praise it they did. Sir Arthur Quiller-Couch in the chapter 'On Reading the Bible (I)' in *On the Art of Reading* wrote approvingly of them:

But let me turn to Ireland, where, though not directly derived from our English Bible, a similar scriptural accent survives among the peasantry and is, I hope, ineradicable. I choose two sentences from a book of 'Memories' recently written by the survivor of the two ladies who together wrote the incomparable 'Irish R.M.'. The first was uttered by a small cultivator who was asked why his potato-crop had failed:

'I couldn't hardly say,' was the answer. 'Whatever it was, God spurned them in a boggy place.'

Is that not the accent of Isaiah?

'He will surely violently turn and toss thee like a ball into a large country.'

The other is the benediction bestowed upon the late Miss Violet Martin by a beggar-woman in Skibbereen:

'Sure ye're always laughing! That ye may laugh in the sight of the Glory of Heaven!'

In 1932, when Trinity College, Dublin, offered Edith an honorary Doctorate of Letters, she accepted on condition that Martin's name should be associated with hers, the literary firm of Somerville and Ross being still at work. Sir Robert Tate was the University Orator at the time, and in his Latin oration he skilfully skirted the problem raised by the continued literary career of a woman who had ceased to breathe at a quarter to eight in the morning of the twenty-first of December 1915.

Herbert Greene, to whom the fame and success of Somerville and Ross must have been as unthinkable and as unwelcome as women undergraduates at Oxford, must have found it more painful than anyone else to come to terms with what his beloved made of her life. Tactless and patronizing he may have been, but he was faithful, and never married. In 1932, when Edith was seventy-four and Herbert seventy-five, it was Herbert who made the English translation of the Trinity Orator's Latin speech; what Herbert's feelings were about Martin he concealed, but with exquisite feeling he translated Sir Robert Tate's Latin:

> . . . I recall with veneration to your memory the cousin associated with her in so many works; whom living she loved more than the light of day, and whom, now that she is taken from her sight, she cherishes with no less love as though she were present and helping. Therefore, not only this island of ours, but the greater Ireland, scattered over either half of the world, will confess, and gladly, that for no woman's brow could our academic wreath more worthily be woven.

Edith in her doctoral robes. Her left hand rests on her recently published An Incorruptible Irishman.

The Collis Biography

In his biography of Somerville and Ross, Maurice Collis stated that Edith was a man-hater who was incapable of normal sexual love. His analysis is built up gradually:

> Any sexual union with a man had something revolting about it for Edith. Deep in her was a profound distaste for the opposite sex ... Edith's deepest feelings were concentrated entirely on her own sex [page 32] ... Edith had been deprived of what she required, association with a woman who would be all in all to her and to whom she would be all in all [page 36] ... Edith could only fall in love with a woman [page 37] ... Edith's feeling for Martin, however, was something more overwhelming than tenderness and the development of a common talent. It was a passion, an obsession from the depths of her being [page 38]. ... The fact was that Edith had tried during the wedding [her sister's] to look as cheerful as custom required, but she had a deep-seated dislike of weddings, a dislike amounting to disgust. In declaring the dogs to be disgusted she was revealing her own feelings. ... Why she felt disgusted ... could only be fully explained by a psychiatrist, though perhaps enough has been said earlier in this book to hint at what his explanation might be [page 96].

To reinforce this analysis he quotes, as Edith's diary entry on the night of Martin's death: 'Only goodnight beloved, not farewell', and states that Edith 'frantic with grief' tried to communicate with the dead Martin.

We are offered Edith's reactions to three events in support of this psychiatrical theory: firstly her reaction to the engagement and marriage of her beloved cousin, Ethel Coghill; secondly to the marriage of her sister, Hildegarde; thirdly to the death of Martin. None of the quotations given from Edith Somerville's diaries and letters relating to these events is quoted without distortion. Contexts are not given, parts of sentences are given as whole, and in one instance words that were not Edith Somerville's are given as her own.

On 1 June 1879, Edith had to take to her bed with a throat infection: 'Uncle Jim [her grandfather's brother, the local doctor] came over, and having swept and garnished my throat, 7 ulsters [Edith's word for ulcers] worse than the first took possession of it.' For the next five days

a fever kept Edith in bed. She enters: '2 June – Encore disease. 3 June
– Decay. 4 June – Disorder. 5 June – Disgusting.' On the sixth of June
she began to pick up, and enters: 'Read Tom Sawyer – Felt better –
That unprincipled woman the Twin has been and gone and engaged
herself to Jimmy Penrose. She had to come and 'fess to her injured
Twin – she ought to be ashamed of herself.' Though she was taken
out for a drive next day, Edith spent most of the following day in bed:
'The Twin came up bringing her sheaf with her. I only wonder I
didn't have a relapse at the sight of them – when she knew I was
simply broken in wedding presents, and she can't go shares in her own
– Mean Beast – Moreover she exposes me to public obloquy as the
remaining Twin and deprived me of two nights sleep.' The following
day, the 8th, Edith staggered downstairs, having been in bed for seven
days. She writes: 'Crawled downstairs like a moribund caterpillar.'

Edith's rushing, colloquial style, with its liberal use of the dash, has
been misread here. Ethel's 'sheaf' was the list of wedding presents,
made to avoid duplication, carried about to relations and friends by
Victorian brides-to-be. Ethel and Edith, as 'The Twins' up till then,
had given wedding gifts together. There had been many weddings that
year, and Edith, as she says, was 'broke' through buying gifts half
shares with Ethel. The sentence: 'She can't go shares in her own –
Mean Beast' means that Edith will have to pay for Ethel's gift on her
own. Leaving out the dash between 'her own' and 'Mean Beast' gives
the erroneous and suggestive sentence – 'She can't go shares in her
own Mean Beast', which contrives to imply that Ethel proposed to
divide her attentions between Jimmy Penrose and Edith, and that
Edith, in her possessiveness, objected to the fraction rather than the
whole. The quotation: 'Crawled downstairs like a moribund caterpillar' is used to suggest that Edith was made physically ill by Ethel's
revelation, whereas – as we see from the full context given above –
Edith had been physically ill and bedridden for the week previous to
Ethel's news of her engagement.

In December 1880, the preparations for Ethel's wedding involved
the entire village, and all households were engaged in the decoration
of the bridal route and the preparation of food and accommodation
for those coming as guests from afar. Edith and her mother Adelaide
were driven to distraction. But although Edith heads the description
of the day of the wedding 'The hideous day', she got through it with
some brio:

> For a wonder, it was fine though very cold. Got to the church
> early. The Cobbs had decorated the CJ pew beautifully. Jack and
> Hugh carried her tail from the carriage to the church. The
> coastguards having made a sailwalk right up to the door. No end
> of people there. Mr Bushe and Jack read the service and they both
> spoke up awfully well, and there was no hitch anywhere. When it

was over Joe and I darted up and played the wedding march while they signed in the pew ... [amusing description of breakfast, etc.] The O'Donovans have got up an impromptu dance for tomorrow night. Very spirited and worthy conduct. After the outer world had gone we all changed and went up the river in the coastguard boat. Sang somewhat. Up here for tea. Egerton, Louie, Frank, Bessy and Mr & Miss Hewson and Jack came up afterwards. Some music and finally Joe went through his repertoire of songs, with a different 'make-up' in the way of hat and stick for each. Mr Hewson did the Dublin Cries and when Frank said 'the menagerie has gone through all their tricks' they went home.

Using only the closing description of these after-tea entertainments Maurice Collis writes that Edith 'makes it clear that the evening's festivities ... made her think of animals in a menagerie going through their tricks'.

Through some carelessness in the preparation of the wedding feast for Ethel and Jimmy, the food made several people ill, including Edith and her mother Adelaide. However, Edith could never resist any opportunity to dance with her favourite dancing partner, Claude Coghill (Joe), and forced herself up out of bed to go to a ball arranged by the O'Donovans at Lissard, in honour of the wedding.

The description of the wedding is here given in full. The Mr and Mrs Leger mentioned in parenthesis were two wedding guests staying over in Castletownshend who bored her – for what seemed sixteen years:

> December 31, Friday. Fine. Awfully sick last night.
> (combination of the worst qualities of Mr and Mrs Leger – both
> for sixteen years etcetera) – stayed in bed all day, very mean.
> Bock [her cousin Ada, daughter of Dr Jim] came up before lunch,
> and there was a running fire of boys all day. Joe in the last stage
> of agony as it had been settled he ought not to go to the dance.
> However at 6.30 he came up saying he had been given leave and
> although feeling at the point of death, I forsook my couch for the
> sake of swaggering with the Prophet [Joe] in the 'Lar-di-dar' – all
> the Castle men and Bessie and Louie came. Bock and Miss Gilford
> came with Mother, Papa and me. Got there about 9. Melian had
> taken the Seal home with her and they had arranged everything
> most wonderfully, beautiful floor, programmes and everything.
> Everyone from the whole county was there. Joe and I in vain
> tried to instil the noble principles of the polonaise figure of the
> quadrille into their benighted minds but none of them would play
> and we had to give it up. CT contributed 14 dancers who did
> their duty as that duty should be done. The feeling of 'the flure'

revived me; and mother, who was also done up by the wedding
came to life in a marvellous way – partook but frugally of supper
remembering last night. The Seal quite the child of the house, in
great form. Went home about 4. Soup before starting. My! it was
pretty stiff, a good dance, but not as good as ours '79–80 –
however one needed something to take the taste of that wedding
out of our mouths, it felt like an aggravated nightmare resulting
from a too heavy supper and simply clung to the roof of yr
mouth.

The aftermath of the wedding and the O'Donovans' ball is described
by Maurice Collis thus:

> She was very sick in the night and stayed in bed all next day.
> However in the evening she got up and went to a dance given by
> the O'Donovans. 'One needed something to take the taste of that
> wedding out of our mouths. It felt like an aggravated nightmare.'

By neglecting to mention that Edith's illness was caused by bad
food, and by placing a full stop after 'nightmare', an apparently direct
quotation has been made to fit a theory.

It is quite common for women to be emotionally upset at the
wedding of their sister or childhood best friend. Edith was upset at the
weddings of her sister Hildegarde and her 'Twin' Ethel Penrose, but
this was to be expected. She did not have a phobia about weddings in
general; being a popular person, she was often a bridesmaid, and in
fact was one, at a wedding she enjoyed very much, in April of the
same year that Ethel was married. Maurice Collis discusses the reason
for Edith being 'disgusted' when her sister Hildegarde married Egerton
Coghill, when there is not a shred of evidence to show that Edith felt
disgusted. Here again his stress is misleading, being placed on only part
of a letter written to Hildegarde by Edith, describing the events after
Hildegarde and Egerton had left (to punt down the Thames on honeymoon). The letter, and also one to Martin describing the wedding,
stresses the dreadful mood that the house dogs got into; normally
petted and talked to as a matter of course, the dogs were swept aside
and ignored. They became mournful and glared at the rushing members of the family from huddles in corners to which they had retired
in umbrage.

The fact that the dogs were moody and disgusted should not be
transferred crudely to Edith. In the morning of the wedding day Hildegarde and Edith had been alone, Edith dressing Hildegarde. They kept
themselves 'stiff with champagne'. They were deeply attached to each
other, and the excess of emotion that caused both of them to cry is
entirely understandable. To the end of her life Edith would refer to
her sister as 'beloved' and just as she addressed letters to Martin 'Dear
Child', so was Hildegarde her 'Dear Child'. The letters to Martin and

(Monday, Dec. 20) unchanged, & they believed that she would have another night like the preceding one — But at 5 a.m. on Tuesday, Dec. 21 — they say the breathing changed, & began to fail, & at a quarter to eight this morning it ceased.

December 21. Tues. E.Œ.S. 1915:

DECEMBER, 1915

THURSDAY a fine morning. Got up early that ... over'd with violets a big E. Took it to church & laid it above her heart. Afterwards was put into the grave with her. a great quantity of beautiful flowers – Hildegarde & I ... away to the Cromleck field, where Martin I have so often sat. It was very windy ... Stayed there while the in ...

FRIDAY has opened – Jim went away, back to Galloway. went up to Lismore by the 12 train with Dooley & Sheila. Got there at ... Trains all late. Ethel & Jim ... Judith only there – found many letters. Notices of Martin in the papers, all alike saying a light has ...

SATURDAY, Christmas Day ... gone out wrote letters. Took the dogs out, walked with Jim & Ethel & Judith many letters. a storm beginning to night.

Received this Week.	Paid this Week

Hildegarde regarding the wedding reveal no disgust on Edith's part. The more intimate letter to Martin was later given to Hildegarde as a wedding anniversary present after both Martin and Egerton were dead, to enable Hildegarde to recall to perfection that most important day. Edith warned Hildegarde that to read it would cause her to cry, as it had her.

Throughout her life Edith's public reserve and control were stoic, probably owing to her early recognition that control and reserve were qualities that men did not expect in women. Her love for her brothers and her father, and her fondness for boys like Sydney de Morgan in her youth, were abundantly expressed. No more inappropriate a word than 'frantic' could be found to describe Edith, even in her deepest grief. At her mother's death in 1895 her reaction of stunned, black gloom made her retreat into inaction, and she would come back into herself after some days of silence.

Her diary is reticent; when overcome, she made no entry. She made no entry in her diary on the night of Martin's death. She did keep, through the weeks of Martin's last illness, a clinical diary of medical detail in a separate volume. It ends: 'the breathing changed, and at a quarter to eight this morning it ceased. December 21, Tuesday E.Œ.S. 1915.' The line 'only goodnight beloved, not farewell' is to be found, in quotation marks, on a loose leaf inserted into the 1916 diary. The leaf has three consoling quotations. One, by Florence Nightingale, advises on how to adjust to the death of a person who is young, another is a prayer taken from a volume of sermons by the Venerable Basil Wilberforce called *New (?) Theology*. The prayer is printed by Maurice Collis without its source. The single line 'only goodnight beloved, not farewell' also comes from this volume, from a sermon called 'Praying for the Departed'. Its context is this:

> The agony of a recent bereavement is keen and passionate and cannot reason coolly; but it is our privilege and our duty not to 'sorrow as those without hope'. The nearer we get to the God within us, the nearer we are to our beloved departed. It will be but a little while and we shall be reunited. The revelation of the survival of the Christ encourages us to alter the agonising 'goodbye' of bereavement into the 'goodnight' of expectation, to say when they depart: 'only goodnight beloved, not farewell'.

At Martin's death, during the days that Edith and Hildegarde were with her at the Glen Vera Nursing Home, it was Hildegarde who openly showed her emotion, weeping and embracing Martin, who was no longer conscious of their presence. Edith, remote, sat for a while gripping Martin's hand. As always needing to do something to alleviate her anguish of mind, she began to draw Martin; an exactly similar reaction occurred in the painter, Sir John Lavery, at his wife's deathbed – he set up his easel and painted her. A few days later, at Martin's funeral, Edith, on the morning of the day, was making a letter 'E' in violets to put on Martin's hands before the coffin was closed. Absorbed in the making of this wreath, she sent for the children at Glen Barra- hane, to show them how it was done. This was not the action of a person so grief-stricken as to be out of control. One of the children to watch her making this wreath, Sylvia Townshend's daughter, recalled her composure. Edith and Hildegarde could not bring themselves to be present at the burial, but went into the orchard field and wept. Edith's devastation at Martin's death was open – she said 'the better part' of her was gone, that Martin had been 'so much more' than a sister. It was Ethel Smyth who forced Edith to state after Martin's death that this best of friendships had not expressed itself in sensual affection.

The ease of their relationship, which their letters show was non-possessive, would suggest that if there was a sexual element in their love, it was an urge weak enough for them to suppress it with good humour. We know that at nineteen Edith Somerville met a man whom she pursued. Within her first week of knowing Hewitt Poole they were exchanging poems and drawings; she pursued him with invitations and gave him a portrait photograph. Martin Ross's first letter to Edith was left unanswered for nine weeks, when Martin wrote again. It was Martin's persistence that made Somerville and Ross, slow starting as it was.

Edith Somerville died on 8 October 1949, in Tally Ho. She had chosen to be buried beside Martin, However, no one knew that although Martin's grave had been sunk into earth with no difficulty, the place allotted for Edith, only a few feet away, was solid rock. The scene of panic on the morning of Edith's funeral was entirely in accord with her blackest humour. A neighbour of Edith's was detailed to procure dynamite to clear the rock, and with considerable difficulty it was obtained from the garda barracks. One result of the explosions was that the cross on Martin's grave was broken at the base and collapsed.

The Books of Somerville and Ross

Books published by Somerville and Ross up to 1915:

An Irish Cousin, Richard Bentley, London, 1889.
Naboth's Vineyard, Spencer Blackett, London, 1891.
Through Connemara in a Governess Cart, W.H. Allen, London, 1892.
In the Vine Country, W.H. Allen, London, 1893.
The Real Charlotte, Ward and Downey, London, 1894.
Beggars on Horseback, Blackwood, Edinburgh and London, 1895.
The Silver Fox, Lawrence and Bullen, London, 1897.
Some Experiences of an Irish R.M., Longmans, Green, London, 1899.
A Patrick's Day Hunt, Arch. Constable, London, 1902.
All on the Irish Shore, Longmans, Green, London, 1903.
Slipper's A.B.C of Fox Hunting, Longmans, Green, London, 1903.
Some Irish Yesterdays, Longmans, Green, London, 1906.
Further Experiences of an Irish R.M., Longmans, Green, London, 1908.
Dan Russel the Fox, Methuen, London, 1911.
The Story of the Discontented Little Elephant, Longmans, Green, London, 1912.
In Mr Knox's Country, Longmans, Green, London, 1915.

Books published by Somerville and Ross after the death of Martin Ross:

Irish Memories, Longmans, Green, London, 1917.
Mount Music, Longmans, Green, London, 1919.
Stray-Aways, Longmans, Green, London, 1920.
An Enthusiast, Longmans, Green, London, 1921.
Wheel-Tracks, Longmans, Green, London, 1923.
The Big House of Inver, Heinemann, London, 1925.
French Leave, Heinemann, London, 1928.
The States Through Irish Eyes, first American edition Houghton Mifflin, Boston and New York, 1930; Heinemann, London, 1931 (Martin Ross does not appear as co-author).
An Incorruptible Irishman, Ivor Nicholson and Watson, London, 1931.
The Smile and the Tear, Methuen, London, 1933.
Notes of the Horn, Peter Davies, London, 1934 (Martin Ross is not named as co-author).
The Sweet Cry of Hounds, Methuen, London, 1936.

Sarah's Youth, Longmans, Green, London, 1938.
Notions in Garrison, Methuen, London, 1941.
Happy Days, Longmans, Green, London, 1946.
Maria, and Some Other Dogs, Methuen, London, 1949.

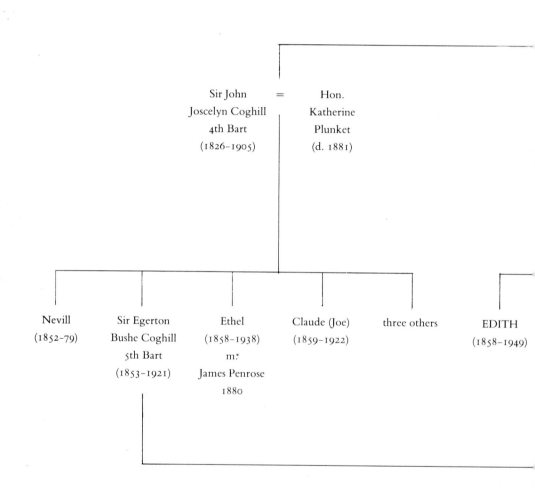

The Somerville
Family Tree

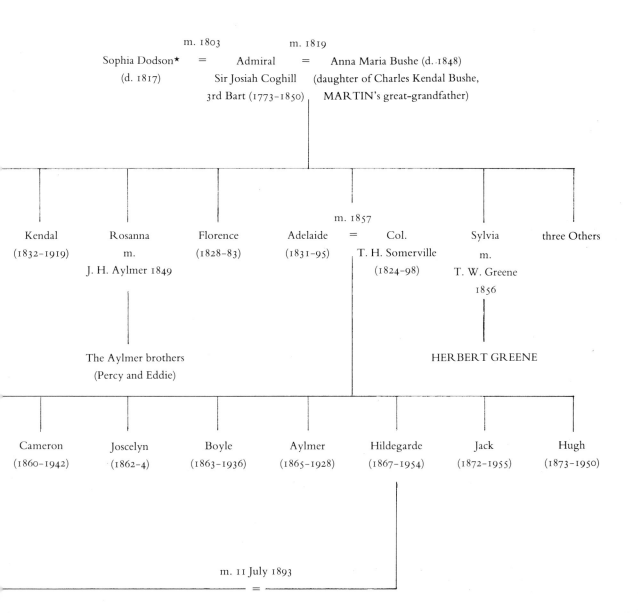

m. 1803   m. 1819

Sophia Dodson★   =   Admiral   =   Anna Maria Bushe (d. 1848)

(d. 1817)   Sir Josiah Coghill   (daughter of Charles Kendal Bushe,

3rd Bart (1773–1850)   MARTIN's great-grandfather)

m. 1857

Kendal   Rosanna   Florence   Adelaide   =   Col.   Sylvia   three Others

(1832–1919)   m.   (1828–83)   (1831–95)   T. H. Somerville   m.

J. H. Aylmer 1849   (1824–98)   T. W. Greene

1856

The Aylmer brothers   HERBERT GREENE

(Percy and Eddie)

Cameron   Joscelyn   Boyle   Aylmer   Hildegarde   Jack   Hugh

(1860–1942)   (1862–4)   (1863–1936)   (1865–1928)   (1867–1954)   (1872–1955)   (1873–1950)

m. 11 July 1893

=

★ Who had daughters Caroline, Josephine and Emmeline. Emmeline m. 1839 Rev. Charles Bushe,
son of Charles Kendal Bushe, Rector of Castlehaven.

Acknowledgements and Sources

I should like to thank the following for their help in the preparation of this book: Margaret Bonfiglioli; Philomena Byrne; Jonathan Cavendish; Thomas Charles-Edwards; the late Canon Claude Chavasse; Judith Chavasse; Captain P. M. B. Chavasse; the late Sir Patrick Coghill; Sir Toby and Lady Coghill; Deirdre Coleman; Clare Craven; Professor John Cronin, Q.U.B.; the Rev. Nicholas Cummins; Stephen Davies; Rosemary ffolliott; Faith Garson; Bea Jackson; Mrs Katharine Johnston; Mary Kelly, Assistant Librarian, Q.U.B.; the late Hannah Leary; the late Contessa Sylvia Lovera di Maria; Anne Minihane; John Peacock; Franta Provaznik; Dr Hilary Robinson; Eithne Ryan, Headmistress of Alexandra College; Rose Marie Salter-Townshend; Jeanne Sheehy; Colonel and Mrs Brian Somerville; Mr and Mrs Christopher Somerville; Diana Somerville; Michael Somerville; Miss M. H. Stuart, Librarian of Alexandra College; Eirian Wain; Philip Wilkinson; Gordon Wheeler, Sub-Librarian, Q.U.B.

I am indebted to many relations of Edith Somerville for their generosity and courtesy over a long period, particularly Diana Somerville, goddaughter and niece, and Katharine Johnston, née Coghill, niece, who read drafts of this book and made many helpful comments while enduring a long inquisition cheerfully. I wish to thank Mary Kelly for her kind assistance and after-care when I worked on the papers of Somerville and Ross at Q.U.B. John Peacock, photographer, Oxford, has worked with me for seven years in the location, rescue and restoration of photographs in various stages of evanescence; I gratefully acknowledge his skill and good humour in the face of decay and disorder. Hilary Robinson has always been generous in co-operation and I must acknowledge her help particularly with Chapters 7 and 3, which include work that we have done together. Without the co-operation of my husband and sons this book would not have been finished.

I have to thank the late Colonel H. D. Gallwey for permission to use in Chapter 1 material that I first published in *The Irish Genealogist*, Vol. V., no. 6 (1979).

I am grateful to the executors of the estate of Somerville and Ross for permission to quote from their published and unpublished works.

The following books by Somerville and Ross are currently in print in Britain: *The Real Charlotte* and *The Big House at Inver*, both by Quartet; *The Irish R.M. Complete* and *An Enthusiast*, both by Sphere. A selection, *The Irish R.M.*, is in print in the U.S.A., published by Penguin Books.

I would also like to thank the owners of the following illustrations and manuscripts for permission to use them in this book.

ILLUSTRATION SOURCES

Collection of Margaret Bonfiglioli: Pencil drawings on page 50 (top) and page 52 (bottom).

Collection of the late Canon Claude Chavasse: Chancellor portrait of Edith Somerville, page 31.

Coghill Family Archive, from Plate Albums 4 and 5: Photographs on pages 7, 9, 13, 17, 18, 19, 20, 21, 23, 24, 27, 28, 33, 39, 48, 57, 58, 59, 60, 61, 62, 65, 68, 69, 70, 71, 77, 96, 97, 104, 116, 141, 143, 146, 147, 148, 154, 157, 165, 195, 197, 199, 202, 208, 211; paintings on page 87, 'A Religious Procession' and 'Gathering the Harvest'.

Collection of Faith Coghill: Anatomical studies from a bound volume, page 86.

Collection of Katharine Coghill (Mrs Terence Johnston): Egerton Coghill by Edith Somerville, page 91; photographs on pages 131, 150, 220.

Collection of Rosemary ffolliott: Photographs on pages 35, 36, 37.

Collection of Gifford Lewis: Pencil drawings by Edith Somerville on pages 44, 45, 50, 51, 53, 90, 101, 103, 105, 106, 109, 118; montage on page 190; photograph by Elliott and Fry on page 125; photographs by author on pages 113, 152, 166, 167, 176.

Anne Minihane, photographer, Skibbereen: Copy of Cummins portrait, courtesy of Rev. Nicholas Cummins, Rector of the Parish of Altar; photograph of the graves of Somerville and Ross, page 239.

Franta Provaznik, photographer, Oxford: Panorama from Knockdrum, page 10; copies of anatomical studies by Edith Somerville, page 86.

Queen's University of Belfast, Special Collections: Drawings from the Welsh tour, pages 79, 81; three wash drawings from *In the State of Denmark*, pages 92-3; two line drawings from *A Patrick's Day Hunt*, page 98; portrait photograph of Martin Ross, page 124; a page from Somerville's Irish exercise book, page 172; *Irish Homestead* front cover, page 174; automatic writing by Geraldine Cummins, page 181; deathbed study of Martin Ross by Edith Somerville, page 185; automatic writing by Edith Somerville, page 191; diary entry, page 193; M.W.F.L. membership card, page 213; diary entries, pages 236, 237.

Collection of Rose Marie Salter-Townshend: Photographs on pages 142, 144, 145, 192.

From the albums of Admiral Boyle Somerville (courtesy of his son Colonel Brian Somerville): pages 32, 47, 62, 112, 117, 153, 159, 163.

Collection of Colonel Brian Somerville: Painting of Rineen, detail, page 87; Edith Somerville in her doctoral robes, page 230.

Collection of Christopher Somerville: Düsseldorf portrait, page 43; 1894 Paris studio portrait, page 78; Somerville painting out of doors, page 88; painting 'Retrospect', page 89; four Kodaks from Rea races, page 94; wash drawing 'Emmie and Cameron playing cards', Summer 1895, page 99.

Collection of Diana Somerville: Photographs on pages 128, 129.

Edith Somerville's scrapbooks (part of the Coghill Family Archive): pages 71, 75, 83, 99, 123, 125, 126, 132, 133, 135, 148, 149, 153, 170, 176, 178, 205, 207, 227, 228.

MANUSCRIPT SOURCES

Coghill Family Archives

Letters of Edith Somerville to her sister Hildegarde, Lady Coghill.

Letters of Edith Somerville to her nephew Professor Nevill Coghill.

The Buddh Dictionary.

Miscellaneous papers.

Collection of Rosemary ffolliott: Letters of Hewitt Poole to his wife, Mia Jellett.

The Henry W. and Albert A. Berg Collections, the New York Public Library, Astor, Lenox and Tilden Foundations: The correspondence of Edith Anna Œone Somerville and Violet Florence Martin; Martin Ross correspondence with Augusta, Lady Gregory.

The Library, the Queen's University of Belfast: The diaries of Edith Somerville and Violet Martin; notebooks and miscellaneous papers, including Somerville's papers accumulated as President of the M.W.F.L. and some of her correspondence with Ethel Smyth.

Somerville Papers, Drishane House: Diaries of Adelaide Somerville, miscellaneous papers.

Index